D1605976

DISCOURSE ON THE SCIENCES AND ARTS

(FIRST DISCOURSE)

AND POLEMICS

JEAN-JACQUES ROUSSEAU
DISCOURSE ON THE SCIENCES AND ARTS

(FIRST DISCOURSE)

AND POLEMICS

THE COLLECTED WRITINGS OF ROUSSEAU

Vol. 2

EDITED BY

ROGER D. MASTERS AND CHRISTOPHER KELLY

TRANSLATED BY

JUDITH R. BUSH, ROGER D. MASTERS,

AND CHRISTOPHER KELLY

DARTMOUTH COLLEGE
PUBLISHED BY UNIVERSITY PRESS OF NEW ENGLAND
HANOVER AND LONDON

DARTMOUTH COLLEGE
Published by University Press of New England, Hanover, NH 03755
© 1992 by the Trustees of Dartmouth College
All rights reserved
Printed in the United States of America   5 4 3 2 1
CIP data appear at the end of the book

This project has been supported by the French Ministry of Culture—Direction du Livre et de la
Lecture, Pro Helvetia, and the National Endowment for the Humanities Translation Fund.

Frontispiece: Engraving by Coteau, based on a plaster cast of Rousseau's head;
lithographed by Villain. Private Collection.

Contents

Contents

PREFACE

Although Jean-Jacques Rousseau is a significant figure in the Western tradition, there is no standard edition of his major writings available in English. Unlike those of other thinkers of comparable stature, moreover, many of Rousseau's important works either have never been translated or have become unavailable. The present edition of the *Collected Writings of Rousseau* is intended to meet this need.

Our goal is to produce a series that can provide a standard reference for scholarship that is accessible to all those wishing to read broadly in the corpus of Rousseau's work. To this end, the translations seek to combine care and faithfulness to the original French text with readability in English. Although, as every translator knows, there are often passages where it is impossible to meet this criterion, readers of a thinker and writer of Rousseau's stature deserve texts that have not been deformed by the interpretive bias of the translators or editors.

Wherever possible, existing translations of high quality have been used, although in some cases the editors have felt minor revisions were necessary to maintain the accuracy and consistency of the English versions. Where there was no English translation (or none of sufficient quality), a new translation has been prepared.

Each text is supplemented by editorial notes that clarify Rousseau's references and citations or passages otherwise not intelligible. Although these notes do not provide as much detail as is found in the critical apparatus of the Pléiade edition of the *Oeuvres complètes*, the English-speaking reader should nevertheless have in hand the basis for a more careful and comprehensive understanding of Rousseau than has hitherto been possible.

For Volume 2, we have focused on Rousseau's first major work, the *Discourse on the Sciences and Arts*, and the polemical exchanges between Rousseau and his critics that immediately followed its publication in 1750. Most of the attacks on the *First Discourse* have never been translated and are not widely known even in French; they provide a panorama of French intellectual life at the middle of the eighteenth century. Most of Rousseau's replies to these attacks have rarely been translated. The volume concludes with Rousseau's preface to his play, *Narcissus: Or the Lover of Himself* (in which Rousseau summed up the controversy in 1753). As a result, this volume provides a unique perspective on Rousseau's emergence as a major thinker during the years between 1750 and 1753.

October 1991   R.D.M.

                                           C.K.

Chronology of Works in Volume 2

1712
June 28: Jean-Jacques Rousseau born in Geneva.

1728
Rousseau leaves Geneva; ultimately settles in Chambéry with Mme. de Warens and pursues his self-education.

1742
Rousseau first arrives in Paris; meets leading musicians, writers, and scientists and, after two years as secretary to the French ambassador to Venice, returns to Paris and collaborates with Diderot.

1749
October: The Academy of Dijon proposes the topic "Has the restoration of the sciences and arts tended to purify morals?" for its prize competition. Rousseau reads the announcement in the *Mercury of France* while walking to Vincennes to visit Diderot, who has been imprisoned there.

1750
July: The Academy of Dijon awards Rousseau the prize for his *Discourse on the Sciences and Arts*.

1751
January: Probable date of the publication of the *Discourse on the Sciences and Arts* (later called *First Discourse*).

June: Publication of the "Observations on the *Discourse*" and "Letter to Raynal" in the *Mercury*.

September: Publication of King Stanislaus's "Reply" in the *Mercury*.

October: Publication of Rousseau's "Observations" and Gautier's "Refutation" in the *Mercury*.

November: Publication of "Letter to Grimm."

December: Publication of Bordes's *Discourse on the Advantages of the Sciences and Arts* in the *Mercury*. Bordes had delivered his discourse to the Academy of Lyon in June.

1752
April: Publication of Rousseau's "Final Reply" in answer to Bordes.

May: Publication of Rousseau's "Letter about a New Refutation."

August: Disclaimer of the Academy of Dijon.

1753

January or February: Publication of "Preface to *Narcissus*."

Summer: Rousseau works on the "Preface to a Second Letter to Bordes."

November: Academy of Dijon announces contest for the prize in moral philosophy on the subject "What is the source of inequality among men, and whether it is authorized by natural law."

1754

Rousseau works on *Discourse on the Origins of Inequality* (*Second Discourse*) and article on "Political Economy" for Volume 5 of the *Encyclopedia*.

1755

Publication of *Second Discourse* and "Political Economy."

1762

Publication of *Émile* and *Social Contract*. Rousseau's condemnation by the Parlement of Paris and his flight.

1772

Rousseau begins *Rousseau, Judge of Jean-Jacques* (the *Dialogues*).

1778

July 2: Rousseau dies at Ermenonville.

Introduction

Rousseau's Discourse on the
Sciences and Arts

In the two centuries since the publication of his political writings, Jean-Jacques Rousseau has been condemned and praised, studied seriously and dismissed as eccentric. Although he is often considered one of the most important political philosophers of the eighteenth century, his doctrines have been described as "necessarily inconsistent with each other"; praised as the clearest apostle of popular democracy, his political thought has been attacked as "totalitarian."[1] Whatever the judgment, most of those who have debated the meaning, character, and value of Rousseau's work have admitted its historical and current importance.

Rousseau himself claimed that his political thought forms a "system" directly addressing the perennial issues of human nature and history. Late in his life, Rousseau claimed that all of his writings were essentially devoted to the "principle that nature made man happy and good, but that society depraves him and makes him miserable."[2] Nor was this "principle" invented after the fact in order to bring unity to his ideas.[3] In January 1762, shortly before the *Social Contract* was published, Rousseau explained the inspiration for his philosophic career in a now famous letter to Malesherbes:

> I was going to see Diderot, then prisoner at Vincennes; I had in my pocket a *Mercury of France* that I leafed through on the way. I fell on the question of the Academy of Dijon, which gave rise to my first writing. If ever something was like a sudden inspiration, it is the movement which occurred to me at that reading; suddenly I felt my mind dazzled by a thousand lights. . . . Oh Monsieur, if I had ever been able to write a quarter of what I saw and felt under that tree, with what clarity would I have shown all the contradictions of the social system; with what force would I have exposed all the abuses of our institutions, with what simplicity would I have demonstrated that man is naturally good, and that it is by these institutions that men become wicked.[4]

How could it be, then, that an author who claimed to have developed a political "system" based on a single "principle" discovered in a moment of "illumination" has so confused readers?

The Intellectual Background

To understand Rousseau's political thought—and especially the *First Discourse* and the controversy it generated—it is well to begin with a brief summary of the eighteenth-century setting. In politics, the years prior to the French Revolution were the epoch of "enlightened despotism," symbolized by Frederick the Great of Prussia. The powers of traditional rulers, essentially unlimited by constitutional restraints, often seemed to be used arbitrarily. Despite criticisms, the French monarchy was incapable of fundamental reform because of its inability to challenge the vested rights of the aristocracy. Unmindful of the revolt that was to usher in an Age of Democratic Revolution at the end of the century, European rulers fought a series of limited wars, which only further obscured the coming internal upheavals. One can almost speak of a calm before the storm: "Après moi, le déluge."

In intellectual circles, however, calm was hardly in evidence. To understand the ferment of thought in eighteenth-century France, it is necessary to distinguish three main factors that form the philosophic background of Rousseau's political writings. The first of these was the "Great Tradition" of Western thought—what might be called the doctrine of the "establishment"—derived from the medieval inheritance of which St. Thomas Aquinas was the greatest representative. The orthodox segments of French society—church, king, and nobility—continued to insist on the unquestioned truth of Christian dogma, on the necessary and divinely sanctioned character of monarchy, and on the inherently rational character of the natural law that defined man's secular, moral, and social duties.

By the eighteenth century, however, these orthodox beliefs had begun to decay into mere ritual for many. In the preceding century, a powerful challenge to the traditional synthesis of reason and faith had already emerged. The naturalistic and secular philosophies of Bacon, Descartes, Hobbes, Spinoza, and Locke (the first four of whom are referred to in the *First Discourse*) can be called the second major factor in the intellectual background of Rousseau's thought.

These seventeenth-century thinkers had, broadly speaking, questioned the rational basis of the established notions of natural law, political justice, and religion. Their religious beliefs were unorthodox: atheism, deism, or Socinianism. They insisted that social and political justice needs a more solid basis than traditional philosophy and theology, which are too easily led astray by prejudice, custom, and error. The alternative was found in nature, both in the sense of physical nature as the source of all ideas (Hobbes's materialism and Locke's epistemology) and in the sense of an individualistic, presocial status as the reference point for natural law (hence, the importance of the "state of nature" for Hobbes, Spinoza, and Locke). By adopting such radical bases for their philosophical speculations, the seventeenth-century philosophers hoped to avoid the uncertainties of traditional metaphysical disputes. Patterning their thought on natural science (or "natural philosophy," as it was called in the age of Newton), they aspired to a new kind of knowledge, free from the errors of the orthodox teachings.

This profound criticism of the Great Tradition did not go unnoticed in the eighteenth century. On the contrary, there arose a movement dedicated to the diffusion of the new, nontheological rationalism modeled on the study of natural phenomena. This movement is the third element in the intellectual background of Rousseau's work; usually called the Enlightenment, its chief proponents are often described as the philosophes. Optimistic and skeptical all at once, critical of the prejudices and narrow-mindedness of those established in power, the philosophes believed that the mass of men could be "enlightened" by the spread of education and sound reasoning (such as was to be made possible by the massive *Encyclopedia* edited by Diderot at the same time Rousseau was writing). Once the erroneous beliefs of the age had been swept away, a more rational, just, and happy society could be established. Progress on earth was possible.[5]

While societies continued to be ruled by those who dogmatically maintained the established traditions of religion, politics, and morality, these traditions were undermined by the skeptical criticism diffused by the philosophes. The "Age of Enlightened Despotism" contained an inherent contradiction, since the enlightenment tended to destroy the foundations of absolute monarchy. Rousseau's thought, to which we now turn, lays bare the root of this contradiction.

Rousseau: Classic or Modern?

Although Rousseau is perhaps the most famous thinker of the eighteenth century, the curious paradox of his fame cannot be overemphasized: in his first major work, Rousseau radically rejected the outlook of the age he is often taken to represent. The decisive characteristic of eighteenth-century thought was the growing belief in enlightenment and progress, symbolized by Diderot's *Encyclopedia*. And yet, at a time when he was Diderot's best friend, Rousseau wrote a blistering attack on the enlightenment in his *Discourse on the Sciences and Arts* (or the *First Discourse*);[6] the spread of the arts and sciences, far from being a good thing as most supposed, was challenged by Rousseau as a corrupting influence on society.

Because he attacks the basic preconceptions of his contemporaries, the spirit behind Rousseau's thought must be questioned: was Rousseau inspired by a classical or by a modern conception of man, nature, and society? Since the *First Discourse* so explicitly argues that popular enlightenment is morally corrupting, it might be assumed that Rousseau depends solely on premodern traditions to prove that his own age—modernity—is in error. Nevertheless, Rousseau's *Second Discourse*[7] is based upon the principles introduced by Hobbes and Locke, who may be considered among the founders of the modern philosophical perspective. One need only mention the reputation of Rousseau as a forerunner of modern democracy (as well as his asserted responsibility for modern totalitarianism) to indicate that it is by no means easy to specify the underlying character of Rousseau's philosophy. Within the *First Discourse* itself, Rousseau praises modern thinkers such as Bacon, Newton, and Descartes.

The Attack on the Enlightenment: The First Discourse

The structure of the *First Discourse* is simple. If one disregards the brief foreword and preface added for publication, the work consists of a short introductory passage and two main parts. The first part is explicitly devoted to "historical inductions" intended to prove the proposition that "our souls have been corrupted in proportion to the advancement of our sciences and arts toward perfection."[8] Having asserted that the society of his time is morally depraved, Rousseau formulates the relationship between corruption and enlightenment as a phenomenon that "has been observed in all times and in all places."[9] He proceeds to give examples of what might be called a "law" of history, since it is as predictable as the tides: Ancient Egypt, Greece, Rome, and Constantinople, as well as modern China, have all been corrupted by the spread of knowledge, whereas the Persians, Scythians, Germans, early Romans, and Swiss were both virtuous and unenlightened; Sparta was moral and Athens corrupt. Admittedly, individuals may be both wise and virtuous, but the prime exemplar of such enlightened virtue, Socrates, was a bitter critic of the arts and sciences.[10] Fabricius, the early Roman hero, would have been horrified had he returned to see the corruption of Rome caused by literature and the arts.

In the second part of the *Discourse*, Rousseau turns to an analysis of the "sciences and arts in themselves" to explain the apparent contradiction between virtue and enlightenment. Human knowledge, whether of astronomy, rhetoric, geometry, physics, or morals, depends decisively on the prior existence of "our vices": the sciences are both symptoms of corruption and inherently dangerous. Rousseau specifies these dangers in detail. First, because error is a more likely consequence of speculation than is truth, study is not likely to achieve its proclaimed aim of knowledge. Second, the pursuit of the arts and sciences is a waste of time for a citizen. The discoveries of truly great scientists, like Newton, Descartes, and Bacon, do not directly teach the citizen to be virtuous; a fortiori, there is even less value in the works of the "crowd of writers" who try to disseminate philosophy and who serve only to destroy faith and virtue. Third, enlightenment always produces luxury, fatal both to sound morals and to political power. Rousseau lists a series of conquests of rich and enlightened nations by poorer and warlike peoples. He shows that luxury, by corrupting men, also corrupts taste; Rousseau contrasts the degradation of overly civilized men with the "simplicity of the earliest times." Fourth, the arts and sciences destroy the military virtues needed by any political community for its self-defense; Rousseau again adduces historical examples to buttress his assertion that modern soldiers, while brave, lack true force and strength. Finally, the spread of the arts, by forcing men to recognize and honor talent, produces rewards based on appearances rather than recompenses for actions. As a result, inequality among men develops on an artificial basis, unrelated to true virtue.

Rousseau then praises the academies (like that of Dijon), declaring that their functions mitigate the dangers of the arts, letters, and sciences, and again attacks the "crowds" of authors who diffuse learning.[11] Those who cannot go far in the sciences should be artisans,[12] whereas those who can make truly great intellectual advances—the "preceptors of the human race"—need no teachers: the functions of the philosophes and encyclopedists, who try to spread knowledge, are either unnecessary or pernicious. Rousseau concludes that the true philosophers, such as Newton, Descartes, and Bacon, should become advisers to kings; only when political power and scientific knowledge work in harmony can the arts and sciences be profitable. As for the common man, Rousseau concludes that he should avoid study and knowledge, devoting himself to the practice of his true duty: "Let us leave to others the care of informing peoples of their duties, and limit ourselves to fulfilling well our own. . . . O virtue! . . . is it not enough in order to learn your laws to commune with oneself and listen to the voice of one's conscience in the silence of the passions? That is true philosophy."[13]

It takes little reflection to see that the *First Discourse* can be criticized as being self-contradictory: Rousseau criticizes the arts and sciences, yet he writes an erudite discourse for an academy of arts and sciences. Rousseau himself saw this problem: "How can one dare blame the sciences before one of Europe's most learned Societies, praise ignorance in a famous Academy, and reconcile contempt for study with respect for the truly learned? I have seen these contradictions, and they have not rebuffed me."[14] Given this assertion, the superficial inconsistency of the *First Discourse* can hardly be the ground for rejecting Rousseau's position; rather one must look for an underlying principle that could explain the paradox.

The reconciliation of "these contradictions" cited by Rousseau can be found in the conception of knowledge developed in classical antiquity, most notably by Plato.[15] According to many ancient philosophers, there is a fundamental distinction between the opinions of most men and true knowledge, accessible only to a few. The opinions of a given society at a given time are held uncritically by the average citizen, but he who would devote his life to the pursuit of wisdom must be willing to question such commonly held beliefs. Philosophy presupposes doubt; by examining popular notions with an open mind, one can come to understand the universal truths behind them.

The character and bearing of this classical dichotomy of knowledge and opinion may be clearer if some of the main points of Plato's thought are indicated. According to the *Republic*, the best political order that could be wished for would be rule by a "philosopher-king." But for Plato this is a paradox: Socrates speaks of his fear that the idea of a philosopher-king will be laughed at as ridiculous and impossible.[16] It is paradoxical to talk of a philosopher who is king because the philosopher is motivated by a disinterested search for truth, whereas the king or ruler is concerned with radically different matters, such as material welfare and power, about which he must be partisan. Indeed, to realize the best political regime, Plato asserts that philosophers would have to be compelled to rule.[17] True philosophy—the impartial quest for wisdom—is essentially opposed to politics.

The opposition between politics and philosophy, derived from the distinction between knowledge and opinion, has far-reaching implications. Philosophy is the highest human activity, but it is an activity open to few. For the rest of the human species—the "ordinary men"—

philosophy is dangerous because it depends on a doubting of common opinions (like the belief that the laws and customs of one's own country are always right and just). Politics and political virtue are the standard for most; patriotism is a positive good because only within a particular, "historical" society can the average man have an idea of what is good or bad.

The stability and soundness of popular opinion require a small community, relatively independent of foreign pressures and composed of patriotic citizens who prefer the public good to private gain. But political virtue is, by itself, insufficient; the best society must also permit (and, indeed, require) a few men to study philosophy. These few must be able to doubt without shaking the beliefs of the many. When a society of virtuous patriots tolerates the existence of philosophers and permits them to direct its political destinies, the goodness of the citizens can be combined with the superior knowledge of which some men are capable. Any other solution, which attempts to merge knowledge with popular opinion, will produce neither stability nor wisdom.[18]

This restatement of Plato's conception of philosophy and politics, however imperfect, should at least indicate the classical elements in Rousseau's thought. Rousseau always criticized the political trend toward large states based on commercial economies, clearly in evidence by the eighteenth century. In the name of "virtue" he consistently emphasized the superiority of the small city-state of classical antiquity, mirrored in his native city of Geneva. He argued that it is impossible for the citizens of a large society to know each other and to concern themselves with the common good; men devoted to private economic enterprises cannot place the public interest above their own selfish desires. The only truly sound political community must be based on patrotism and virtue, like Sparta and republican Rome.

Rousseau consequently preferred the political conceptions of the ancients to those of the moderns: "Ancient Political thinkers incessantly talked about morals and virtue, those of our time talk only of business and money."[19] To achieve justice, one must go back to the classical conception of a small political unit animated by patrotism. If political improvement is possible, it is not that reform, based on a diffusion of scientific knowledge, that philosophes contemplated. Since popular enlightenment is intrinsically corrupting, the education of the mass of men should be oriented toward the strengthening of healthy opinions, virtue, and patrotism.

This does not mean that philosophy or science is, as such, "bad." The few men capable of a disinterested search for truth are "the preceptors of the human race"; they alone can "raise monuments to the glory of human intellect."[20] But the role of the philosopher is that of an adviser to the ruler, not that of a popular educator. The philosophes failed to see that there is an insoluble contradiction between philosophy and politics, a contradiction that can be resolved (insofar as such a resolution is possible) only on the grounds of classical thought.

Rousseau's Critics and the Unity of His "System"

The publication of the *First Discourse* was the occasion of immediate and widespread controversy. At the outset, public attention was drawn to the essay by the announcement of the Academy of Dijon's prize in the *Mercury of France*. Since the editor, the Abbé Raynal, was an acquaintance of Rousseau's, it is perhaps not surprising that the "Observations on the Discourse Which Was Awarded the First Prize at Dijon" encouraged the author to develop his ideas further in response to the objections and queries. Rousseau's reply, the "Letter to Raynal," sets the tone for much that will follow:

I know in advance the great words that will be used to attack me: enlightenment, knowledge, laws, morality, reason, propriety, consideration, gentleness, amenity, politeness, education, etc. To all that I will reply only with two other words, which ring even more loudly in my ear, Virtue, truth. I will write constantly, Truth, virtue! If anyone perceives only words in this, I have nothing more to say to him.[21]

Rousseau "knows in advance" the nature of the debate—and he has taken the high ground, the ancient combination of ethical principle (virtue) and philosophic wisdom (truth) characterizing Plato's Socrates in his attack on the sophists.

The first major reply to Rousseau came from an unusual quarter: King Stanislaus I of Poland, cousin of the French king. The "Reply . . . by the King of Poland," published in the *Mercury* in September 1751, could be said to represent the position of the "establishment" in more ways than one. For those in power in eighteenth-century Europe, as today, the moral effects of the sciences and arts are inherently positive: "The more the sciences are cultivated in a State, the more the State flourishes."[22] Not only does learning contribute to morals by making it easier for men to "do well," but ignorance is often associated with vice and crime.

For King Stanislaus, the effects of the sciences and arts are not limited to a secular definition of politics and morality: "The more the Christian . . . studies revelation, the stronger his faith becomes."[23] Individual scientists are defended from the charge of moral corruption on the grounds that they are often poor, without power and without concern for material gain; the scientific community is defended from the charge of moral corruption on the grounds that vice arises from wealth and the human tendency to "abuse" all things, not from knowledge and science in themselves.

Rousseau's answer, the *Observations*, adopts a deferential but firm tone in rejecting the king's criticisms. In the *Confessions*, Rousseau indicates that this response is a unique work in that it shows how to combine pride and respect while defending the truth against a king. [24] Admitting from the outset that he views science as "very good in itself,"[25] Rousseau makes three basic points. First, the socially corrupting effects of the scientific community as a whole do not mean that individual scientists or writers are necessarily corrupt; second, there is no fundamental contradiction between Rousseau's act of writing and his criticism of those who write, for even the Church Fathers used the tools of pagan science and philosophy to defend their faith against paganism; and finally, the essential distinction that needs to be drawn is between true science or philosophy and the false claimants to those titles.

Beneath the direct rejoinders, however, one begins to glimpse more clearly the broader theory on which Rousseau's argument rests. Perhaps the most essential element in this perspective is the assertion that history has a direction or tendency, the tendency for developed or civilized societies to become corrupt: "It is with sadness that I am going to pronounce a great and deadly truth. It is only one step from knowledge to ignorance, and alternation from one to the other is frequent in Nations. But once a people has been corrupted, it has never been seen to return to virtue."[26] History tends toward corruption, if only because political or social virtue cannot be regained once they have been lost:

You would try in vain to destroy the sources of evil. You would take away in vain the nourishment of vanity, idleness, and luxury. You would even return men in vain to that first equality, preserver of innocence and source of all virtue. Their hearts once spoiled will be so forever. There is no remedy short of some great revolution—almost as much to be feared as the evil it might cure—and which is blameworthy to desire and impossible to foresee.[27]

It is "equality," not education or religion, that serves to preserve "innocence" and instill "virtue." Although a "great revolution" might restore equality and virtue, it is "blameworthy to desire" because such a revolution is impossible to control and extremely likely to aggravate the problem. Under these conditions, especially in the monarchies dominating most of Europe, the sciences and arts are unavoidable features that may even mitigate some of the ills of which they are symptoms.

Rousseau's reply to the king of Poland did not, of course, silence his critics. In the following months, a series of essays appeared rebutting the *First Discourse* and attacking its author. Because they provide a panorama of intellectual life in the middle of the eighteenth century, it is instructive to read the arguments of Rousseau's critics (most never before translated into English) as well as his rejoinders. While it is not possible to analyze each in detail here, a word on each of the attacks on Rousseau and his way of answering it will indicate the character of the debate.

The "Refutation of the Observations of Jean-Jacques Rousseau of Geneva" makes explicit the conventional position of the Great Tradition described above and exemplified by King Stanislaus's original reply. The *First Discourse* is "a web of contradictions" because enlightenment and the sciences are "sparks of the Divinity" that God "made for man"; their abuses are due to human sin rather than to the sciences and arts themselves.[28] Rousseau did not specifically answer this rejoinder, which illustrates how eighteenth-century Catholicism could be used to justify the development of education in the arts and sciences.

The "Refutation" by Canon Joseph Gautier, a professor of mathematics and history at Lunéville, illustrates the position of the academics of the day. Following the structure of the *First Discourse* and rebutting it point by point, Gautier insists not only that the sciences and arts are necessary and helpful, but that the abuses associated with them stem from ubiquitous flaws in human nature rather than from faults peculiar to the cultivation of the mind. Rousseau's response, a classic of polemic writing, was to publish a letter to his friend Grimm in which he explains why he will not answer Gautier directly. By rebutting Gautier without recognizing him as a serious critic, the *Letter to Grimm* shows Rousseau's capacity for sarcasm and irony: after belittling Gautier's reasoning, Rousseau wonders whether Gautier wasn't secretly in agreement with the *First Discourse* and wrote against it merely to defend his professional interests. In short, Rousseau suggests, Gautier is either a fool because his arguments are so weak or a knave because he knows better but is dissembling for selfish reasons. In suggesting these options, Rousseau rejects Gautier's insistence that there is an easy harmony between the self-interest of intellectuals and political responsibility.

The next major critic was not so easily dismissed. Unlike the earlier critics, who attempted to reconcile the tradition and the enlightenment, this critic was a self-conscious partisan of modernity. The "Discourse on the Advantages of the Sciences and Arts" by Charles Bordes, a friend of Rousseau's, focuses on history and culture as setting humans apart from other species. More important, Bordes stresses the distinctness of modern politics, in which the sciences and arts make possible larger and more powerful states than existed in antiquity: "Here a new order of things is developing. It is no longer a question of those small domestic kingdoms closed in the walls of a city . . . it is a vast and powerful monarchy" based on science and technology.[29] In short, Bordes presents the views of the serious intellectuals of the day, for whom Rousseau's argument challenges not only the progress of modernity over the ancients but the progress of humans over other animals.

In the "Final Reply," Rousseau takes this criticism seriously.[30] Emphasizing again that the sciences and arts are the "masterpieces" of human reason, Rousseau points out the difference between philosophy and its effects on society. In so doing, he suggests a double preference for antiquity: Ancient philosophy is preferable to that of the moderns because it was destined for the few, on the assumption that humans differ fundamentally in intellect; ancient politics is politically preferable to that of the moderns because it was republican, on the assumption that citizens do not differ fundamentally in their capacity for civic virtue.

The last criticism to which Rousseau responded is not merely the most detailed of the attacks on the *First Discourse* but also probably the most representative of the phenomenon in question. Although the rejoinder to Bordes was intended to close the debate, Rousseau felt compelled to answer a "Refutation of the Discourse Which Won the Prize of the Academy of Dijon in the Year 1750, by an Academician of Dijon Who Denied It His Vote." This attack, published in 1752, goes through Rousseau's text point by point in the manner of a teacher correcting the essay of an ill-prepared student. Precisely because the arguments were neither substantial nor novel, the fact that the author claimed to be a member of the Academy of Dijon called for a rejoinder.

The academy itself, to defend its decision and its reputation, then published a disavowal, making it clear that the author of the refutation—Claude-Nicolas Lecat, secretary of the Academy of Sciences of Rouen—was not one of its members. Although Rousseau himself had no way of knowing this at the time of writing his rejoinder, Lecat's combination of dishonesty and pedantry reflects precisely the defects of eighteenth century letters that were the immediate target of the *First Discourse*.

Two texts provide a summary of the debate and the place of the *Discourse on the Sciences and Arts* in Rousseau's thought more broadly. In the fragmentary "Preface to a Second Letter to Bordes," started as a reply to Bordes's rejoinder to the "Final Reply" but never completed or published, Rousseau indicates for the first time the deeper intentions behind his criticism of the sciences and arts. This short manuscript is invaluable as a demonstration of the "unity" of Rousseau's "sad but great System," which Bordes had been the first contemporary to notice.[31] Making explicit the extent to which he had hidden a more complex argument in the *First Discourse*, Rousseau admits using the techniques of esoteric writing in the service of a comprehensive philosophic alternative to both the Great Tradition and its challenge by the philosophes.

After repeating the duality of "truth and virtue" as his principles,[32] Rousseau suggests for the first time that his "system" will attack the very legitimacy of established government:

> If the Discourse of Dijon alone excited so many murmurs and caused so much scandal, what would have happened if I had from the first instant developed the entire extent of a System that is true but distressing, of which the question treated in this Discourse is only a Corollary? A declared enemy of the violence of the wicked, I would at the very least have passed for the enemy of public tranquillity. . . .
>
> Some precautions were thus at first necessary for me, and it is in order to be able to make everything understood that I did not wish to say everything. It was only gradually and always for few Readers that I developed my ideas. It is not myself that I treated carefully, but the truth, so as to get it across more surely and make it useful. I have often taken great pains to try to put into a Sentence, a line, a word tossed off as if by chance the result of a long sequence of reflections. Often, most of my Readers must have found my discourses badly connected and almost entirely rambling, for lack of perceiving the trunk of which I showed them only the branches.[33]

Since the blunt statement of the truth would have destroyed "public tranquillity," Rousseau admits to having written for "few Readers"—the true philosophers—who are to see a "System that is true but distressing." If nothing else, the "Preface to a Second Letter to Bordes" demonstrates that Rousseau had developed a coherent theoretical position several years before the publication of the *Discourse on Inequality* in 1755.[34]

The principles of Rousseau's system include, of course, a violent attack on contemporary forms of social, economic, and political inequality as unnatural and illegitimate. The *First Discourse*'s attack on the sciences and arts as manifestations of and supports for this inequality is a corollary of this system. Its foundation is developed in the assertion of natural goodness in the *Second Discourse*. The paradoxical combination of an elitist view of science and an egalitarian view of politics, which is only fully apparent when one considers Rousseau's mature political writings as the presentation of a coherent philosophical position, becomes more evident as Rousseau summarizes the entire controversy arising from the Academy of Dijon's prize.

This understanding of the place of the *First Discourse* in Rousseau's system is confirmed by the preface to Rousseau's play, *Narcissus: Or the*

Lover of Himself, which concludes the present volume. The publication of this play provided an occasion to justify the paradox of a writer who had attacked writers by publishing an academic discourse against the scholarship of academicians. The preface, written in the fall of 1752, summarizes Rousseau's view of the arts and sciences by emphasizing the place of drama and popular letters rather than philosophy as such. In so doing, Rousseau focuses in a practical way on his concern for the effects of intellectual life on the average citizen—and therewith the egalitarian view of human nature that became the explicit basis of Rousseau's challenge to authority in the *Second Discourse* and *Social Contract*.

Rousseau's Originality

To use contemporary terms, Rousseau's principles are "democratic" and "revolutionary." But whereas democrats or revolutionaries often imply that historical progress will inevitably result if corrupt regimes are swept away, Rousseau rejects such an optimistic view of history—and yet still favors a republican or egalitarian form of government. In other words, the revolutionary side of Rousseau's thought takes on added power precisely because he accepts the view of history usually adopted by traditionalists; the argument that many societies will inevitably be ruled by despots and tyrants only makes the assertion of political freedom all the more striking.

Rousseau's originality thus lies in his attempt to combine a view of human nature derived from moderns like Hobbes and Locke with a view of history derived from ancients like Plato and Aristotle. In his later writings, Rousseau shows how he proposes to replace the aggressive or rational egoism of Hobbes and Locke with the more passive and instinctive self-preservation of isolated animals. And while sharing the ancients' skepticism toward radical historical progress, Rousseau modifies it by presenting scientific principles that show how to construct a legitimate and free government, at least in some instances.

If Rousseau is considered in terms of his conceptions of human nature and of history, which are fundamental to all political thought, the coherence of his "political system" becomes clearer. Unlike most writers, he not only saw why prior political philosophers had been divided by these basic issues, he also transformed the terms of the debate in his attempt to resolve it. In short, Jean-Jacques Rousseau is one of the few political theorists who goes to the root of most of the perennial questions and who thereby contributed new concepts if not a new frame of reference to our understanding of politics.

Note on the Text

This translation is an effort to provide an English version that corresponds word for word (as far as possible) with the French texts of Rousseau and his critics. Wherever possible, words have been translated consistently both within and between Rousseau's political writings. Although this goal may cause some awkwardness, it has the advantage of permitting the reader to come to his own conclusions with the smallest danger that the translation will have imposed a particular interpretation.

The translation of the *First Discourse* was originally published by St. Martin's Press (1964) and is reproduced here with permission. As a basic text for the *First Discourse*, the excellent critical edition of George R. Havens (*Jean-Jacques Rousseau: Discours sur les sciences et les arts* [New York: Modern Language Association of America, 1946]) was used. Translations have then been compared with the texts in volume 3 of the Pléiade edition of Rousseau's *Oeuvres Complètes* (edited by Jean Starobinski) and volume 2 of the Intégrale edition of Rousseau's *Oeuvres complètes*, edited by Michel Launay (Paris: Seuil—l'Intégrale, 1971), neither of which was published until after St Martin's Press had published the translation of the *First Discourse*.

Most of the essays written by Rousseau's critics and his rejoinders to them were newly translated for the present edition by Judith R. Bush under a generous grant from the National Endowment for the Humanities. The "Discourse on the Advantages of the Sciences and Arts" was translated by Roger D. Masters. The "Refutation" by Lecat and Rousseau's preface to *Narcissus* were translated by Christopher Kelly. Many of these texts are not available in the Pléiade and have been based on Launay's edition of Rousseau's *Oeuvres complètes*, in the Collection l'Intégrale published by Editions du Seuil. To facilitate locating the original French text, the running heads will indicate pages in the Pléiade (*Pl., III. 100*) or Launay's edition (*Int., II. 100*).

In order to provide consistency throughout, a few minor modifications in previously published translations have been necessary.

We would like to thank the Beinecke Rare Book Library of Yale University for permission to consult the first editions of the discourses and a manuscript translation of the *Second Discourse* written by John Farrington of Clapham, England, in 1756. Farrington's version, which is superior to the other translations we have found, suggested solutions to several difficult problems. We would also like to thank Richard P. Duval for assistance in translating Rousseau's Latin quotations in the discourses.

We thank the following publishers for permission to reprint quotations from the works indicated: Thomas Nelson (Frederick Watkins, trans., *Rousseau: Political Writings*); E. P. Dutton, Everyman's Library (Richard Crawley, trans., *Thucydides' The History of the Peloponnesian War*).

DISCOURSE

Which Won the Prize

of the Academy of Dijon

In the year 1750

On the Question proposed by that Academy:

*Has the restoration of the sciences &
arts tended to purify morals?*

By a Citizen of Geneva

Barbarus hic ego sum quia non intelligor illis.
Ovid.[1]

GENEVA

Barillot & Son

Satyr, you do not know it.

Foreword

WHAT IS CELEBRITY? Here is the unfortunate work to which I owe mine. Certainly this piece, which won me a prize and made me famous, is at best mediocre, and I dare add that it is one of the slightest of this whole collection.[2] What an abyss of miseries the author would have avoided if only this first written work had been received as it deserved to be! But a favor that was unjustified to begin with inevitably brought upon me, by degrees, a harsh penalty[3] that is even more unjustified.

Preface

HERE IS ONE of the greatest and finest questions ever debated. This Discourse is not concerned with those metaphysical subtleties that have prevailed in all parts of Literature and from which the Announcements of Academic competitions are not always exempt; rather, it is concerned with one of those truths that pertain to the happiness of mankind.

I foresee that I will not easily be forgiven for the side I have dared to take. Running counter to everything that men admire today, I can expect only universal blame; and the fact of having been honored by the approval of a few Wise men does not allow me to count on the approval of the Public. But then my mind is made up; I do not care to please either the Witty or the Fashionable. At all times there will be men destined to be subjugated by the opinions of their century, their Country, their Society. A man who plays the free Thinker and Philosopher today would, for the same reason, have been only a fanatic at the time of the League.[4] One must not write for such Readers when one wants to live beyond one's century.

Another word and I am done. Little expecting the honor I received, I had, since submitting it, reworked and expanded this Discourse, to the point of making in a sense another work of it; today I consider myself obliged to restore it to the state in which it was honored. I have merely jotted down some notes and left two easily recognized additions of which the Academy might not have approved.[5] I thought that equity, respect, and gratitude required of me this notice.

DISCOURSE

Decipimur specie recti.[6]

HAS THE RESTORATION of the Sciences and Arts tended to purify or corrupt Morals?[7] That is the subject to be examined. Which side should I take in this question? The one, Gentlemen, that suits a decent man who knows nothing and yet does not think any the less of himself.

It will be difficult, I feel, to adapt what I have to say to the Tribunal before which I appear. How can one dare blame the sciences before one of Europe's most learned Societies, praise ignorance in a famous Academy, and reconcile contempt for study with respect for the truly Learned? I have seen these contradictions, and they have not rebuffed me. I am not abusing Science, I told myself; I am defending Virtue before virtuous men. Integrity is even dearer to good People than erudition to Scholars. What then have I to fear? The enlightenment[8] of the Assembly that listens to me? I admit such a fear; but it applies to the construction of the discourse and not to the sentiment of the Orator. Equitable Sovereigns have never hesitated to condemn themselves in doubtful disputes; and the position most advantageous for one with a just cause is to have to defend himself against an upright and enlightened Opponent who is judge of his own case.[9]

This motive which encourages me is joined by another which determines me: having upheld, according to my natural intellect, the cause of truth, whatever the outcome there is a Prize which I cannot fail to receive; I will find it at the bottom of my heart.

FIRST PART

It is a grand and beautiful sight to see man emerge from obscurity somehow by his own efforts; dissipate, by the light of his reason, the darkness in which nature had enveloped him; rise above himself; soar intellectually into celestial regions; traverse with Giant steps, like the Sun, the vastness of the Universe; and—what is even grander and more difficult—come back to himself to study man and know his nature, his duties, and his end. All of these marvels have been revived in recent Generations.

Europe had sunk back into the Barbarism of the first ages. The Peoples of that Part of the World which is today so enlightened lived, a few centuries ago, in a condition worse than ignorance. A nondescript scientific jargon, even more despicable than ignorance, had usurped the name of knowledge, and opposed an almost invincible obstacle to its return. A revolution was needed to bring men back to common sense; it finally came from the least expected quarter. The stupid Moslem, the eternal scourge of Letters, brought about their rebirth among us. The fall of the Throne of Constantine brought into Italy the debris of ancient Greece.[10] France in turn was enriched by these precious spoils. Soon the sciences followed Letters; the Art of writing was joined by the Art of thinking—an order which seems strange but which is perhaps only too natural; and people began to feel the principal advantage of commerce with the muses, that of making men more sociable by inspiring in them the desire to please one another with works worthy of their mutual approval.

The mind has its needs as does the body. The needs of the body are the foundations of society, those of the mind make it pleasant. While Government and Laws provide for the safety and well-being of assembled men, the Sciences, Letters, and Arts, less despotic and perhaps more powerful, spread garlands of flowers over the iron chains with which men are burdened, stifle in them the sentiment of that original liberty for which they seemed to have been born, make them love their slavery, and turn them into what is called civilized peoples. Need raised Thrones; the Sciences and Arts have strengthened them. Earthly powers, love talents and protect those who cultivate them.* Civilized peoples, cultivate talents: happy slaves, you owe to them that delicate and refined taste on which you pride yourselves; that softness of character and urbanity of morals which make relations among you so amiable and easy; in a word, the semblance of all the virtues without the possession of any.

By this sort of civility, the more pleasant because it is unpretentious, Athens and Rome once distinguished themselves in the much vaunted days of their magnificence and splendor. It is by such civility that our century and our Nation will no doubt surpass all times and all Peoples. A philosophic tone without pedantry; natural yet engaging manners, equally remote from Teutonic simplicity and Italian pantomime: these are the fruits of the taste acquired by good education and perfected in social intercourse.

How sweet it would be to live among us if exterior appearance were always the image of the heart's disposition; if decency were virtue; if our maxims served as our rules; if true Philosophy were inseparable from the

---

*Princes always view with pleasure the spread, among their subjects, of the taste for Arts of amusement and superfluities which do not result in the exportation of money. For, besides fostering that pettiness of soul so appropriate to servitude, they very well know that all needs the Populace gives itself are so many chains binding it. Alexander, desiring to keep the Ichthyophagi dependent on him, forced them to give up fishing and to eat foodstuffs common to other Peoples; but the American Savages who go naked and live on the yield of their hunting have never been subjugated. Indeed, what yoke would one impose on men who need nothing?

title of Philosopher! But so many qualities are too rarely combined, and virtue seldom walks in such great pomp. Richness of attire may announce a wealthy man, and elegance a man of taste; the healthy, robust man is known by other signs. It is in the rustic clothes of a Farmer and not beneath the gilt of a Courtier that strength and vigor of the body will be found. Ornamentation is no less foreign to virtue, which is the strength and vigor of the soul. The good man is an Athlete who likes to compete in the nude. He disdains all those vile ornaments which would hamper the use of his strength, most of which were invented only to hide some deformity.

Before Art had molded our manners and taught our passions to speak an affected language, our morals were rustic but natural, and differences of conduct announced at first glance those of character. Human nature, basically, was no better, but men found their security in the ease of seeing through each other, and that advantage, which we no longer appreciate, spared them many vices.

Today, when subtler researches and a more refined taste have reduced the Art of pleasing to principles, a base and deceptive uniformity prevails in our morals, and all minds seem to have been cast in the same mold. Incessantly politeness requires, propriety demands; incessantly usage is followed, never one's own genius. One no longer dares to appear as he is; and in this perpetual constraint, the men who form this herd called society, placed in the same circumstances, will all do the same things unless stronger motives deter them. Therefore one will never know well those with whom he deals, for to know one's friend thoroughly, it would be necessary to wait for emergencies—that is, to wait until it is too late, as it is for these very emergencies that it would have been essential to know him.

What a procession of vices must accompany this uncertainty! No more sincere friendships; no more real esteem; no more well-based confidence. Suspicions, offenses, fears, coldness, reserve, hate, betrayal will hide constantly under that uniform and false veil of politeness, under that much vaunted urbanity which we owe to the enlightenment of our century. The name of the Master of the Universe will no longer be profaned by swearing, but it will be insulted by blasphemies without offending our scrupulous ears. Men will not boast of their own merit, but they will disparage that of others. An enemy will not be grossly insulted, but he will be cleverly slandered. National hatreds will die out, but so will love of Fatherland.[11] For scorned ignorance, a dangerous Pyrrhonism will be substituted.[12] There will be some forbidden excesses, some dishonored vices, but others will be dignified with the name of virtues; one must either have them or affect them. Whoever wants to praise the sobriety of the Wise men of our day may do so; as for me, I see in it only a refinement of intemperance as unworthy of my praise as their cunning simplicity.*

Such is the purity our morals have acquired. Thus have we become good People. It is for Letters, the Sciences, and the Arts to claim their share of such a wholesome piece of work. I will add only one thought: an Inhabitant of some faraway lands who wanted to form a notion of European morals on the basis of the state of the Sciences among us, the perfection of our Arts, the decency of our Entertainments, the politeness of our manners, the affability of our speech, our perpetual demonstrations of goodwill, and that tumultuous competition of men of all ages and conditions who seem anxious to oblige one another from Dawn to Dark; that Foreigner, I say, would guess our morals to be exactly the opposite of what they are.

When there is no effect, there is no cause to seek. But here the effect is certain, the depravity real, and our souls have been corrupted in proportion to the advancement of our Sciences and Arts to perfection. Can it be said that this is a misfortune particular to our age? No, Gentlemen; the evils caused by our vain curiosity are as old as the world. The daily ebb and flow of the Ocean's waters have not been more steadily subject to the course of the Star which gives us light during the night[13] than has the fate of morals and integrity been subject to the advancement of the Sciences and Arts. Virtue has fled as their light dawned on our horizon, and the same phenomenon has been observed in all times and in all places.

Consider Egypt, that first school of the Universe, that climate so fertile under a bronze sky, that famous country from which Sesostris departed long ago to conquer the World.[15] Egypt became the mother of Philosophy and the fine Arts, and soon after, she was conquered by Cambyses,[16] then by the Greeks, the Romans, the Arabs, and finally the Turks.

Consider Greece, formerly populated by Heroes who twice conquered Asia, once at Troy and once in their own hearths. Nascent Letters had not yet brought corruption into the hearts of its Inhabitants, but the progress of the Arts, the dissolution of morals, and the yoke of the Macedonian[17] followed each other closely; and Greece, always learned, always voluptuous, and always enslaved, no longer experienced anything in her

---

*"I like," says Montaigne, "to argue and discuss, but only with a few men and for myself. For to serve as a spectacle to the Great and to show off competitively one's wit and one's babble is, I find, a very inappropriate occupation for an honorable man." It is the occupation of all our wits, save one.[14]

revolutions but a change of masters. All the eloquence of Demosthenes could never revive a body enervated by luxury and the Arts.[18]

It is in the time of Ennius and Terence[19] that Rome, founded by a Shepherd and made famous by Farmers, begins to degenerate. But after Ovid, Catullus, Martial, and that crowd of obscene Authors whose names alone alarm decency, Rome, formerly the Temple of Virtue, becomes the Theatre of crime, the shame of Nations, and the plaything of barbarians. That World Capital finally falls under the yoke she had imposed on so many Peoples, and the day of her fall was the eve of the day one of her Citizens was given the title Arbiter of Good Taste.[20]

What shall I say about that Metropolis of the Eastern Empire which, by its position, seemed destined to be the metropolis of the whole world, that refuge of the Sciences and Arts when they were banned from the rest of Europe perhaps more through wisdom than barbarism. All that is most shameful in debauchery and corruption, most heinous in betrayals, assassinations and poisons, most atrocious in the combination of all crimes, forms the fabric of the History of Constantinople. Such is the pure source from which we received the Enlightenment of which our century boasts.

But why seek in remote times proofs of a truth for which we have existing evidence before our eyes. In Asia there is an immense country where honors for Letters lead to the highest offices of the State. If the Sciences purified morals, if they taught men to shed their blood for their Fatherland, if they aroused courage, the Peoples of China would be wise, free, and invincible. But if there is no vice that does not dominate them, no crime with which they are not familiar; if neither the enlightenment of Government Officials, nor the supposed wisdom of Laws, nor the multitude of Inhabitants of that vast Empire were able to save it from the yoke of the ignorant and coarse Tartar, what purpose did all its Learned men serve? What benefit has resulted from the honors bestowed on them? Could it consist in being populated by slaves and wicked men?

Contrast these pictures with that of the morals of those few Peoples who, preserved from this contamination of vain knowledge, have by their own virtues created their own happiness and an example for other Nations. Such were the first Persians, an extraordinary Nation where one learned virtue as one learns Science among us, which conquered Asia with such ease, and which alone had the glory of having the history of its institutions taken for a Philosophic Novel.[21] Such were the Scythians, about whom we have been left magnificent praises. Such were the Germans, whose simplicity, innocence, and virtues a writer—tired of tracing the crimes and foul deeds of an educated, opulent, and voluptuous

People—took comfort in describing.[22] Such had been Rome itself at the time of its poverty and ignorance. Such to this day, finally, is that rustic nation so much praised for its courage, which could not be destroyed by adversity, and for its fidelity, which could not be corrupted by bad example.*

It is not through stupidity that the latter have preferred other exercises to those of the mind. They were not unaware that in other lands idle men spent their lives debating about the sovereign good, vice and virtue; and that proud reasoners, giving themselves the highest praises, lumped all other Peoples together under the contemptuous name of barbarians. But they considered their morals and learned to disdain their doctrine.**

Could I forget that in the very heart of Greece rose that City as renowned for its happy ignorance as for the wisdom of its Laws, that Republic of demi-Gods rather than men, so superior did their virtues seem to humanity? O Sparta! you eternally put to shame a vain doctrine! While the vices which accompany the fine Arts entered Athens together with them, while a Tyrant there so carefully collected the works of the Prince of Poets,[25] you chased the Arts and Artists, the Sciences and Scientists away from your walls.

The outcome showed this difference. Athens became the abode of civility and good taste, the country of Orators and Philosophers. The elegance of Buildings there corresponded to that of the language. Marble and canvas, animated by the hands of the most skillful Masters, were seen everywhere. From Athens came those astonishing works that will serve as models in all corrupt ages. The Picture of Lacedaemon is less brilliant. "There," said other Peoples, "men are born virtuous and the very air of the Country seems to instill virtue." Of its inhabitants nothing is left to us except the memory of their heroic actions. Should such monuments be worth less to us than the curious statues Athens has left us?[26]

Some wise men, it is true, resisted the general torrent and kept themselves from vice while dwelling with the Muses. But listen to the judg-

---

*I dare not speak of those happy Nations which do not even know by name the vices we have so much trouble repressing, those savages in America whose simple and natural regulations Montaigne does not hesitate to prefer not only to the Laws of Plato, but even to everything Philosophy could ever imagine as most perfect for the government of Peoples. He cites numerous striking examples for anyone who would know how to appreciate them. But just think, he says, they don't wear pants!"[23]

**In good faith, will someone tell me what opinion the Athenians themselves must have had concerning eloquence when they so carefully kept it away from that upright Tribunal against whose Judgments the Gods themselves never appealed? What did the Romans think of medicine when they banished it from their Republic? And when a remnant of humanity brought the Spanish to forbid their Lawyers to enter America, what idea must they have had of Jurisprudence? Could one not say that they believed they atoned, by this one Act, for all the evils they had caused those unfortunate Indians.[24]

ment that the first and most unhappy of them made of the Learned men and Artists of his time.

"I examined the Poets," he says, "and I consider them to be men whose talent deceives themselves and others, who claim to be wise men, who are taken to be such, and who are nothing of the kind.

"From Poets," continues Socrates, "I turned to Artists. No one knew less of the Arts than I; no one was more convinced that Artists possessed some very beautiful secrets. However, I perceived that their condition is no better than that of the Poets, and that they are all under the same prejudice. Because the most skillful among them excel in their Specialty, they consider themselves the wisest of men. This presumption altogether tarnished their knowledge in my eyes. So it was that, putting myself in the place of the Oracle and asking myself which I would rather be, what I am or what they are, to know what they have learned or to know that I know nothing, I answered myself and the God: I want to remain what I am.

"We do not know, neither the Sophists, nor the Poets, nor the Orators, nor the Artists, nor I, what is the true, the good, and the beautiful. But between us there is this difference: although those men know nothing, they all think they know something; whereas, if I know nothing, at least I am not in doubt of it. Hence all that superior wisdom attributed to me by the oracle reduces itself solely to my firm conviction that I am ignorant of what I do not know."[27]

There you have the Wisest of men according to the Judgment of the Gods and the most learned Athenian according to the opinion of all Greece, Socrates, Eulogizing ignorance. Can it be believed that if he were reborn among us, our Learned men and Artists would make him change his mind? No, Gentlemen, this just man would continue to scorn our vain Sciences; he would not help to enlarge that mass of books by which we are flooded from all sides; and, as he did before, he would leave behind to his disciples and our Posterity no other precept than the example and memory of his virtue. Thus is it noble to teach men!

What Socrates had begun in Athens, Cato the Elder[28] continued in Rome, inveighing against those cunning and subtle Greeks who seduced the virtue and enervated the courage of his fellow citizens. But the Sciences, Arts, and dialectic again prevailed: Rome was filled with Philosophers and Orators; military discipline was neglected, agriculture was scorned, Sects were embraced and the Fatherland forgotten. The sacred names of liberty, disinterestedness, obedience to Laws were replaced by the names of Epicurus, Zeno, Arcesilaus.[29] "Since Learned men have begun to appear among us," said their own philosophers, "good People have been eclipsed."[30] Until then, the Romans had been content to practice virtue; all was lost when they began to study it.

O Fabricius! What would your noble soul have thought if, restored to life to your own misfortune, you had seen the pompous appearance of that Rome saved by your valor and better glorified by your worthy name than by all its conquests? "Gods," you would have said, "what has become of those thatched roofs and those rustic hearths where moderation and virtue used to dwell? What disastrous splendor has succeeded Roman simplicity? What is this strange language? What are these effeminate morals? What is the meaning of these statues, these Paintings, these buildings? Madmen, what have you done? Have you, the Masters of Nations, made yourselves slaves of the frivolous men you conquered? Are these Rhetoricians who govern you? Is it to enrich Architects, Painters, Sculptors, and Comedians that you watered Greece and Asia with your blood? Are the spoils of Carthage the booty of a flute player? Romans, hasten to tear down these Amphitheatres, break these marble statues, burn these paintings, chase out these slaves who subjugate you and whose fatal arts corrupt you. Let other hands win fame by vain talents; the only talent worthy of Rome is that of conquering the world and making virtue reign in it. When Cineas took our Senate for an Assembly of Kings,[31] he was dazzled neither by vain pomp nor by affected elegance. He did not hear that frivolous eloquence which is the study and charm of futile men. What then did Cineas see of such majesty? O Citizens, he saw a sight that could never be produced by your wealth or all your arts, the most noble sight that has ever appeared beneath the heavens, the Assembly of two hundred virtuous men, worthy of commanding Rome and governing the Earth."

But let us leap over the interval of space and time and see what has happened in our countries and under our own eyes; or rather, let us set aside odious pictures which would offend our delicacy, and spare ourselves the trouble of repeating the same things under different names. It was not in vain that I called up the shade of Fabricius; and what did I make that great man say that I might not have put into the mouth of Louis XII or Henry IV?[32] Among us, it is true, Socrates would not have drunk the hemlock; but he would have drunk from an even more bitter cup: insulting ridicule and scorn a hundred times worse than death.

Behold how luxury, licentiousness, and slavery have in all periods been punishment for the arrogant attempts we have made to emerge from the happy ignorance in which eternal wisdom had placed us. The heavy veil with which she covered all her operations seemed to warn us adequately that she did not destine us for vain studies. Is there even one of her lessons from which we have known how to profit, or which we have neglected with impunity? Peoples, know once and for all that nature wanted to keep you from being harmed by science just as a mother wrests a dangerous weapon from her child's hands; that all the secrets she hides from you are so many evils from which she protects you, and that the difficulty you find in educating yourselves is not the least of her benefits. Men are perverse; they would be even worse if they had the misfortune to be born learned.

How humiliating for humanity are these reflections! How mortified our pride must be! What! could probity be the daughter of ignorance? Could science and virtue be incompatible? What conclusions might not be drawn from these prejudices? But to reconcile these apparent contradictions it is only necessary to examine closely the vanity and emptiness of those proud titles that dazzle us, and that we so freely give to human learning. Let us therefore consider the Sciences and Arts in themselves. Let us see what must result from their progress; and let us no longer hesitate to agree on all points where our reasoning will be found to coincide with historical inductions.

Second Part

It was an ancient tradition, passed from Egypt to Greece, that a God who was hostile to the tranquillity of mankind was the inventor of the sciences.* [33] What must the Egyptians themselves, in whose country the sciences were born, have thought of them? They were able to see at first hand the sources that produced them. In fact, whether one leafs through the annals of the world or supplements uncertain chronicles with philosophic research, human learning will not be found to have an origin corresponding to the idea we like to have of it. Astronomy was born from superstition; Eloquence from ambition, hate, flattery, and falsehood; Geometry from avarice; Physics from vain curiosity; all, even Moral philosophy, from human pride. Thus the Sciences and Arts owe their birth to our vices; we would be less doubtful of their advantages if they owed it to our virtues.

The defect of their origin is recalled to us only too clearly in their objects. What would we do with Arts without the luxury that nourishes them? Without the injustices of men, what purpose would Jurisprudence serve? What would History become, if there were neither Tyrants nor

*The allegory in the fable of Prometheus is easily seen; and it does not seem that the Greeks who riveted him on the Caucasus thought any more favorably of him than did the Egyptians of their God Thoth. "The satyr," an ancient fable relates, "wanted to kiss and embrace fire the first time he saw it; but Prometheus cried out to him: Satyr, you will mourn the beard on your chin, for fire burns when one touches it." [34] This is the subject of the frontispiece. [35]

Wars nor Conspirators? In a word, who would want to spend his life in sterile speculations if each of us, consulting only the duties of man and the needs of nature, had time for nothing except his Fatherland, the unfortunate, and his friends? Are we destined then to die fixed to the edge of the well where the truth has hidden?[36] This reflection alone should rebuff, from the outset, any man who would seriously seek to educate himself by the study of Philosophy.

What dangers there are! What false paths when investigating the Sciences! How many errors, a thousand times more dangerous than the truth is useful, must be surmounted in order to reach the truth? The disadvantage is evident, for falsity is susceptible of infinite combinations, whereas truth has only one manner of being. Besides, who seeks it sincerely? Even with the best intentions, by what signs is one certain to recognize it? In this multitude of different sentiments, what will be our *Criterium* in order to judge it properly?* And hardest of all, if by luck we finally find it, who among us will know how to make good use of the truth?

If our sciences are vain in the object they have in view, they are even more dangerous in the effects they produce. Born in idleness, they nourish it in turn; and irreparable loss of time is the first injury they necessarily cause society. In politics as in morality, it is a great evil to fail to do good, and every useless citizen may be considered a pernicious man. Answer me then, illustrious Philosophers—you who taught us in what proportions bodies attract each other in a vacuum; what are, in the orbits of planets, the ratios of areas covered in equal time intervals; what curves have conjugate points, points of inflexion, and cusps; how man sees everything in God; how soul and body could be in harmony, like two clocks, without communicating; which stars could be inhabited; what insects breed in an extraordinary manner[37]—answer me, I say, you from whom we have received so much sublime knowledge: had you taught us none of these things, would we consequently be fewer in number, less well governed, less formidable, less flourishing or more perverse? Reconsider, then, the importance of your products; and if the works of the most enlightened of our learned men and our best Citizens provide us with so little that is useful, tell us what we must think of that crowd of obscure Writers and idle men of Letters who uselessly consume the substance of the State.

Did I say idle? Would God they really were! Morals would be

*The less one knows, the more he thinks he knows. Did the Peripatetics have doubts about anything? Did Descartes not construct the Universe with cubes and vortices? And even today, is there in Europe any trivial Physicist who does not boldly explain the profound mystery of electricity, which will perhaps be forever the despair of true Philosophers?

healthier and society more peaceful. But these vain and futile declaimers go everywhere armed with their deadly paradoxes, undermining the foundations of faith, and annihilating virtue. They smile disdainfully at the old-fashioned words of Fatherland and Religion, and devote their talents and Philosophy to destroying and debasing all that is sacred among men. Not that at bottom they hate either virtue or our dogmas; they are enemies of public opinion, and to bring them to the foot of altars it would suffice to send them among Atheists. O passion to gain distinction, of what are you not capable?

The misuse of time is a great evil. Other evils that are even greater accompany Letters and Arts. Luxury, born like them from the idleness and vanity of men, is such an evil. Luxury rarely develops without the sciences and arts, and they never develop without it. I know that our Philosophy, always rich in peculiar maxims, holds contrary to the experience of all centuries that luxury produces the splendor of States; but having forgotten the necessity for sumptuary laws, will our philosophy still dare deny that good morals are essential to the stability of Empires, and that luxury is diametrically opposed to good morals? Granted that luxury is a sure sign of wealth; that it even serves, if you like, to increase wealth. What conclusion must be drawn from this paradox so worthy of our time; and what will become of virtue when one must get rich at any price? Ancient Political thinkers incessantly talked about morals and virtue, those of our time talk only of business and money. One will tell you that in a given country a man is worth the price he would fetch in Algiers; another, following this calculation, will discover some countries where a man is worth nothing and others where he is worth less than nothing.[38] They evaluate men like herds of cattle. According to them a man is worth no more to the State than the value of his domestic consumption. Thus one Sybarite would have been worth at least thirty Lacedaemonians. Guess, then, which of these two republics, Sparta or Sybaris, was subjugated by a handful of peasants and which made Asia tremble.

The Monarchy of Cyrus was conquered with thirty thousand men by a Prince who was poorer than the least significant Persian Satrap; and the Scythians, the most miserable of Peoples, successfully resisted the most powerful Monarchs of the Universe. Two famous republics competed for World Empire: one of them was very rich, the other had nothing, and it was the latter which destroyed the former. The Roman Empire, in turn, after devouring all the wealth of the Universe, was the prey of people who did not even know what wealth was. The Franks conquered the Gauls, and the Saxons England, with no other treasures than their bravery and poverty. A group of poor Mountaineers, whose greed was limited to a few sheepskins, after taming Austrian pride crushed that opulent and formidable House of Burgundy which made Europe's Potentates tremble. Finally, all the power and wisdom of the successor of Charles V, supported by all the treasures of the Indies, were shattered by a handful of herring-fishers.[39] Let our political thinkers deign to suspend their calculations in order to think over these examples, and let them learn for once that with money one has everything, except morals and Citizens.

Precisely what, then, is at issue in this question of luxury? To know whether it is more important for Empires to be brilliant and transitory or virtuous and durable. I say brilliant, but with what luster? Ostentatious taste is rarely combined in the same souls with the taste for honesty. No, it is not possible that Minds degraded by a multitude of futile concerns could ever rise to anything great, and even if they should have the strength, the courage would be lacking.

Every Artist wants to be applauded. The praises of his contemporaries are the most precious part of his reward. What will he do to obtain praise, therefore, if he has the misfortune to be born among a People and at a time when the Learned, having themselves become fashionable, have enabled frivolous youth to set the tone; when men have sacrificed their taste to the Tyrants of their liberty* when, because one of the sexes dares approve only what is suited to the weakness of the other, masterpieces of dramatic Poetry are dropped and marvels of harmony rejected.[41] What will an artist do, Gentlemen? He will lower his genius to the level of his time, and will prefer to compose ordinary works which are admired during his lifetime instead of marvels which would not be admired until long after his death. Tell us, famed Arouet,[42] how many vigorous and strong beauties have you sacrificed to our false delicacy, and how many great things has the spirit of gallantry, so fertile in small things, cost you?

Thus the dissolution of morals, a necessary consequence of luxury, leads in turn to the corruption of taste. And if, by chance, among the men distinguished by their talents, there is one who has firmness in his soul and refuses to yield to the genius of his times and disgrace himself by childish works, woe to him. He will die in poverty and oblivion.

---

*I am very far from thinking that this ascendancy of women is in itself an evil. It is a gift given them by nature for the happiness of the human Race. Better directed, it could produce as much good as today it does harm. We do not adequately suspect the advantages that would result for society if a better education were given to that half of the human Race which governs the other. Men will always be what is pleasing to women; therefore if you want them to become great and virtuous, teach women what greatness of soul and virtue are. The reflections occasioned by this subject and made long ago by Plato greatly deserve to be better developed by a writer worthy of following such a master and defending so great a cause.[40]

Would that this were a prediction I make and not an experience I relate! Carle, Pierre,[43] the moment has come when that brush destined to increase the majesty of our Temples with sublime and saintly images will fall from your hands, or will be prostituted to ornament carriage panels with lascivious paintings. And you, rival of Praxiteles and Phidias, you whose chisel the ancients would have commissioned to make Gods capable of excusing their idolatry in our eyes; inimitable Pigalle,[44] your hand will be reduced to sculpting the belly of a grotesque figure or it must stay idle.

One cannot reflect on morals without delighting in the recollection of the simplicity of the image of the earliest times. It is a lovely shore, adorned by the hands of nature alone, toward which one incessantly turns one's eyes and from which one regretfully feels oneself moving away. When innocent and virtuous men enjoyed having Gods as witnesses of their actions, they lived together in the same huts; but soon becoming evil, they tired of these inconvenient spectators and relegated them to magnificent Temples. Finally, they chased the Gods out in order to live in the Temples themselves, or at least the Temples of the Gods were no longer distinguishable from the houses of the citizens. This was the height of depravity, and vices were never carried further than when they could be seen, so to speak, propped up on columns of marble, and engraved on corinthian capitals at the entry of Great men's Palaces.

While living conveniences multiply, arts are perfected and luxury spreads, true courage is enervated, military virtues disappear, and this too is the work of the sciences and of all those arts which are exercised in the shade of the study. When the Goths ravaged Greece, all the Libraries were saved from burning only by the opinion, spread by one among them, that they should let the enemy keep belongings so well suited to turn them away from military exercise and amuse them with idle and sedentary occupations. Charles VIII found himself master of Tuscany and the Kingdom of Naples virtually without having drawn his sword; and his whole Court attributed this unhoped for ease to the fact that the Princes and Nobility of Italy enjoyed themselves becoming ingenious and learned more than they exerted themselves becoming vigorous and warlike. In fact, says the sensible man who relates these two anecdotes,[45] all examples teach us that in such military regulations, and in all regulations that resemble them, study of the sciences is much more apt to soften and enervate courage than to strengthen and animate it.

The Romans admitted that military virtue died out among them to the degree that they became connoisseurs of Paintings, Engravings, Jeweled vessels, and began to cultivate the fine arts. And, as if that famous country were destined to serve unceasingly as an example to other peoples, the rise of the Medicis and the revival of Letters brought about anew, and perhaps for always, the fall of that warlike reputation which Italy seemed to have recovered a few centuries ago.

The ancient Greek republics, with that wisdom which shone through most of their institutions, forbade their Citizens the practice of those tranquil and sedentary occupations which, by weighing down and corrupting the body, soon enervate the vigor of the soul. What view of hunger, thirst, fatigues, dangers, and death can men have if they are crushed by the smallest need and rebuffed by the least difficulty? Where will soldiers find the courage to bear excessive work to which they are totally unaccustomed? With what kind of spirit will they make forced marches under Officers who do not even have the strength to travel on horseback? Let no one raise as an objection the renowned valor of all those modern warriors who are so scientifically disciplined. I hear their bravery on a single day of battle highly praised, but I am not told how they bear overwork, how they endure the rigor of the seasons and the bad weather. Only a little sun or snow, or the lack of a few superfluities is necessary to dissolve and destroy the best of our armies in a few days. Intrepid warriors, admit for once the truth you so rarely hear: you are brave, I know; you would have triumphed with Hannibal at Cannae and at Trasimene; with you Caesar would have crossed the Rubicon and enslaved his country; but it is not with you that the former would have crossed the Alps and the latter conquered your ancestors.

Fighting does not always win wars, and for Generals there is an art superior to that of winning battles. A man who runs intrepidly into the line of fire is nonetheless a very bad officer. Even in the soldier, a little more strength and vigor would perhaps be more necessary than such bravery, which does not preserve him from death; and what does it matter to the State whether its troops perish by fever and cold or by the enemy's sword.

If cultivating the sciences is harmful to warlike qualities, it is even more so to moral qualities. From our earliest years a foolish education adorns our mind and corrupts our judgment. I see everywhere immense institutions where young people are brought up at great expense, learning everything except their duties. Your children will not know their own language, but they will speak others that are nowhere in use; they will know how to write Verses they can barely understand; without knowing how to distinguish error from truth, they will possess the art of making them both unrecognizable to others by specious arguments. But they will not know what the words magnanimity, equity, temperance, humanity, courage are; that sweet name Fatherland will never strike their ear; and if they hear of God, it will be less to be awed by him than to be afraid of him.* I would like it as well, said a Wise man, if my pupil spent his time playing court tennis; at least his body would be more fit.[47] I know children must be kept busy and that, for them, idleness is the danger most to be feared. What then should they learn? That is surely a fine question! Let them learn what they ought to do as men** and not what they ought to forget.

Our gardens are adorned with statues and our Galleries with paintings. What would you think these masterpieces of art, exhibited for public admiration, represent? The defenders of the Fatherland? or those even greater men who have enriched it by their virtues? No. They are pictures of all the aberrations of the heart and reason, carefully drawn from ancient Mythology and presented to our children's curiosity at an early age—doubtless so that they may have models of bad actions before their eyes even before they know how to read.

What brings about all these abuses if not the disastrous inequality introduced among men by the distinction of talents and the debasement of virtues? That is the most evident effect of all our studies and the most dangerous of all their consequences. One no longer asks if a man is upright, but rather if he is talented; nor of a Book if it is useful, but if it is well written. Rewards are showered on the witty, and virtue is left with-

---

*Pens. Philosoph.

**Such was the education of the Spartans according to the greatest of their Kings. It is, says Montaigne, worthy of great consideration that the excellent regulations of Lycurgus, in truth monstrously perfect, were concerned with the sustenance of children as if this were their main care; and in the very home of the Muses, so little mention is made of doctrine that it is as if those noble youths disdained all other yokes, and, instead of our Teachers of science, could only be given Teachers of valor, prudence, and justice.

Now let us see how the same Author speaks of the ancient Persians. Plato relates, he says, that the eldest son of their Royal line was educated thus: after his birth he was not given to women, but to Eunuchs who, because of their virtue, had the highest influence with the King. They took charge of making his body handsome and healthy, and at the age of seven taught him to ride and hunt. When he reached fourteen, they placed him in the hands of four men: the wisest, most just, most temperate, and most valiant in the Nation. The first taught him Religion; the second to be always truthful; the third to conquer his cupidity; the fourth to fear nothing. All, I will add, were to make him good, none to make him learned.

Astyages, in Xenophon, asks Cyrus to give an account of his last Lesson. It is this, he says: in our school a big boy with a small tunic gave it to one of his smaller schoolmates, and took away the latter's tunic, which was bigger. When our Tutor made me judge of this dispute, I ruled that things should be left in this condition since both parties seemed to be better fitted in this way. Whereupon I was reproved for having done wrong, for I had stopped to consider suitability when I should first have provided for justice, which demands that no one be compelled in matters concerning his belongings. And he says that he was punished for it, just as we are punished in our villages for having forgotten the first aorist tense of τύπτω.[48] My Schoolmaster would have to give me a fine harangue, *in genere demonstrativo*, before he could persuade me that his school matches that one.[49]

out honors. There are a thousand prizes for fine discourses, none for fine actions. But let someone tell me whether the glory attached to the best of the discourses which will be crowned by this Academy is comparable to the merit of having founded the prize?

The wise man does not chase after riches, but he is not insensitive to glory, and when he sees it so poorly distributed, his virtue, which a little emulation would have animated and made useful to society, languishes and dies out in misery and oblivion. In the long run, this is what must everywhere be the result of the preference given to pleasing talents rather than useful ones, and what experience since the revival of the sciences and arts has only too well confirmed. We have Physicists, Geometers, Chemists, Astronomers, Poets, Musicians, Painters; we no longer have citizens; or if a few of them are left, dispersed in our abandoned countryside, they perish there indigent and despised. Such is the condition to which those who give us bread and who give milk to our children are reduced, and such are the sentiments we have for them.

I admit, however, that the evil is not as great as it could have become. By placing salutary herbs beside various harmful plants, and by placing within several injurious animals the antidote for their wounds, eternal providence has taught Sovereigns, who are its ministers, to imitate its wisdom. Following this example, that great Monarch,[50] whose glory will only acquire new luster from age to age, drew out of the very bosom of the sciences and arts, sources of a thousand disorders, those famed societies simultaneously responsible for the dangerous trust of human knowledge and the sacred trust of morals—trusts which these societies protect by the attention they give both to maintaining within themselves the total purity of their trusts, and to requiring such purity of the members they admit.

These wise institutions, reinforced by his august successor and imitated by all the Kings of Europe, will at least serve as a check on men of letters, all of whom, in aspiring to the honor of being admitted to Academies, will keep watch over themselves and try to make themselves worthy by means of useful works and irreproachable morals. Those Academies which will choose, for the prize competitions honoring literary merit, subjects suited to revive love of virtue in the hearts of Citizens, will show that such love reigns among them, and will give the People that very rare and sweet pleasure of seeing learned societies devote themselves to disseminating throughout the human Race not merely pleasant enlightenment but also salutary teachings.

Do not, therefore, raise an objection which for me is only a new proof. So many precautions show only too well the necessity of taking them, and remedies are not sought for nonexistent evils. Why must even these, by their inadequacy, have the character of ordinary remedies? So many establishments created for the benefit of the learned are thereby all the more able to deceive concerning the objects of the sciences and to direct minds toward their cultivation. It seems, to judge by the precautions taken, that there are too many Farmers and that a lack of Philosophers is feared. I do not want to attempt here a comparison between agriculture and philosophy; it would not be tolerated. I shall only ask: what is Philosophy? What do the writings of the best known philosophers contain? What are the Teachings of these lovers of wisdom? To listen to them, would one not take them for a troop of charlatans, each crying from his own spot on a public square: Come to me, I alone do not deceive. One holds that there are no bodies and that everything is appearance. Another that there is no substance other than matter, nor any God but the world. This one suggests that there are neither virtues nor vices and that moral good and evil are chimeras. That one that men are wolves and can devour one another with clear conscience.[51] O great Philosophers, why don't you save these profitable Teachings for your friends and children; you would soon reap the reward, and we would have no fear of finding among ourselves any of your sectarians.

Such are the marvelous men on whom the esteem of their contemporaries was showered during their lifetime and for whom immortality was reserved after their death! Such are the wise maxims we have received from them and that we will transmit from age to age to our descendants. Has Paganism, abandoned to all the aberrations of human reason, left posterity anything to compare with the shameful monuments prepared for it by Printing under the reign of the Gospel? The impious writings of Leucippus and Diagoras died with them. The art of perpetuating the extravagances of the human mind had not yet been invented. But thanks to Typography* and the use we make of it, the dangerous reveries of Hobbes and Spinoza will remain forever. Go, famous writings of which

---

*Considering the awful disorders Printing has already caused in Europe, and judging the future by the progress that this evil makes day by day, one can easily predict that sovereigns will not delay in taking as many pains to banish this terrible art from their States as they once took to establish it. The Sultan Achmet, bowing to the importunities of some supposed men of taste, had consented to establish a Printing Press at Constantinople. But the press had hardly begun to operate when it had to be destroyed and the equipment thrown in a well. It is said that Caliph Omar, consulted on what should be done with the library of Alexandria, replied in these terms: If the Books in this library contain things opposed to the Koran, they are bad and must be burned. If they contain only the doctrine of the Koran, burn them anyway-they are superfluous. Our Learned men have cited this reasoning as the height of absurdity. However, imagine Gregory the Great in place of Omar, and the Gospel in place of the Koran, the Library would still have been burned, and it would be perhaps the finest deed in the life of that Illustrious Pontiff.

the ignorance and simplicity of our Forefathers would have been incapable; escort to our descendants those even more dangerous works which reek of the corruption of morals in our century, and together carry to coming centuries a faithful history of the progress and advantages of our sciences and arts. If they read you, you will not leave them any doubt about the question we discuss today; and unless they be more foolish than we, they will raise their hands to Heaven and say with bitterness of heart: "Almighty God, thou who holds all Spirits in thy hands, deliver us from the enlightenment and fatal arts of our forefathers, and give back to us ignorance, innocence, and poverty, the only goods that can give us happiness and are precious in thy sight."

But if the development of the sciences and arts has added nothing to our true felicity, if it has corrupted our morals, and if the corruption of morals has impaired purity of taste, what shall we think of that crowd of elementary Authors who have removed the difficulties that blocked access to the Temple of the Muses and that nature put there as a test of strength for those who might be tempted to learn? What shall we think of those Compilers of works who have indiscreetly broken down the door of the Sciences and let into their Sanctuary a populace unworthy of approaching it; whereas it would be preferable for all who could not go far in the career of Letters to be rebuffed from the outset and directed into Arts useful to society. He who will be a bad versifier or a subaltern Geometer all his life would perhaps have become a great cloth maker. Those whom nature destined to be her disciples needed no teachers. Verulam,[52] Descartes, Newton, these Preceptors of the human Race had none themselves; indeed, what guides would have led them as far as their vast genius carried them? Ordinary Teachers would only have restricted their understanding by confining it within the narrow capacity of their own. The first obstacles taught them to exert themselves, and they did their utmost to traverse the immense space they covered. If a few men must be allowed to devote themselves to the study of the Sciences and Arts, it must be only those who feel the strength to walk alone in their footsteps and go beyond them. It is for these few to raise monuments to the glory of human mind. But if we wish nothing to be beyond their genius, nothing must be beyond their hopes. That is the only encouragement they need. The soul gradually adapts itself to the objects that occupy it, and it is great events that make great men. The Prince of Eloquence was Consul of Rome, and the greatest, perhaps, of Philosophers Chancellor of England.[53] If the one had held only a chair in some University and the other obtained only a modest pension from an Academy, can it be believed, I say, that their work would not have reflected their status? Therefore may Kings not disdain to allow into their councils the men most capable of advising them well; may they renounce the old prejudice, invented by the pride of the Great, that the art of leading People is more difficult than that of enlightening them, as if it were easier to engage men to do good willingly than to constrain them to do it by force. May learned men of the first rank find honorable asylum in their courts. May they obtain there the only recompense worthy of them: that of contributing by their influence to the happiness of the People to whom they will have taught wisdom. Only then will one see what can be done by virtue, science, and authority, animated by noble emulation and working together for the felicity of the human Race. But so long as power is alone on the one side, intellect and wisdom alone on the other, learned men will rarely think of great things, Princes will more rarely do fine ones, and the People will continue to be vile, corrupt, and unhappy.

As for us, common men not endowed by Heaven with such great talents and not destined for so much glory, let us remain in our obscurity. Let us not chase after a reputation which would escape us, and which in the present state of things would never be worth what it cost, even if we had all the qualifications to obtain it. What good is it to seek our happiness in the opinion of another if we can find it within ourselves? Let us leave to others the care of informing Peoples of their duties, and limit ourselves to fulfilling well our own. We do not need to know more than this.

O virtue! Sublime science of simple souls, are so many difficulties and preparations needed to know you? Are not your principles engraved in all hearts, and is it not enough in order to learn your Laws to return into oneself and listen to the voice of one's conscience in the silence of the passions? That is true Philosophy, let us know how to be satisfied with it; and without envying the glory of those famous men who are immortalizd in the Republic of Letters, let us try to put between them and us that glorious distinction noted between two great Peoples long ago: that the one knew how to speak well, the other to act well.[54]

Observations on the Discourse
which was awarded the first prize at Dijon [1]

The author of the academic Discourse which won the prize of the Academy of Dijon is invited by persons who take an interest in the good and the true that prevail in it to publish that more complete treatise he had projected and subsequently suppressed.

They think the reader would find in it clarifications and modifications of several general propositions, open to exceptions and restrictions. All of that could not be included in an academic discourse, limited to a short space. Perhaps that type of style also does not allow such details, and besides would appear too mistrustful of the enlightenment and equity of its judges.

That is what some well-intentioned persons wanted to give to understand to certain readers bristling with objections and perhaps ill-humored at seeing luxury attacked too vigorously. They have protested because the author seems, they say, to prefer the situation in which Europe was before the renewal of the sciences, a state worse than ignorance because of the false knowledge or scholastic jargon that prevailed.

They add that the author prefers rusticity to politeness, and that he delivers a mortal blow to all learned men and artists. He should have indicated his starting point, they continue, in designating the epoch of decadence, and in going back to that first epoch, compare the morals of that time with ours. Lacking that, we do not see how far back it is necessary to go, unless it is to the time of the apostles.

They say further, in relation to luxury, that as a good policy it is known that it should be forbidden in small States, but that the case of a kingdom like France, for example, is altogether different. The reasons for that are known.

In the end, this is what they object. What practical conclusion can be reached from the thesis the author upholds? If he is granted everything he asserts about the injury from too many learned men, and principally poets, painters, and musicians, as well as the opposite effect of too few farmers, that, I say, can be granted to him without difficulty. But what use can one draw from it? How can this disorder be remedied, either on the side of the princes or that of private individuals? Can the former interfere with the freedom of their subjects relative to the professions they enter? And as for luxury, the sumptuary laws they can pass never resolve the problem entirely. The author is not unaware of all that could be said about that.

But what touches most closely the generality of readers is to know what they themselves can derive from this in their capacity as simple private individuals, and that indeed is the important point, since if one could successfully bring every private individual to cooperate voluntarily on what the public good requires, this unanimous cooperation would make a sum more complete, and without comparison more solid, than all the imaginable regulations that could be made by the powers that be.

There is a vast career opened to the author's talent, and since the press rolls on and very likely will roll on (whatever he could say about it) and always in the service of the frivolous and worse rather than that of truth, isn't it just for everyone who has better views and the requisite talent to contribute all the counterweight of which he is capable?

Moreover, there are cases where one is more accountable to the public for a second piece of writing than one was for the first. There are not many readers to whom one can apply the proverb: *the good listener needs only a hint*. It is impossible to shed too much light on truths which clash so directly with the general taste, and it is important to take away any foothold from chicanery.

There are also many readers who would appreciate them [these truths] more in a very unified style, rather than in that ceremonial garb required by academic discourses. And the author, who appears to disdain all vain finery, will doubtless prefer it, liberated as he will be in that way from a form that is always constricting.

P.S. We learn that an academician from one of the good cities in France is preparing a discourse in refutation of the author's. He will doubtless include in it an article against the total suppression of printing, which many people found very exaggerated.

Letter to M. the Abbé Raynal
Author of the Mercury of France

I owe thanks, sir, to those who have passed on to you the observations that you so kindly convey to me, and I will try to benefit from them; however, I will admit that I find my Censors a little hard on my logic, and I suspect they would have proved less scrupulous if I had shared their opinion. It seems to me at least that if they themselves had a little of that rigorous exactness they require of me, I would have had no need of the clarifications for which I am going to ask them.

The Author seems, they say, *to prefer the situation in which Europe was before the renewal of the Sciences, a State worse than ignorance because of the false knowledge or jargon that prevailed.* The Author of this observation seems to have me say that false knowledge or scholastic jargon is preferable to Science; yet it is I myself who said it was worse than ignorance. But what does he mean by that word "situation?" Does he apply it to enlightenment or to morals, or does he confuse those things I went to such pains to distinguish? Besides, since this is the heart of the question, I admit it was very awkward of me only to have seemed to take a position on it.

They add that *the Author prefers rusticity to politeness.*

It is true that the Author prefers rusticity to the proud and false politeness of our century, and he stated the reason why. *And that he delivers a mortal blow to all learned men and artists.* So be it, since that is what they want, I agree to suppress all the distinctions I made.

He should have indicated his starting point, they continue, *in designating the epoch of decadence.* I did more than that. I made my proposition general: I assigned this first level of the decadence of morals to the first moment of the cultivation of Letters in all the countries of the world, and I found that the progress of these two things was always in proportion. *And in going back to that first epoch, compare the morals of that time with ours.* That is what I would have done at greater length in a large volume.

Lacking that, we do not see how far back it is necessary to go, unless it is to the time of the Apostles? I do not see why that would pose a problem, if the fact were true. But I ask the Censor to be fair: Does he wish I had said that the time of the most profound ignorance was that of the Apostles?

They say further, in relation to luxury, that as good policy it is known that it should be forbidden in small States, but that the case of a Kingdom like France, for example, is altogether different. The reasons for that are known. Don't I have cause to complain here too? These reasons are the ones to which I tried to respond. Well or badly, I responded. Now there is hardly any greater indication of scorn for an Author than to answer him with nothing but the same arguments he refuted. Must I show them the problem they have to resolve? Here it is: *What will become of virtue when one must get rich at any price?** That is what I asked them and am still asking them.

As for the two observations that follow, the first of which begins with the words: *In the end, this is what they object* and the other with these: *but what touches most closely*, I beg the Reader to spare me the trouble of transcribing them. The Academy had asked me whether the restoration of the Sciences and Arts had tended to purify morals. That was the question I had to resolve. Yet here they make it a crime for me not to have resolved another one. Surely this criticism is at the very least most peculiar. However, I almost have to apologize to the Reader for having anticipated it, because that is what he could believe in reading the last five or six pages of my discourse.

Moreover, if my Censors persist in wanting more practical conclusions, I promise them some that are very clearly spelled out in my first reply.

On the uselessness of sumptuary Laws to root out luxury once it is established, they say that *the Author is not unaware of all that could be said about that*. How true. I am not unaware of the fact that when a man is dead there is no point in calling Doctors.

It is impossible to shed too much light on truths which *clash* so very *directly with the general taste, and it is important to take away any foothold from chicanery.* I do not entirely share this opinion, and I believe that playthings should be left to children.

There are also many Readers who would appreciate them more in a very unified style than in that ceremonial garb required by Academic Discourses. I strongly share the taste of those Readers. This, then, is one point on which I can agree with the feeling of my critics, as I do from now on.

I do not know who the adversary is with whom I am threatened in the *Post-Script*. Whoever it may be, I cannot resolve to reply to a work before reading it, nor to consider myself defeated before being attacked.

Besides, whether I reply to the criticisms that have been announced or whether I am satisfied to publish the expanded work that is requested,

*Discourse, page 38.[1]

I warn my Censors that they may well not find in it the modifications for which they hope. I foresee that when it is a question of defending myself, I will follow without scruple all the consequences of my principles.[2]

I know in advance the great words that will be used to attack me: enlightenment, knowledge, laws, morality, reason, propriety, consideration, gentleness, amenity, politeness, education, etc. To all that I will reply only with two other words, which ring even more loudly in my ear. Virtue, truth, I will write for myself constantly; Truth, virtue! If anyone perceives only words in this, I have nothing more to say to him.

Reply to the Discourse
which was awarded the prize of the Academy of Dijon
by the King of Poland [1]

The *Discourse* of the citizen of Geneva has surprising things in it, and one will be equally surprised, perhaps, to see it rewarded with a prize by a famous academy.

Is it his private sentiment which the author wanted to establish? Isn't it only a paradox with which he wanted to amuse the public? Whichever it is, to refute his opinion, it is necessary only to examine how it is proved, restore anonymity to the truths he adopted, and confront him with himself. Could I, in using his principles to combat him, defeat him with his own weapons and make him triumph in his own defeat?

His way of thinking announces a virtuous heart. His manner of writing reveals a cultivated mind. But if he effectively unites science and virtue, and the one (as he attempts to prove) is incompatible with the other, how has his doctrine not corrupted his wisdom? Or how has his wisdom not convinced him to remain in ignorance? Has he given virtue preference over science? Why, then, display such vast and sought after erudition to us with so much affectation? Did he prefer science, on the contrary, to virtue? Why then preach the latter at the expense of the former to us with so much eloquence? Let him begin by reconciling such singular contradictions, before he combats commonly held notions. Before he attacks others, let him be consistent with himself.

Would he have claimed only to exercise his mind and make his imagination shine? Let us not envy him the frivolous advantage of having succeeded in doing so. But in this case, what is to be concluded about his discourse? What one concludes after reading an ingenious novel. In vain does an author give fictions the colors of truth. One sees perfectly well that he does not believe what he pretends to want to persuade.

As for me, who flatter myself neither with having enough capacity to understand something about it to the detriment of my morals, nor with having enough virtue to be able to do much honor with it to my ignorance, in raising myself against such an untenable opinion, I have no other interest than to maintain that of the truth. The author will find an impartial adversary in me. I even seek his approval of me for attacking him; all my efforts in this combat having no other object than to reconcile his mind and his heart, and procure the satisfaction of seeing united in his soul the sciences I admire and the virtues he loves.

I

The sciences serve to make known the true, the good, and the useful of all kinds, a precious knowledge which, by enlightening minds, ought naturally to contribute to purifying morals.

The truth of this proposition needs only to be presented to be believed. Thus I will not stop to prove it. I am interested only in refuting the ingenious sophisms of those who dare to combat it.

Right from the beginning of his discourse, the author offers us the most beautiful spectacle. He shows us man at grips, so to speak, with himself, in some manner leaving the nothingness of his ignorance, dissipating by the efforts of his reason the shadows in which nature had enveloped him; rising up by the mind to the highest spheres of the celestial regions; subjecting the movements of the stars to his calculation, and measuring with his compass the vast expanse of the universe; then returning to the depths of his heart, and rendering an account to himself of the nature of his soul, its excellence, its lofty destiny.

How honorable such an admission, wrested by the truth, is to the sciences! How well it shows their necessity and advantages! How costly it must have been to the author to be forced to make it, and still more to retract it!

Nature, he says, is beautiful enough by itself. It can only lose by being embellished. Happy are the men, he adds, who know how to profit from its gifts without knowing them. It is to the simplicity of their mind that they owe the innocence of their morals. What fine morality is recited to us here by the censor of the sciences and the apologist of morals! Who would have expected that such reflections had to follow from the principles he has just established!

Nature is beautiful in itself, no doubt. But isn't it to discover its beauties, to penetrate its secrets, to unveil its operations that learned men use their research? Why is such a vast field open to our gaze? Does the mind, which was made to explore it and which acquires more strength and breadth in this exercise so worthy of its activity, have to be reduced to a few fleeting perceptions or to stupid admiration? Will morals be less pure because reason will be more enlightened? And as the torch that is given to us to guide us adds light, will our path become less easy to find and more difficult to follow? What would happen to all the gifts the Creator has given to man if, limited to the organic functions of his senses, he could only examine what he sees, reflect on what he hears, discern by smell the relations objects have to him, supplement by touch what is lacking to sight, and judge by taste what is beneficial or harmful to him? Without reason which illuminates and leads us, indistinguishable from the animals, governed by instinct, would we not soon become as like them in our actions as we already are in our needs? It is only with the help of reflection and study that we can be successful in regulating the palpable things within our grasp, correcting the errors of our senses, subjecting the body to the empire of the mind, leading the soul, that spiritual and immortal substance, to the knowledge of its duties and of its end.

Since it is principally by their effects on morals that the author makes a point of discrediting the sciences, in order to avenge them from such a false imputation, I would have only to relate here the advantages society owes to them. But who could enumerate the numberless goods they bring and the infinite amenities they spread? The more the sciences are cultivated in a State, the more the State flourishes. Without them, everything would languish.

What does the artisan not owe them, for everything that contributes to the beauty, solidity, proportion, and perfection of his works? The farmer, for the different ways of forcing the earth to reward his labors with the offerings he anticipates from it? The physician, for discovering the nature of illnesses and the property of remedies? The jurist, for discerning the spirit of the laws and the diversity of duties? The judge, for unraveling the artifices of cupidity from the simplicity of innocence, and deciding with equity concerning the goods and the life of men? Every citizen, whatever his profession or condition, has duties to fulfill. And how can they be fulfilled unless they are known. Without knowledge of history, politics, and religion, how can those in charge of the government of States be able to maintain order, subordination, security, and abundance in them?

Curiosity, natural to man, inspires in him the desire to learn. His needs make him feel the necessity of doing so. His employments impose on him the obligation of doing so, his progress makes him taste the pleasure of doing so. His first discoveries increase his eagerness to know. The more he knows, the more he feels there is knowledge to be acquired. And the more knowledge he has acquired, the easier it is for him to do good.

Hasn't the citizen of Geneva experienced this? Let us be wary of believing his modesty about it. He claims one would be more virtuous if one were less learned. It is the sciences, he says, that make us know evil. We would be ignorant of so many crimes without them, he cries. But is ignorance of vice a virtue, then? Is it doing good to be ignorant of evil? And if it is abstaining from evil because one is ignorant of it that is called being virtuous, let him at least agree that there is no great merit in it. It is exposing oneself to not being virtuous for long. It is being so only until some object comes to solicit the natural inclinations or some occasion comes to awaken the dormant passions. It seems to me like seeing a false brave man, who displays his valor only when there are no enemies. If an enemy appears and he must prepare for defense, his courage fails and virtue vanishes. If the sciences acquaint us with evil, they also acquaint us with the remedy for it. A clever botanist knows how to separate healthful plants from poisonous herbs. Whereas the common man, who is equally ignorant of the virtue of the former and the poison of the others, crushes them underfoot without distinction, or picks them indiscriminately. A man enlightened by the sciences distinguishes among the large number of objects that offer themselves to his knowledge, those which deserve his aversion or his seeking. In the deformity of vice and the turmoil that follows it, in the charms of virtue and the peace that accompanies it, he finds the basis for his respect and taste for the one, his horror and scorn for the other. He is wise by choice; he is solidly virtuous.

But it is said there are countries where without science, without study, without detailed knowledge of the principles of morality, they are better practiced than in others where they are better known, more praised, more highly taught. Without strictly examining here those parallels so often made between our morals and those of the Ancients or foreigners—odious parallels that contain less zeal and equity than envy of one's compatriots and ill-humor for one's contemporaries, isn't it rather to climate, temperament, absence of opportunity, lack of a goal, the economy of the government, customs, laws, to every other cause except the sciences that one ought to attribute the difference in morals sometimes noted in different countries and at different times? Isn't constantly recalling that much-praised primitive simplicity, always representing it as the inseparable companion of innocence, drawing a portrait in the mind to delude oneself? Where did anyone ever see men without faults, without desires, without passions? Don't we carry within ourselves the seed of all the vices? And if there were times, if there are still climates where certain crimes are unknown, aren't other disorders seen there? Aren't there even more monstrous ones among those peoples whose stupidity is praised? Just because gold does not tempt their greed, because honors do not arouse their ambition, do they know less pride and injustice? Are they less given to the baseness of envy, less carried away by the rage for revenge? Are their coarse senses inaccesible to the attraction of pleasures? And to what excesses will be taken voluptuousness which has no rules and knows no limits? But even when there are fewer crimes in these savage countries than in certain civilized ones, are there as many virtues? Does one see there above all those sublime virtues, that purity of morals, that magnanimous disinterestedness, those supernatural actions engendered by religion?

Haven't the many great men who have defended it through their works, who have caused it to be admired through their morals, drawn from study those superior understandings that have triumphed over errors and vices? It is false wit and presumptuous ignorance that bring about doubts and prejudices. It is pride and obstinacy that produce schisms and heresies. It is Pyrrhonism and incredulity that favor independence, revolt, passions, all the heinous crimes. Such adversaries do honor to religion. To defeat them, it has only to appear; by itself, it is capable of confounding them all. Its only fear is not being well enough known. It needs only to be explored in depth to win respect. One loves it as soon as one knows it. As one explores it more deeply, one finds new motives for believing it and new ways to practice it. The more the Christian examines the authenticity of its claims, the more reassured he is about the belief he holds. The more he studies revelation, the stronger his faith becomes. It is in the divine Scriptures that he discovers its origin and excellence. It is in the scholarly writings of the Church Fathers that he follows its development century by century. It is in the books of moral philosophy and the sacred annals that he sees the examples of it and applies them to himself.

What! Will ignorance take away from religion and virtue such pure enlightenment, such powerful supports! And will a scholar from Geneva stridently teach that irregularity of morals is due to that same religion! It would be more amazing to hear such a strange paradox if it were not known that the peculiarity of a system, however dangerous it is, is only an additional reason for whoever has only the private mind as guide. Studied religion is the infallible guide to good morals for all men. I go further. The very study of nature contributes to uplifting the sentiments and regulating behavior. It leads back naturally to the admiration, love, gratitude, and submission that every reasonable soul feels is due to the Almighty. In the regular course of those immense globes that pass over our heads, the astronomer discovers an infinite Power. In the exact proportion of all the parts composing the universe, the geometer perceives the effect of a limitless intelligence. In the sequence of the seasons, the linking of causes and effects, the vegetation of plants, the organization of animals, the constant uniformity and astonishing variety of the different phenomena of nature, the physicist cannot mistake their author, preserver, arbiter, and master.

From these reflections, the true philosopher—coming down to practical consequences and returning into himself after vainly seeking in all objects surrounding him that perfect happiness to which he constantly aspires and finding nothing on earth that answers the immensity of his desires—feels that he is made for something greater than everything that is created. He naturally turns back toward his first principle and his final end. He is fortunate if being open to grace, he learns to seek the happiness of his heart only in the possession of his God!

II

Here the anonymous author himself gives an example of the abuse one can make of erudition and the influence prejudices have over the mind. He goes digging back in the most remote centuries. He returns to the oldest part of antiquity. He wears himself out with arguments and research to find votes of support to accredit his opinion. He cites witnesses who attribute the decadence of kingdoms and empires to the cultivation of the sciences and arts. He imputes to learned men and artists luxury and softness, the usual sources of the strangest revolutions.

But Egypt, Greece, the republic of Rome, and the empire of China, which he dares call as witness in favor of ignorance, with disregard for the sciences and to the detriment of morals, ought to have recalled to his memory those famous legislators who illumined with the breadth of their understanding and guided with the wisdom of their laws those great States whose first foundations they set down; those celebrated orators who sustained them on their road to destruction by the victorious force of their sublime eloquence; those philosophers, those wise men who, by their learned writings and moral virtues, did honor to their country and immortalized their name.

What a mass of striking examples I could offer in opposition to the small number of daring writers he cited! I would only have to open the records of world history. How many incontestable testimonies, august monuments, immortal works there are by which history attests that the sciences contributed everywhere to the happiness of men, the glory of empires, the triumph of virtue.

No, it is not from the sciences, but from the bosom of wealth that softness and luxury have always been born. And in no time has wealth been the share of the learned. For one Plato in opulence, for one Aristippus accredited at court, how many philosophers are there reduced to a cloak and beggar's sack, draped in their own virtue, and ignored in their solitude! How many, like Homer and Diogenes, Epictetus and Aesop, in poverty! The learned have neither the taste nor the leisure to amass great wealth. They love study, they live in mediocrity. And a laborious and moderate life, spent in the silence of retreat, occupied with reading and work, is assuredly not a voluptuous and criminal life. The conveniences of life, albeit often the fruit of the arts, are not thereby the lot of artists. They work only for the rich, and it is the idle rich who profit from and abuse the fruits of their industry.

The most highly touted effect of the sciences and arts, the author continues, is that politeness introduced among men that he enjoys confounding with artifice and hypocrisy, a politeness, according to him, which serves only to hide faults and mask vices. Would he wish, then, for vice to appear openly, for indecency to be joined to disorder and scandal to crime? If in fact that politeness in manners were only a refinement of amour-propre to veil weaknesses, would it not still be an advantage for society that the vicious person would not dare to show himself for what he is and would be forced to borrow the trappings of seemliness and modesty? It has been said, and it is true, that hypocrisy, odious as it is in itself, is still an homage that vice pays to virtue. It at least protects weak souls from the contagion of the bad example.

But it is to misunderstand the learned to blame them for the influence in the world of that supposed politeness which is accused of dissimulation. It is possible to be polite without dissimulating. It is certainly possible to be both without being very learned. And more commonly still, it is possible to be very learned without being terribly polite.

Love of solitude, the taste for books, limited desire to appear in what is called high society, limited disposition to present oneself graciously in it, limited hope of pleasing or shining in it, boredom inseparable from frivolous and almost intolerable conversations for minds accustomed to thinking: everything contributes to making great social gatherings as foreign to the learned man as he is foreign to them. What impression does he make in groups? Look at him, with his dreamy gaze, his frequent distractions, his mind occupied, his studied expressions, his sententious discourses, his profound ignorance of the most recognized fashions and the most common usages. By the ridicule he brings to them and finds in them, by the constraint he endures and causes in them, he soon bores and is bored. He leaves ill-satisfied, and people are very happy to see him leave. He inwardly censures all those he is leaving; they mock aloud at the one who leaves. And while he bemoans their vices, they laugh about his faults. But all those faults, after all, are quite indifferent for morals. And it is to those faults that more than one learned man, perhaps, has the obligation for not being as vicious as those who criticize him.

But before the reign of the sciences and arts, the author adds, one saw more extensive empires, more rapid conquests, more famous warriors. If he had spoken less as an orator and more as a philosopher, he would have said one then saw more of those audacious men who, carried away by violent passions and carrying a troop of slaves along behind them, attack tranquil nations, subjugate peoples who were ignorant of the profession of war, subjecting countries where the arts had raised no barriers to their sudden excursions. Their valor was nothing but ferocity, their courage nothing but cruelty, their conquests nothing but inhumanity. They were impetuous torrents which ravaged all the more when they encountered fewer obstacles. Also, as soon as they were gone, the only thing left behind were the traces of their fury. No form of government, no law, no administrative regulation, no bond held together and united vanquished people to them.

Compare those times of ignorance and barbarism to those fortunate centuries when the sciences spread the spirit of order and of justice everywhere. Today we see wars that are less frequent but more just, actions less astonishing but more heroic, victories less bloody but more glorious, conquest less rapid but more assured, warriors less violent but more formidable, knowing how to vanquish with moderation,treating the vanquished with humanity. Honor is their guide, glory their recompense. However, says the author, in battles one sees a great difference between poor countries, which are called barbarian, and rich peoples, which are called civilized. It certainly seems that the citizen of Geneva has never been in a position to note from close range what happens in battles. Is it surprising that barbarians are less cautious and expose themselves more? Whether they vanquish or are vanquished, they can only win if they survive their defeats. But it is that the hope of base interest, or rather brutal despair, inspires in these bloodthirsty men the feelings that duty excites in those generous souls that give themselves up to their fatherland. With the difference which the author was unable to observe, that the valor of the latter, colder, more thoughtful, more moderate, more knowledgeably conducted, is for that very reason always more certain of success.

But finally Socrates, the famous Socrates himself cried out against the sciences of his time. Must one be surprised at this? The indomitable pride

of the stoics, the effeminate softness of the epicureans, the absurd arguments of the Pyrrhonians, the taste for dispute, empty subtleties, numberless errors, monstrous vices infected philosophy at that time and dishonored philosophers. It was the abuse of the sciences, not the sciences
themselves, which this great man condemned, and we condemn it after
him. But the abuse made of something supposes the good use that can
be made of it. What is not abused? And because an anonymous author[2],
for example, has once abused the fecundity of his mind and the deftness
of his pen to defend a bad cause, must he be forbidden to use it on other
occasions and for other other subjects more worthy of his genius? To
correct a few excesses of intemperance, must all the grapevines be uprooted? The intoxication of the mind has thrust some learned men into
strange aberrations. I agree about that, and deplore it. By the discourses
of some, in the writings of others, religion has degenerated into hypocrisy, piety into superstition, theology into error, jurisprudence into chicanery, astronomy into judicial astrology, physics into atheism. Plaything
of the most bizarre prejudices, attached to the most absurd opinions,
infatuated with the most senseless systems, what deviations does the human mind follow when, given over to presumptuous curiosity, it wants
to go beyond the limits set for it by the same hand that gave the sea its
boundaries. In vain the waves roar, rise up, thrust themselves with fury
on the resisting shores. Soon constrained to turn back on themselves,
they return to the bosom of the ocean, and leave on the shore only a light
foam that evaporates in a moment, or some shifting sand that flees under
our steps. It is the natural image in the natural world of the vain efforts
of the mind when, excited by the thrusts of a dominant imagination,
carried away by every doctrinal breeze, with an audacious flight it wants
to rise above its sphere, and tries to penetrate what it is not allowed to
understand.

But the sciences, far from authorizing such excesses, are full of maxims
that reprove them. And the truly learned man who never loses sight of
the torch of revelation, who always follows the infallible guide of legitimate authority, proceeds with safety, walks with confidence, advances
with great strides in the career of the sciences, makes himself useful to
society, honors his fatherland, completes his journey in innocence, and
ends it with glory.

Observations by Jean-Jacques Rousseau of Geneva On the Reply Made to his Discourse[1]

I owe thanks rather than a reply to the Anonymous Author who has just honored my Discourse with a Reply. But what I owe to gratitude will not make me forget what I owe to truth; and I will not forget, either, that whenever reason is at issue, men return to the right of Nature and resume their original equality.

The Discourse to which I have to reply is full of things that are very true and very well proved, to which I cannot find any Reply. For although I am called Scholar in it, I would be very angry to be counted among those who know how to respond to everything.

My defense will be no less easy because of that. It will be confined to comparing to my sentiment the truths raised in objection. For if I prove that they do not attack it, that will, I believe, be sufficient defense of it.

I can reduce to two principal points all the Propositions established by my Adversary. One comprises the praise of the Sciences, the other deals with their abuses. I shall examine them separately.

It appears from the tone of the Reply that one would have been glad if I had said much more that was bad about the Sciences than I in fact did. It is assumed that the praise of the sciences found at the beginning of my Discourse was painful for me to write. It is an admission wrested by truth, and which I lost no time retracting, according to the Author.

If this admission is a praise wrested by truth, it must then be believed that I thought the good I said about the sciences. The good the Author himself says about them is not contrary to my sentiment, then. This admission, it is said, is wrested by force. So much the better for my cause; for that shows that truth is stronger than inclination in me. But on what basis can this praise be judged to be forced? Would it be because it is badly done? It would bring the sincerity of authors to a terrible trial to judge them by this new principle. Would it be because it is too short? It seems to me I could easily have said fewer things in more pages. It is, it is said, because I retracted it. I do not know where I made that mistake. And all I can respond is that I did not intend to do so.

Science is very good in itself, that is evident. And to say the opposite would be to repudiate good sense. The Author of all things is the source of truth; knowing everything is one of his divine attributes. In a sense, then, it is to share in the supreme intelligence to acquire knowledge and expand one's enlightenment. In this sense I praised learning and it is in this sense that my Adversary praises it. He enlarges more about the various kinds of usefulness Man can derive from the Arts and Sciences. And I would willingly have said as much if that had been my subject. Thus we are in perfect agreement on this point.

But how can it be that the Sciences, whose source is so pure and whose end so praiseworthy, engender so many impieties, so many heresies, so many errors, so many absurd systems, so many contradictions, so many follies, so many bitter Satires, so many wretched Novels, so many licentious Poems, so many obscene Books; and in those who cultivate them so much pride, so much avarice, so much spitefulness, so many cabals, so many jealousies, so many lies, so many heinous deeds, so many calumnies, so many cowardly and shameful flatteries? I said that it is because Science—as beautiful and sublime as it is—is not made for man; that he has too limited a mind to make much progress in it, and too many passions in his heart not to put it to bad use; that it is enough for him to study his duties well, and that each person has received all the enlightenment he needs for this study. My Adversary admits from his side that the Sciences become harmful when they are abused, and that in fact many do abuse them. In that respect, we are not saying very different things, I believe. I add, it is true, that they are abused very much and that they are always abused; and it does not seem to me that the opposite was maintained in the Reply.

I can assert then that our principles, and consequently all the propositions that can be deduced from them, are not at all opposed, and that is what I had to prove. However, when we come to conclude, our two conclusions turn out opposite. Mine was that since the Sciences do more harm to morals than good to society, it would have been desirable for men to pursue them with less ardor. My Adversary's is that although the Sciences do much harm, one must not give up cultivating them because of the good they do. I defer, not to the Public, but to the small number of true Philosophers to determine which of these two conclusions is to be preferred.

I have some slight Observations to make about a few passages in this Reply which appeared to me to be slightly lacking in the correctness I willingly admire in the others, and which may have contributed by that to the mistaken conclusion the Author draws from them.

The work begins with a few personal remarks which I will not address except insofar as they pertain to the question. The Author honors me with several praises, and that assuredly opens my way to a fine career. But there is too little proportion between these things. A respectful silence about the objects of our admiration is often more suitable than indiscreet praise.*

My Discourse, it is said, is somewhat surprising.** It seems to me that this would demand some clarification. It is also surprising to see it awarded first prize. Yet it is no marvel to see mediocre writings awarded prizes. In every other sense, this surprise would honor the Academy of Dijon as much as it insults the integrity of Academies in general; and it is easy to sense how much I will use that to benefit my cause.

In very pleasantly organized Sentences, I am accused of a contradiction between my conduct and my doctrine. I am reproached for having cultivated myself the studies I condemn.*** Since Science and Virtue are incompatible, as it is asserted I strive to prove, I am asked in a rather urgent tone how I dare to use one while declaring myself in favor of the other.

It is very clever to implicate me in the question that way. That personal remark cannot fail to throw confusion in my Reply, or rather in my Replies, for unfortunately I have more than one to make. Let us try at least to have accuracy make up for lack of pleasantness.

1. That the cultivation of the Sciences corrupts the morals of a nation is what I have dared maintain, what I dare believe I have proved. But how could I have said that in each particular Man, Science and Virtue are incompatible, I who exhorted Princes to invite the truly Learned to their

*All Princes, good and bad, will always be basely and indifferently praised as long as there are Courtiers and People of Letters. As for Princes who are great Men, they must have praises that are more moderate and better chosen. Flattery offends their virtue, and praise itself can be a disservice to their glory. I at least know well that Trajan would be much greater in my eyes if Pliny had never written.[2] If Alexander had been in fact what he affected to appear to be, he would never have thought about his portrait or his Statue. But for his Panegyric, he would have allowed only a Lacedemonian to make it, at the risk of having none. The only eulogy worthy of a King is one that emerges not from the mercenary lips of an Orator but from the voice of a free People.

** It is the question itself that might be surprising: a great and fine question if ever there was one, and one which might not be asked again for a long time. The French Academy has just proposed a subject very similar to it for the eloquence prize for the year 1752. It must be maintained that *Love of Letters Inspires Love of Virtue*. The Academy did not judge it appropriate to leave such a subject as an open question; and for this occasion that wise Company doubled the time it previously allotted to Authors, even for the most difficult subjects.

***I cannot justify myself as many others do by saying that our education is not dependent on ourselves and that we are not consulted about being poisoned. I threw myself into study very willingly, and it was with even more conviction that I abandoned it, when I perceived the turmoil into which it threw my soul with no benefit for my reason. I no longer want any part of a deceiving profession, where one believes he is doing a great deal for wisdom while doing everything for vanity.

Court and to place their trust in them, so that for once one might see what Science and Virtue joined for the happiness of the human race can do. These truly Learned are few in number, I admit, for to make good use of Science, great talents and great Virtues must be joined. Now that can barely be hoped for in a few privileged souls, but should not be expected in an entire people. One cannot conclude, therefore, from my principles that a man cannot be learned and virtuous all at once.

2. Still less can I be personally accused of this supposed contradiction even if it really existed. I adore Virtue; my heart bears witness to this. It also tells me only too much how far it is from this love to the practice that makes a man virtuous. Besides, I am far from having Science, and farther still from affecting it. I would have thought that the ingenuous admission I made at the beginning of my Discourse would protect me from this imputation; I feared rather that I would be accused of judging things I did not know. It is readily sensed that it was impossible for me to avoid both these reproaches simultaneously. For all I know they would eventually be joined together if I did not hasten to refute this one, however little it may be warranted.

3. On this subject, I could relate what the Church Fathers said of the worldly Sciences they scorned and which they nonetheless used to combat the Pagan Philosophers. I could cite the comparison they made to the Egyptian vases stolen by the Israelites.[3] But I will be satisfied for my final Reply to ask this question: If someone came to kill me and I were fortunate enough to seize his weapon, would I be forbidden to use it to chase him out of my house before throwing it away?

If the contradiction for which I am criticized does not exist, it is therefore not necessary to assume that I only wanted to amuse myself with a frivolous paradox; and that appears to me all the less necessary because the tone I chose, bad as it may be, is at least not one that is used in games of wit.

It is time to stop discussing what concerns me. Nothing is ever gained by talking about oneself, and it is an indiscretion which the Public rarely forgives, even when one is forced to do it. Truth is so independent of those who attack it and those who defend it, that the Authors who dispute over it ought mutually to forget each other. That would save a lot of paper and ink. But this rule so easy to practice with me is not so at all in relation to my Adversary; and that is a difference which does not favor my reply.

Observing that I attack the Sciences and Arts by their effects on morals, to respond to me the Author enumerates all the uses derived from them in every station. It is as if, to vindicate an accused person, one was satisfied to prove that he is very healthy, that he is very skillful, or that he is very rich. So long as it is acknowledged that the Arts and Sciences make us dishonest people, I will not disagree that they are very useful to us in other ways. It is one more conformity they will have to the majority of vices.

The Author goes further and claims in addition that we need to study in order to admire the beauties of the universe, and that the spectacle of nature—exposed, it seems, to the eyes of all for the instruction of the simple, itself requires much education in the Observers in order to be perceived by them. I admit that this proposition surprises me: would it be ordained that all men be Philosophers or would it be ordained that Philosophers alone believe in God? The Scriptures exhort us in a thousand places to adore the greatness and goodness of God in the marvels of his works. I do not think they prescribed anywhere that we study Physics or that the Author of Nature is less well adored by me who knows nothing than by the person who knows both the cedar and the hyssop, both the nose of the fly and that of the Elephant.

One always believes one has said what the Sciences do when one has said what they ought to do. That seems very different to me, however: the study of the Universe ought to exalt man toward his Creator, I know, but it exalts only human vanity. The Philosopher, who flatters himself that he fathoms the secrets of God, dares associate his supposed wisdom with eternal wisdom: he approves, he blames, he corrects, he prescribes laws to nature and limits to the Divinity. And while occupied with his vain systems, he goes to great lengths to arrange the mechanisms of the world, the Farmer—who sees the rain and the sun in turn fertilize his field—admires, praises, and blesses the hand from which he receives these blessings, without concerning himself about the manner in which they come to him. He does not seek to justify his ignorance or his vices by his incredulity. He does not censure God's works and does not attack his master to show off his own adequacy. The blasphemous statement of Alphonse X will never enter the mind of the common man. That blasphemy was reserved for a learned mouth.[4]

Curiosity, natural to man, it continues, *inspires in him the desire to learn.* He ought to work to control it then, along with all his natural inclinations. *His needs make him feel the necessity of doing so.* In many respects, knowledge is useful. Yet savages are men, and they do not feel that necessity. *His employments impose on him the obligation of doing so.* They oblige him much more often to renounce study in order to attend to his duties.* *His progress makes him taste the pleasure of doing so.* For that very reason he ought to be wary of it. *His first discoveries increase his eagerness to know.* This happens in fact to those who have talent. *The more he knows, the more he feels there is knowledge to be acquired.* That is to say that the use of all the time he loses is to stimulate him to lose still more. But there are scarcely more than a few men of genius for whom the sight of their own ignorance grows as they learn, and it is only for them that study can be good. Hardly have those small minds learned something than they believe they know everything, and there is no kind of foolishness which this persuasion does not make them say and do. *The more knowledge he has acquired, the easier it is for him to do good.* It is apparent that in talking like this, the Author heeded his heart far more than he observed men.

He proposes further that it is good to know evil in order to learn to flee it. And he suggests that one can be sure of one's virtue only after testing it. These maxims are at least dubious and subject to much discussion. It is not certain that in order to learn to do good, one is obliged to know in how many ways one can do evil. We have an internal guide, far more infallible than all the books, and which never abandons us in need. It would suffice to lead us innocently, if we would listen to it. And how could one be obliged to test one's strengths in order to confirm one's virtue if it is one of the practices of virtue to flee occasions for vice?

The wise man is continually on his guard and always mistrusts his own strength. He reserves all his courage for times of need and never exposes himself to danger inappropriately. The braggart is the person who incessantly boasts about more than he can do, and who—after he has dared and insulted everyone—is beaten at the first encounter. I ask which of these two portraits better resembles a Philosopher at grips with his passions.

I am reproached for the affectation of selecting my examples of virtue from the ancients. It appears quite likely that I would have found still more if I could have gone even further back. I also cited one modern people, and it is not my fault if I found only one. I am reproached further in a general maxim for making odious parallels which, it is said, contain less zeal and equity than envy of my compatriots and ill-humor for my contemporaries. Yet no one, perhaps, loves his country and his compatriots as much as I. Moreover, I have only one thing to say in response. I stated my reasons and they must be weighed. As for my intentions, judgment of them must be left to that one alone to whom this belongs.

---

*It is a bad sign for a society to require so much Science in those who lead it. If men were what they ought to be, they would scarcely need to study to learn the things they have to do.

I should not remain silent here about a considerable objection that has already been raised against me by a Philosopher*: *Isn't it, I am told here, to climate, temperament, absence of opportunity, lack of a goal, the economy of the government, Customs, Laws, to every other cause except the Sciences that one ought to attribute the difference in morals sometimes noted in different countries and at different times?*

This question contains large objects and would require clarifications too extensive to be suited to this essay. Besides, it would involve examining the very hidden but very real relationships that are found between the nature of the government and the genius, morals, and knowledge of the citizens. And this would thrust me into delicate discussions which could take me too far. Moreover, it would be quite difficult for me to talk about government without giving my Adversary too great an advantage. And taking everything into consideration, these researches are good ones to undertake in Geneva and in other circumstances.

I turn to an accusation much more serious than the preceding objection. I will transcribe it as it was written, for it is important to place it faithfully before the Reader's eyes.

The more the Christian examines the authenticity of its Claims, the more reassured he is about the belief he holds. The more he studies revelation, the stronger his faith becomes. It is in the divine Scriptures that he discovers its origin and excellence. It is in the scholarly writings of the Church Fathers that he follows its development century by century. It is in the Books of moral philosophy and the sacred annals that he sees examples of it and applies them to himself.

What! Will ignorance take away from Religion and virtue such powerful supports and will a Scholar from Geneva openly teach that irregularity of morals is due to it! It would be more amazing to hear such a strange paradox if it were not known that the peculiarity of a system, however dangerous it is, is only an additional reason for someone who has only the private mind as a guide.[6]

I dare to ask the Author how he could ever have given such an interpretation to the principles I have established? How could he have accused me of blaming the study of Religion, I who blame above all the study of our vain Sciences because it turns us away from the study of our duties? And what is the study of the Christian's duties if not his religion itself?

No doubt I should have expressly blamed all those childish subtleties of Scholasticism with which, on the pretext of elucidating the principles of Religion, its spirit is destroyed by substituting scientific pride for

* Preface to the *Encyclopedia*.[5]

Christian humility. I should have protested with greater strength against those indiscreet Ministers who were the first to lay hands on the Ark in order to prop up with their feeble knowledge an edifice sustained by the hand of God. I should have been indignant at those frivolous men who, with their wretched hair-splitting, debased the sublime simplicity of the Gospel, and reduced the doctrine of Jesus Christ to syllogisms. But my purpose today is to defend myself, not to attack.

I see that it is history and facts that ought to end this dispute. If I knew how to set forth in a few words what the Sciences and Religion had in common from the beginning, perhaps that would serve to settle the question on this point.

The people God chose never cultivated the Sciences, and it was never advised to study them. However, if that study were good for anything, that people would have had more need of it than any other people. On the contrary, its Leaders always made efforts to keep it as separate as possible from the idolatrous and learned Nations surrounding it; a precaution less necessary for it from one side than from the other, for this weak and uncouth People was far easier to seduce by the deceits of the priests of Baal than by the Sophisms of the Philosophers.

After frequent dispersions among the Egyptians and the Greeks, Science still had a thousand difficulties developing in the heads of the Hebrews. Josephus and Philo, who would have been only two mediocre men anywhere else, were prodigies among them. The Sadducees, recognizable by their irreligion, were the Philosophers of Jerusalem. The Pharisees, great hypocrites,* were its Scholars. The latter, although they confined their Science approximately to the study of the Law, made this study with every display and dogmatic conceit. They also observed with very great care all the practices of Religion. But the Gospel teaches us the spirit of this exactness and how much consideration it should have been given. Moreover, they all had very little Science and a great deal of pride. And it was not in that respect that they differed most from our Scholars today.

In the establishment of the new Law, it was not to the Learned that Jesus Christ wished to entrust his doctrine and his ministry. In his choice

---

*Prevailing between these two parties were that hate and mutual scorn that has always prevailed between Scholars and Philosophers, that is to say, between those who make their heads into repertoires of someone else's Science, and those who pride themselves on having their own. Pit the music master and the dancing master in the *Bourgeois Gentilhomme*[7] against one another, and you will have the antiquary and the wit, the Chemist and the Man of Letters, the Jurist and the Doctor, the Geometer and the Versifier, the Theologian and the Philosopher. To judge all those People well, it suffices to turn to them and listen to what each of them says to you, not about himself but about the others.

he followed the predilection he showed on every occasion for the lowly and the simple. And in the instructions he gave to his disciples, there is not one word about study or Science, except to denote the scorn with which he treated all that.

After the death of Jesus Christ, twelve poor fishermen and artisans undertook to instruct and convert the world. Their method was simple. They preached without Art but with an earnest heart; and of all the miracles with which God honored their faith, the most striking was the saintliness of their life. The disciples followed this example and their success was prodigious. The Pagan Priests, alarmed, gave Princes to understand that the state was lost because offerings decreased. Persecutions arose, and the persecutors only accelerated the progress of the Religion they wished to stifle. All the Christians rushed to martyrdom; all the Peoples rushed to Baptism. The history of these earliest times is a continual marvel.

Meanwhile the Priests of the idols, not satisfied to persecute the Christians, began to calumny them. The Philosophers, who did not find their advantage in a religion that preaches humility, joined their Priests. Scoffing and insults showered down from all sides on the new Sect. It was necessary to take up the pen to defend oneself. Saint Justin Martyr* was the first to write the Apology of his faith. The Pagans were attacked in

---

*These first writers who sealed the testimony of their pen with their blood would be rather scandalous Authors today, for they upheld precisely the same sentiment as I do. In his exchange with Tripho, Saint Justin reviews the various Sects of Philosophy he had formerly tried, and he makes them so ridiculous that one feels as if one is reading a *Dialogue* of Lucian. In the Apology of Tertullian,[7] one also sees how greatly offended the first Christians were to be taken for Philosophers.

Indeed, the exposition of the pernicious maxims and impious dogmas of its various Sects would be a very withering detail for Philosophy. The Epicureans denied all providence, the Academics doubted the existence of the Divinity, and the Stoics doubted the immortality of the soul. The less famous Sects did not have better sentiments. Here is a sample of them from Theodorus, the leader of one of the two branches of the Cyrenaics, reported by Diogenes Laertius. *Sustulit amicitiam quod ea neque insipientibus neque sapientibus adsit . . . Probabile dicebat prudentem virum non seipsum pro patria periculis exponere, neque enim pro insipientium commodis amittendam esse prudentiam. Furto quoque et adulterio et sacrilegio cum tempestivum erit daturum operam sapientem. Nihil quippe horum turpe natura esse. Sed auferatur de hisce vulgaris opinio, quae e stultorum imperatorumque plebecula conflata est . . . sapientem publice absque ullo pudore ac suspicione scortis congressurum.*[9]

These opinions are peculiar to him, I know. But is there a single one of all the Sects that did not fall into some dangerous error. And what shall we say about the distinction between the two doctrines so eagerly received by all the Philosophers, and by which they professed in secret sentiments contrary to those they taught publicly? Pythagoras was the first to make use of the esoteric doctrine. He did not reveal it to his disciples until after lengthy tests and with the greatest mystery. He gave them lessons in Atheism in secret and solemnly offered Hecatombs to Jupiter. The Philosophers were so comfortable with this method that it spread rapidly in Greece and from there in Rome, as may be seen in the works of Cicero, who along with his friends laughed at the immortal Gods to whom he so

turn. To attack them was to defeat them. The first successes encouraged other writers. On the pretext of exposing the turpitude of Paganism, people threw themselves into mythology and erudition.* They wanted to display Science and wit, Books came out in droves, and morals began to loosen.

Soon people were no longer satisfied with the simplicity of the Gospel and the faith of the Apostles. It was necessary always to have more wit than one's predecessors. They split hairs on all the dogmas; everyone wanted to maintain his opinion, no one wanted to yield. The ambition to be the Leader of a Sect emerged; heresies swarmed on all sides.

Anger and violence did not delay in joining the dispute. These gentle Christians, who only knew how to present their throats to the knife, became furious persecutors among themselves, worse than the idolaters. All were implicated in the same excesses, and the side of truth was not maintained with more moderation than that of error.

Another evil, more dangerous still, was born from the same source. It is the introduction of ancient Philosophy into Christian doctrine. By virtue of studying the Greek Philosophers, people believed they saw relationships to Christianity. They dared to believe that Religion cloaked in the authority of Philosophy would thereby become more respectable. There was a time when it was necessary to be a Platonist in order to be Orthodox. Little more would have been necessary for Plato first and then Aristotle to be placed on the altar beside Jesus Christ.

The Church rose up more than once against these abuses. Its most illustrious defenders often deplored them in terms full of strength and energy. Often they attempted to banish from it all that worldly Science which sullied its purity. One of the most illustrious Popes even reached the point of over-zealousness of maintaining that it was a shameful thing to subject the word of God to the rules of Grammar.[11]

But they cried in vain. Carried along by the torrent, they themselves were constrained to conform to the practice they condemned. And it was

---

eloquently bore witness on the Rostrum. The esoteric doctrine was not carried from Europe to China, but it was born there too with Philosophy. And to it the Chinese owe the large number of Atheists or Philosophers they have among them. The History of this deadly doctrine, written by an informed and sincere man, would be a terrible blow to ancient and modern Philosophy. But Philosophy will always defy reason, truth, and even time, because it has its source in human pride, stronger than all those things.

*Clement of Alexandria[10] has been justifiably reproached for affecting in his writings profane erudition ill-suited to a Christian. However, it seems that it was excusable then to learn the doctrine against which one had to defend oneself. But who can see without laughing all the trouble our Learned men take today to shed light on the reveries of mythology?

in a very learned manner that most of them declaimed against the progress of the Sciences.

After long disturbances, things finally became more settled. Toward the tenth century, the torch of the Sciences stopped illuminating the earth. The Clergy remained plunged in an ignorance that I do not want to justify, since it covered no less the things it should know than those which are useless to it, but from which the Church at least gained a little more rest than it had experienced until that time.

After the revival of Letters, divisions more terrible than ever did not delay in resuming. Learned Men stirred up the dispute, learned Men sustained it, and the most capable always proved themselves the most obstinate. Conferences among Scholars of the different parties were organized in vain. No one brought to them a love of reconciliation, nor perhaps that of truth. All brought only the desire to shine at the expense of their Adversary. Each wanted to win, none wanted to learn. The stronger imposed silence on the weaker. The dispute always ended with insults, and persecution has always been its fruit. Only God knows when all these evils will end.

The Sciences are flourishing today; Literature and the Arts shine in our midst. How has this benefited Religion? Let us ask that multitude of Philosophers who pride themselves on having none. Our Libraries are bursting with Books of Theology, and Casuists swarm among us. We used to have Saints and no Casuists. Science spreads and faith vanishes. Everyone wants to teach how to do good, and no one wants to learn. We have all become Scholars and we have ceased to be Christians.

No, it is not with so much Art and apparatus that the Gospel has spread through the Universe and that its ravishing beauty has penetrated hearts. One need only meditate on this divine Book, the only one necessary for a Christian, and the most useful of all even for someone who is not, to bring to the soul love for its Author and the will to carry out his precepts. Virtue has never spoken such a sweet language. Never has the most profound wisdom expressed itself with so much energy and simplicity. One never ends a reading of it without feeling that he is better than before. O Ministers of the Law that it sets forth to me, take less trouble to teach me so many useless things. Abandon those Learned Books which can neither convince nor touch me. Prostrate yourselves at the feet of this God of mercy, whom you undertake to make me know and love. Ask him for that profound humility that you ought to preach to me. Do not display before my eyes that prideful Science or that indecent display which dishonor you and revolt me. Be moved yourselves if you want me to be moved. And above all show me in your behavior the practice of that Law in which you claim to educate me. You have no need to know or teach me anything more, and your ministry is fulfilled. In all this, there is no place for Literature or Philosophy. This is the fitting way to follow and preach the Gospel, and this is how its first defenders caused it to triumph over all Nations, *non Aristotelico more*, said the Church Fathers, *sed Piscatorio*.[12]

I feel I am becoming lengthy, but I believed I could not dispense with expanding a little on a point of this importance. Moreover, impatient Readers ought to reflect that criticism is a very convenient thing, for wherever one attacks with a single word, pages are needed for the defense.

I shift to the second part of the Reply, about which I will try to be briefer, although I do not find any fewer observations to make.

It is not from the sciences, I am told, *but from the bosom of wealth that softness and luxury have always been born*. I had not said either that luxury was born from the Sciences, but that they were born together and that one scarcely went without the other. This is how I would arrange this genealogy. The first source of evil is inequality. From inequality came wealth, for those words poor and rich are relative, and everywhere that men are equal, there are neither rich nor poor. From wealth are born luxury and idleness. From luxury come the fine Arts and from idleness the Sciences. *In no time has wealth been the share of the Learned*. For that very reason the evil is greater; the rich and the learned serve only to corrupt each other mutually. If the rich were more learned or the learned richer, the latter would not be such cowardly flatterers and the former would like base flattery less, and they would all be better off. That is what can be seen from the small number of those who have the good fortune to be learned and rich at the same time. *For one Plato in opulence, for one Aristippus accredited at Court, how many Philosophers are there reduced to a cloak and beggar's sack, draped in their own virtue and ignored in their solitude?* I do not disagree that there are a large number of Philosophers who are very poor and certainly very angry at being so. I do not doubt either that it is not to their poverty alone that most of them owe their Philosophy. But if I were willing to assume they are virtuous, would it be on the basis of their morals, which the people does not see, that it would learn to reform its own? *The Learned have neither the taste nor the leisure to amass great wealth*. I consent to believe that they do not have the leisure to do so. *They love study*. A person who would not love his profession would be a madman or very wretched. *They live in mediocrity*. It is necessary to be very biased in their favor to count this as a merit in them. *A laborious and moderate life, spent in the silence of retreat, occupied with reading and work, is assuredly not a voluptuous and criminal life.* Not, at least, in the eyes of men. Everything depends on what is inside. A man can be compelled to live such a life and yet have a very corrupt soul. Besides, what does it matter whether he himself is virtuous and modest if the things he works on nourish idleness and spoil the mind of his fellow citizens? *The conveniences of life albeit often the fruit of the Arts are not thereby the lot of Artists.* It hardly seems to me that they are people to refuse them, especially those involved with completely useless and consequently more lucrative Arts, who are in a better position to procure everything they desire for themselves. *They work only for the rich.* As things are now going, I would not be surprised to see the rich work for them someday. *And it is the idle rich who profit from and abuse the fruits of their industry.* Once again, I do not see that our Artists are such simple and modest people. Luxury cannot prevail among one order of Citizens without soon slipping into all the others in different modifications, and it causes the same devastation everywhere.

Luxury corrupts everything, both the rich person who enjoys it and the wretch who covets it. It cannot be said that it is an evil in itself to wear lace trimmed cuffs, an embroidered coat, and to carry an enameled box. But it is a great evil to attach some importance to such finery, to deem the people who have it happy, and to devote time and effort that every man owes to nobler objects to achieving a position in which to acquire similar things. I have no need to learn the profession of a person who is preoccupied with such thoughts to know how I must judge him.

I have passed over the fine portrait made here of the Learned, and I believe I deserve some credit for this kindness. My Adversary is less indulgent: not only does he accord me nothing he can refuse, but rather than to condemn the ill I think of our vain and false politeness, he prefers to excuse its hypocrisy. He asks me if I would like to have vice show itself openly. Assuredly I would like it. Confidence and esteem would be reborn between the good; one would learn to beware of the wicked; and society would thereby be safer. I prefer to have my enemy attack me with open force than to come up treacherously and strike me from behind. What then! Must scandal be combined with crime? I do not know, but I surely wish that deceit were not combined with it. All the maxims about scandal to which we have been treated for so long are very convenient for the vicious: if one wished to follow them rigorously, one must allow himself to be robbed, betrayed, and killed with impunity, and never punish anyone; for a scoundrel on the rack is a very scandalous thing. But is hypocrisy an homage that vice renders to virtue?[13] Yes, like that of Caesar's assassins, who prostrated themselves at his feet in order to stab him more surely. This thought may well be brilliant, it may well be authorized by the famous name of its Author; it is no more just for all that. Will it ever be said that a thief who puts on the livery of a house to rob it more conveniently pays homage to the master of the house he robs? No, to cover one's wickedness with the dangerous cloak of hypocrisy is not to honor virtue at all. It is to insult it by profaning its emblems. It is to add cowardice and deceit to all the other vices. It is to close forever any return to integrity. There are lofty characters who bring even to crime an undefinable quality of pride and generosity in which there can still be seen some spark of that celestial fire destined to animate beautiful souls. But the vile and groveling soul of the hypocrite is like a cadaver, where one no longer finds fire nor warmth nor resource for life. I call upon experience. Great scoundrels have been seen to return to themselves, end their career soundly, and die saved. But what no one has ever seen is a hypocrite who has become a good man. The conversion of Cartouche might reasonably have been attempted; a wise man would never have undertaken that of Cromwell.[14]

I attributed the elegance and politeness that prevail in our manners to the restoration of Letters and Arts. The Author of the Reply disputes this, and I am astonished by that. For since he makes so much of politeness and since he makes so much of the Sciences, I do not perceive the advantage he will gain from taking away from one of these things the honor of having produced the other. But let's examine his proofs. They boil down to this. *The Learned are not seen to be more polite than other men. On the contrary, they are often much less so. Therefore our politeness is not the work of the Sciences.*

I will note first that it is less a matter here of the Sciences than of Literature, fine Arts, and works of taste. And our fine wits, as little Learned as could be wished, but so polite, so widely accepted, so brilliant, such fops would hardly recognize themselves in the sullen and pedantic bearing that the Author of the Reply confers on them. But let's grant him what precedes. Let's grant, if necessary, that the Learned, the Poets, and the fine wits are all equally ridiculous; that the Gentlemen of the Academy of Letters, the Gentlemen of the Academy of Sciences, the Gentlemen of the French Academy are coarse people who know neither the tone nor the practices of the world, and are excluded by their status from good company. The Author will gain little by that, and will not have more right to deny because of it that the politeness and urbanity which prevail among us are the result of good taste, derived first among the ancients and spread among the peoples of Europe by the pleasing

Books published in every part of it.* Just as the best dancing teachers are not always the people who best present themselves, someone can give good lessons in politeness without wishing or being able to be very polite himself. Those ponderous Commentators whom we are told knew everything about the ancients except for grace and finesse, nevertheless managed in their useful, albeit scorned, works to teach us to feel those beauties they did not feel at all. The same is true of that pleasure in commerce and elegance of morals that are substituted for their purity, and that have been noted among all the peoples where Letters have been in honor, at Athens, Rome, China, wherever politeness of both language and manners always accompanies not the Learned and the Artists but the Sciences and the fine Arts.

Next the Author attacks the praises I gave to ignorance. And taxing me for having spoken more as an Orator than as a Philosopher, he depicts ignorance in turn. And one might well guess that he does not lend it beautiful colors.

I do not deny that he is right, but I do not believe I am wrong. One very exact and very true distinction is all that is necessary to reconcile us.

There is a ferocious** and brutal ignorance which is born of a wicked heart and a false mind, a criminal ignorance which extends to the duties of humanity; which multiplies vices, which degrades reason, debases the soul, and makes men like beasts. This ignorance is the one the Author attacks, and of which he paints a most odious and accurate portrait. There is another reasonable kind of ignorance, which consists in confining one's curiosity to the extent of the faculties which one has received; a modest ignorance, which is born from a lively love of virtue and in-

---

*When what is at issue are objects as general as the morals and manners of a people, one must take care not to narrow one's views always by specific examples. That would be the way never to perceive the sources of things. To know whether I am right to attribute politeness to the cultivation of Letters, one must not look for whether one Learned person or another is polite. But one must examine the relationships there may be between literature and politeness, and then see among which people these things are found together, and among which they are found separately. The same must be done with regard to luxury, liberty, and all the other things which influence the morals of a nation, and about which I hear daily such pathetic reasoning. To examine all this on a small scale and about a few individuals is not to Philosophize, it to waste one's time and one's reflections. For one may know Peter or James through and through and have made very little progress in the knowledge of men.15

**I will be very astonished if one of my critics does not make use of the eulogy I gave of several ignorant and virtuous peoples to confront me with the list of all the bands of Brigands who have infected the earth and who were ordinarily not very Learned men. I exhort them in advance not to tire themselves with this research, unless they deem it necessary in order to show me their erudition. If I had said that it was sufficient to be ignorant in order to be virtuous, it would not be worth the trouble of replying to me. And for the same reason, I will believe myself relieved from replying to those who will waste their time upholding the opposite to me.

spires only indifference toward all things that are not worthy of filling a man's heart and do not contribute to his betterment; a sweet and precious ignorance, the treasure of a soul that is pure and content with itself, which places all its happiness in turning inward, bearing witness to its innocence, and has no need to seek a false and vain happiness in the opinion others may have of its enlightenment. That is the ignorance I praised and the one I request from Heaven as punishment for the scandal I caused the scholarly by my stated scorn for human Sciences.

Compare those times of ignorance and barbarism, says the Author, *to those fortunate centuries when the Sciences spread the spirit of order and justice everywhere.* Those fortunate epochs will be difficult to find; but more easily found are those when, thanks to the Sciences, Order and Justice will no longer be anything but vain words used to deceive the people, and where their appearance will have been preserved with care, in order to destroy them in fact with greater impunity. *Today we see wars that are less frequent but more just.* In any era, how can war be more just on one side without being more unjust on the other? I am unable to conceive of that! *Actions less astonishing but more heroic.* Surely no one will deny my Adversary's right to judge heroism. But does he think that what is not at all astonishing for him is not astonishing for us? *Victories less bloody but more glorious; Conquests less rapid but more assured; warriors less violent but more formidable, knowing how to vanquish with moderation, treating the vanquished with humanity. Honor is their guide, glory their recompense.* I do not deny the author that there are great men among us; it would be too easy for him to provide proof of it. That does not mean that the peoples are not very corrupt. Besides, these things are so vague they could almost be said of all ages. And it is impossible to respond to them because it would be necessary to leaf through Libraries and write volumes to establish proofs for or against.

When Socrates spoke ill of the Sciences, he could not have had in mind, it seems to me, the pride of the Stoics, nor the softness of the Epicureans, nor the absurd jargon of the Pyrronians, because none of those people existed in his time. But this slight anachronism is not unbecoming in my adversary. He has better things to do than check dates, and he is no more obliged to know his Diogenes Laertius by heart than I am to have seen at close range what happens in battles.

I agree then that Socrates was thinking only of bringing into relief the vices of the Philosophers of his time. But I do not know what to conclude from that except that even then vices swarmed along with Philosophers. In reply to that, I am told that it is the abuse of Philosophy, and I do not think I said it was not. What! Must everything that is abused therefore be suppressed? Yes, without any doubt, I will reply without hesitation. All those that are useless. All those the abuse of which does more harm than their use does good.

Let's stop a moment on that last consequence and take care not to conclude from it that today we must burn all Libraries and destroy the Universities and Academies. We would only plunge Europe back into Barbarism, and morals would gain nothing from it.* It is with sadness that I am going to pronounce a great and deadly truth. It is only one step from knowledge to ignorance, and alternation from one to the other is frequent in Nations. But once a people has been corrupted, it has never been seen to return to virtue. You would try in vain to destroy the sources of evil. You would take away in vain the nourishment of vanity, idleness, and luxury. You would even return men in vain to that first equality, preserver of innocence and source of all virtue. Their hearts once spoiled will be so forever. There is no remedy short of some great revolution—almost as much to be feared as the evil it might cure—and which is blameworthy to desire and impossible to foresee.

Then let's allow the Sciences and Arts to soften, in a way, the ferocity of the men they have corrupted. Let's seek to make a wise diversion and try to deceive their passions. Let's offer some food to these tigers so they do not devour our children. The enlightenment of the wicked man is still less to be feared than his brutal stupidity. It at least makes him more circumspect about the evil he could do through knowledge of the evil he himself would receive from it.

I have praised the Academies and their illustrious founders, and I will gladly repeat the eulogy. When the ill is incurable, the Doctor applies palliatives and proportions remedies less to the needs than to the temperament of the sick person. Wise legislators should imitate his prudence. And, no longer able to apply the most excellent policy to sick Peoples, they should give them at least, as Solon did, the best they can handle.

In Europe there is a great Prince and, more important, a virtuous Citizen, who in the fatherland that he adopted and that he makes happy has just founded several institutions for the benefit of Letters.[16] In doing so, he has done something very worthy of his wisdom and his virtue. When it is a matter of political establishments, time and place determine everything. In their own interests, Princes must always favor the Sciences and Arts. I have stated the reason for that. And in the present state of things, they must still favor them today even in the interest of

---

* *Our vices would remain,* says the Philosopher whom I have already cited, *and we would have ignorance in addition.* In the few lines that Author wrote on this vast subject, it is apparent that he turned to look at it and saw far.

Peoples. If there were now among us some Monarch limited enough to think and act differently, his subjects would remain poor and ignorant, and would not be any the less vicious for it. My Adversary neglected to take advantage of an example that is so striking and so apparently favorable to his cause. Perhaps he is the only one who does not know it or who has not thought of it. Let him endure being reminded of it then. Let him not withhold from great things the praises they deserve. Let him admire them as we do, and not use them to insist more strongly against the truths he attacks.

Refutation of the Observations
of Jean-Jacques Rousseau of Geneva[1]

We agree with the illustrious author of the refutation published in the *Mercury*, in that we have found as he does:

1. That Mr. Rousseau, learned, eloquent, and a worthy man all at once, makes a singular contrast with the citizen of Geneva, the orator of ignorance, the enemy of the sciences and arts which he considers a constant source of the corruption of morals.

2. Like the respectable anonymous writer, we thought that the discourse awarded first prize by the Academy of Dijon is a web of contradictions which reveal, despite its author, the truth he vainly tries to betray.

3. Like the philosopher prince, who protects letters as powerfully as he defends their cause, we have said that the Genevan orator had articulated too general an anathema against the sciences and arts, and confounded some abuses to which they are put with their natural effects and legitimate uses.

1. Mr. Rousseau replies to the first point that he studied literature without knowing it; that as soon as he *perceived the turmoil into which it threw his soul, he abandoned it.*[2]

How is it this author does not sense the reply that will be made to him that to have brought it to the point at which he has arrived is not to have abandoned it, or at least to have done so very belatedly. That to appear on the stage of academies to debate, to win the prizes they offer, is even to cultivate literature more than ever? The character Mr. Rousseau plays in his reply is therefore no more serious than the one he affects in his discourse.

I use literature, he says, to fight its cultivation, as the holy fathers used *worldly sciences against the pagans. If someone,* he adds, *came to kill me and I were fortunate enough to seize his weapon, would I be forbidden to use it to chase him out of my house before throwing it away?*[3]

The Church Fathers made good use of the worldly sciences to combat the pagans. Therefore these sciences are good, and they are not what those defenders of religion scorned and blamed. For they would have wanted neither to make use of them nor been able to do so usefully. But it was the bad use made of them by those profane philosophers that they objected to, with reason.

It is a very noble act to disarm one's enemy and drive him out with his own weapons. But Mr. Rousseau is not at all in that situation. He disarmed no one. The weapons he uses are truly his own. He acquired them through his labors, his vigils. It seems from their selection and luster that he received them from Minerva herself. And with manifest ingratitude, he uses them to insult that beneficent divinity. He uses them to annihilate, as far as he is able, what is most respectable, most useful, most likable among thinking men: philosophy, the study of wisdom, the love and cultivation of the sciences and arts. There is therefore no accuracy in the application of the examples Mr. Rousseau cites in his favor, and it is always strange that the learned, eloquent man who preserved all his probity, all his virtues with the exception of gratitude, in acquiring these talents uses them to attempt to prove that they deprave the morals of other people.

I add that there is such a necessary contrast between the cause supported by Mr. Rousseau and the means he uses to defend it, that even supposing he wins it, he would still lose it. For in this hypothesis, and according to his principles, by subjugating us his eloquence and wisdom would lead us to virtue, make us better, and consequently show us, even against the author, that all these talents are of the greatest utility.

2. That these contradictions are very frequent in the discourse of the citizen of Geneva has just been convincingly shown by the reading of my remarks. Mr. Rousseau claims that these contradictions are only apparent. That if he praises the sciences in several places, he does so sincerely and heartily, because then he considers them in themselves, he views them as a kind of participation in the *supreme intelligence*, and consequently as excellent. Whereas everywhere else in his discourse he treats the sciences relative to the genius, to the capacity of man. Since man is too limited *to make much progress in them, too passionate not to put them to bad use,*[4] for his good and that of others he ought to abstain from them. They are not at all proportioned to his nature, they are not at all made for him. He ought to avoid them all like so many poisons.

What! The sciences and arts are *not at all made for man!* Has Mr. Rousseau really thought well about it? Would he have forgotten already the marvels he had them perform on man himself? According to him, and according to the truth, the restoration of the sciences and arts *brought man in a way out of nothingness.* It *dissipated the darkness in which nature had enveloped him.* It *raised him above himself.* It took him *by means of his mind into celestial regions, and what is grander and more difficult,* it made him *come back into himself, to study man and know his nature, his duties, and his end. Europe*, continues our orator, *had sunk back into the barbarism of the first ages. The peoples of that part of the world which is today so enlightened lived, a few centuries ago, in a condition worse than ignorance. . . . A revolution was needed to bring men back to common sense.*[5] The citizen of Geneva exhorts kings to call learned men to their councils. . . . He views *enlightenment and wisdom* as companions, and learned men as suited to *teach* the latter *to the peoples.*[6] Enlightenment, sciences, these sparks of the Divinity are then made for man. And the fruit he draws from them is virtue.

What! Why would this emanation of the supreme wisdom not be proper for man? Why would it become harmful to him? Do we have a greater or more sublime model to follow than the Divinity? Can we go astray under such a guide so long as we confine ourselves to the science of religion and morals, to that of nature, and to the art of applying the latter to the needs and conveniences of life, three kinds of knowledge destined for man by his author himself. How is it possible to dare say, then, that they are not made for him when the author of all things has decided the opposite? *His mind is too limited to make much progress in them.* Whatever progress he will make will always be that much of his imperfections erased, that much gained on the glorious path his creator traces for him. *He has too many passions in his heart not to put them to bad use.* The more passions a man has, the more need he has of the science of morality and philosophy to overcome them. The more, too, he ought to amuse and distract himself by the study and exercise of the sciences and arts. The more passions a man has, the more he has of that fire that makes him fit to make the greatest, most useful discoveries. The more he has of the fire that is the principle of the great man, the hero, that makes him fit for vast enterprises, for the most sublime actions. Therefore, the more passions men have, the more necessary and advantageous for others and for themselves that they cultivate the sciences and the arts.

But the more passions he has, the more likely he is to abuse his talents, the adversary will answer.

The more knowledge he has, the less he will abuse them. Great enlightenment shows too clearly the errors, abuses, their principles, the shame connected to all the irregularities for the learned man who sees them so distinctly to dare surrender to them. In his observations, Mr. Rousseau agrees that true learned men do not abuse the sciences. Since, by his admission, they are without danger when they are truly possessed, and only those who do not possess them well abuse them, they cannot then be cultivated with too much zeal. And it is not the cultivation of the sciences that is to be feared, according to Mr. Rousseau himself, but on the contrary the lack of that cultivation, the imperfect cultivation, the abuse of that cultivation. That is what this author's defense comes down to when it is analyzed. And it can be seen that the distinction thought up to save the contradictions in his discourse is frivolous. And that neither this piece of writing nor the observations that come to its support impair in the least the utility so generally recognized of the sciences and arts, as much to procure our needs and our commodities as to make us worthier people.

3. The citizen of Geneva excludes from society all the sciences and all the arts, without exception. He considers the most complete ignorance as man's greatest good, as the only refuge of probity and virtue, and as a result he opposes to our century, polished by the sciences and arts, the morals of the savages in America, the morals of peoples given up solely to nature, solely to instinct. In his observations, Mr. Rousseau declares he is far from falling into this error, that he acknowledges theology, moral philosophy, and finally the science of salvation. But he acknowledges only those, *porro est unum necessarium.*[7] And he considers all the other sciences, all the other arts as useless, as pernicious to the human race, not in themselves but by the abuse made of them, and because *they are always abused.*[8] It appears in his discourse that he places luxury among these abuses. Here in contrast it is luxury that gives birth to the arts, and the *first source of evil is the inequality* of conditions, the distinction between *poor and rich.*[9]

1. I will refrain from seriously establishing the necessity for this inequality of conditions which is the strongest, most essential bond of society. This trivial truth leaps to the eyes of the least intelligent reader. I am only annoyed to see here, as in the discourse of the citizen of Geneva, that an orator of the high standing of Mr. Rousseau dares bring to the sanctuary of the academies paradoxes that Molière and Delille had the prudence to produce only through the mouths of the Misanthrope and the Savage Harlequin, and as eccentricities or oddities suited to make us laugh.[10] Let us return to the seriousness the subject we are addressing deserves.

The exception Mr. Rousseau makes here in favor of theology, moral philosophy, etc., is already a half retraction on his part. For the sciences of theology, of moral philosophy and salvation, are among the most sublime, the broadest. They are unknown to savages, and one will never be minded to consider as an ignorant person anyone who is perfectly educated in them. Athanasius, Chrysostom, Augustine are still admired in our time for this aspect alone. We have just seen, only a moment ago,

that Mr. Rousseau attributes the science of moral philosophy to the renewal of the sciences and arts. For the former is the art *of coming back to
himself to study man and know his nature, his duties, and his end; marvels
which,* he admits, *have been revived with the sciences.* Now this part of the
arts being essential to all men, the consequence of that is that our orator
will be forced to admit that the restoration of the sciences has procured
for the entire human race that very important utility which he labors here
to make independent and very separate from the sciences, even incompatible with them.

As for the science of salvation, taken in the broadest sense, everyone
knows that in those who are destined to teach it to others, to defend it,
and as it was possessed by the great men I have just named, worthy
models for those of our century, it presupposes knowledge of learned
languages, of philosophy, of eloquence, and finally of all the human sciences, since it is men who are to be saved. And that the art of inculcating
in them the truths necessary for this sublime project ought to use all
known means to affect their senses and convince their reason.

Was it learned men, says Mr. Rousseau, whom Jesus Christ chose to
spread his doctrine throughout the universe? Wasn't it fishermen, artisans, ignorant people?

The apostles were really ignorant men when God chose them as missionaries for his law, and he chose them that way on purpose, to give
greater proof of his power. But when they announced and preached this
doctrine of salvation, can it be said that they were ignorant? Aren't they,
on the contrary, an authentic example by which God declares to the universe that the science of salvation assumes knowledge, even the most
universal, most profound human knowledge? The Supreme Being wants
to make a fisherman and an artisan into a Christian, a follower, and a
preacher of the gospel. So it is that the Holy Spirit animates this artisan
and transforms him into an extraordinary man, who firstly speaks the
known languages, and who by the force of his eloquence converts three
thousand souls with a single sermon. One knows what is presupposed
by eloquence so persuasive and victorious amid a people hardened to the
point of still being in the darkness today in this regard. In our day, eloquence does not truly deserve that term unless it combines the order and
solidity of the geometer with the correctness and precise connection of
arguments of the logician, and covers them with flowers. Unless it fills
this excellent canvas with well-assorted materials, taken from the history
of men, from that of the sciences and that of the arts, whose smallest
details become necessary to an orator. Who has ever doubted that the art
of oratory was the art assuming and requiring the most knowledge? And

who will believe that the eloquence that came from the hand of God and given to the apostles for the greatest, the most necessary of all expeditions, was inferior to that of our rhetoricians? Grace and miracles came to the assistance of eloquence, it will be said. Grace and miracles are, no doubt, the main part of a work that human eloquence alone could never have been capable of executing. But it is no less a reality from the Scripture that the holy missionaries of the gospel animated by the spirit of God possessed that divine eloquence, superior to any human faculty, worthy too of the spirit that is the source of all Enlightenment. All nations were dumbfounded to see and hear simple Israelite artisans, not only speak all languages but also suddenly possess the science of the holy scripture, explain and apply it in a striking manner to the subject of their mission, and finally discourse with the learning, the fire, and the enthusiasm of the prophets.

Assuming it is exactly true, then, that the science of salvation is the only one that ought to occupy us, one sees that this science includes and requires all other human knowledge. The learned Church Fathers set the example for us. And Saint Augustine tells us expressly *that it would be shameful and having dangerous consequences for a Christian, believing himself grounded in the authority of the holy scriptures, to reason so pitifully about natural things that he was exposed to the ridicule and scorn of infidels.*

But although the science of salvation is the first and most essential of all, the most rigorous casuists will agree that it is not the only one necessary. And what would happen to society, what would happen to each man in particular if everyone became a Carthusian, a hermit? What would happen to the small number there are today of solitaries solely occupied with their salvation if other men did not work to house them, furnish them, feed them, and cure them of their illnesses? It is then for them as well as for us that farmers, architects, carpenters, locksmiths, etc., work. It is then for them as well as for us that the manufactures of cloth, glass, and pottery arise and produce their works. That the iron, copper, tin, gold, and silver mines are dug and exploited. It is then for them as well as for us that the fisherman throws in his nets, that the cook learns the art of preparing foods, that the navigator goes to the different parts of the earth seeking pepper, clove, cassia, manna, rhubarb, quinine. Therefore we would all want for the things that are most necessary for life and for its preservation if we were solely occupied with the matter of our salvation, and we would fall back into a condition worse than that of the first men, the Savages. *Into a condition worse* than that barbarism which the citizen of Geneva already finds *worse than ignorance.*[11]

The happy people is the one that resembles the republic of the ants, all of whose hardworking subjects are equally eager to achieve the common good of society. Work is the friend of virtue, and the most hard-working people ought to be the least vicious. The most vast, most noble, most useful work, most worthy of a great state, is trading by sea, which removes our excess and exchanges it for our necessities. Which enables us to have what all the peoples on earth have that is beautiful, good, and excellent. Which instructs us about their vices and their follies, so that we can avoid them; about their virtues and wise customs so that we can adopt them. Even the sciences and arts owe their greatest discoveries to navigation, which returns to them with interest what it borrows from them. In war as in peace, the navy is one of the greatest sources of power of a people. Its expenditures are immense, but they do not go out of the State, they enter general circulation. Therefore, they do not entail any real diminution of finances. How well our neighbors know all these truths, and how well they know how to use them! France, situated so advantageously to communicate with all the seas, all parts of the world, this object is worthy of your attention. Make conquests upon Neptune, using your skill in taming its caprices. They will remain with you, along with the immense sums with which your numerous armies often enrich foreign peoples, sometimes your own enemies.

I well know, says Mr. Rousseau, that the politics of a State, the conveniences and (he did not dare add) needs of life, require the cultivation of the sciences and arts. But I maintain that at the same time, they make us dishonest people.

We have amply proved the opposite in the course of this refutation. We will add here that far from probity and the matter of salvation being incompatible with the cultivation of the sciences, the arts, commerce, and with zeal for labor spread among all the subjects of a State, I think on the contrary that the decent man, the Christian, is obligated to give himself to all these talents.

Can one attain one's salvation without fulfilling all of one's duties? And are the duties of man in society limited to meditation, the reading of sacred books, and some exercises in piety? Would a baker who spends his day in prayer and leaves me wanting for bread be attaining his salvation? Would a surgeon who goes to hear a sermon rather than set my broken leg accomplish a very meritorious action before God? The duties of our station are therefore part of those which are essential to the matter of our salvation, and the necessity for all these stations is demonstrated by the needs for which they were invented.

I will agree on the necessity and excellence of all those useful arts, Mr. Rousseau will say, but what are the literary arts good for, what is philosophy good for except to flatter and to foment men's pride?

As soon as you admit the necessity for manufactured goods of all kinds, for our clothing, lodgings, furnishings; as soon as you admit the arts that use metals, minerals, plants for thousands of needs, as well as those which attend to preserving and restoring our health; you can no longer do without mechanics, chemistry, and physics, which contain the principles of all these arts, engender them, direct them, and enrich them every day. As soon as you agree about the necessity for navigation, you must have geographers, geometers, and astronomers. And how could you deny the necessity for all these arts, for all these sciences, and for their natural connection, and for the mutual strength they offer one another? As soon as you really want men to live in society, and to have them obey laws, you must have orators who announce the law to them and persuade them to follow it; moral poets even, who add to the persuasiveness of eloquence the even more powerful charms of harmony.

2. We have defended the necessity and utility of all the sciences, criticized by the citizen of Geneva, disapproved of with some exceptions by the observations of Mr. Rousseau. Let us examine now the abuse he claims is made of them.

We agree that the sciences are sometimes abused. Mr. Rousseau adds that they are *abused a great deal* and even *always abused*.

It would suffice to notice that Mr. Rousseau is reduced, in his justification, to maintaining that the sciences always do evil, that they are *always abused*, to feel the hopelessness of his cause. For any other writer, the citation of this proposition alone would constitute its refutation. But Mr. Rousseau's talents give probability and credit to what is least susceptible to these, and he deserves that we show him consideration by supporting with proofs the very truths that need none.

A continuous and general abuse of the sciences ought to manifest itself 1. by the fact, 2. by the very nature of the sciences, considered in themselves or taken relative to our genius, our talents, and our morals. Now the author agrees that the sciences are excellent in themselves, and we have proved, point 2, that relative to ourselves they are in no way incompatible with good morals. That on the contrary they tend to make us better. What remains for us to examine is the question of fact.

To demonstrate that the sciences and arts deprave morals, it is not enough to cite the depraved morals of a learned century. It would not even be enough to cite men of learning without probity. It is necessary to prove that the depravity comes from science itself, and I dare assert that will never be done.

1. Because most of the examples of the dissolution of morals one can cite have no connection with the sciences and arts, however familiar they have been in the centuries or to the persons who are the objects of the citations.

2. Because the very people who have abused such excellent things had this misfortune only through the depravity they had in their hearts, well before their acquired talents were used to manifest it externally.

What was simultaneously more wicked and more enlightened than Nero? What century was more refined than his? Here if ever ought to be the triumph of the citizen of Geneva's induction. But what! Will he dare to say that all the horrors with which this monster terrified the Romans were due to the enlightenment and talents of Nero or of his century? Let him show us, then, some signs of these rare talents, in the art of having his friends, his tutor, his mother slaughtered. Let him make us perceive, then, some connection between that barbarity which extinguished in him all the feelings of nature, humanity, and gratitude, and that sublime and precious enlightenment which he received from the lessons of the philosopher who was the most intelligent and best man of his century. It is only too evident that Nero at his prime was a young tiger in chains and tamed as it were by education, the sciences, and the fine arts. But whose natural ferocity being only half extinguished with so much help, revives with age, passions, and absolute power. The tiger breaks his chains, and free then as in the forest, he surrenders himself to the carnage for which nature formed him. Nero the tyrannical and cruel is therefore the sole product of a barbarous and indomitable nature, and not that of the sciences and arts, which only delayed and possibly even diminished the deadly ravages of his ferocity. What I state here about Nero can be generalized. To be wicked, it suffices to let nature act, to follow one's instincts. To be good, beneficent, and virtuous, it is necessary to turn inward. It is necessary to think and reflect. And that is what the sciences and fine arts make us do.

That those who have really abused the sciences and arts did so only through a depravity they had from nature, and which does not come at all from that cultivation, is what is evident to whoever pays attention to the goal of the sciences and arts, which we will be permitted to recall here. The very first, the object of science, religion, and morals, is to direct the movements of heart with respect to God and one's neighbor. The second, which is the object of the science of nature, is to give to the mind the correctness and sagacity necessary for the research and reasoning required by that science, which in itself is the study of the works of the creator, and constantly represents to us his greatness, his power, his wisdom, at the same time as it offers us the ground from which we draw what will meet our needs. Finally, the third goal, the particular object of the arts, is to reduce the preceding theory to practice, and to labor to procure for ourselves the needs and conveniences of life.

How will one prove that talents made to mold the heart to goodness and virtue, direct the mind to the truth, and train the powers of the body in necessary and useful labors do just the opposite of what is intended? Without a nature depraved excessively, how is it possible to abuse means so precious and made deliberately to lead us to such laudable ends? And isn't it visible that it is this prior depravity, and not those means, that are the causes of the abuses when they occur? Finally, that it is not the sciences and arts that have depraved the morals of these unfortunates, but on the contrary their naturally perverse morals that have corrupted their knowledge, their talents, or their legitimate uses.

Mr. Rousseau agrees on the usefulness of the science of religion and morals. Therefore it is against that of nature and of the arts that apply it that his declamations are aimed.

One proposes vainly in opposition to Mr. Rousseau that developed nature offers us everywhere the marvels brought about by the Creator, raises us up toward this principle of all things, and in particular of religion and good morals. In vain the scholarly compilations of Niluwentyt, Derham, Pluche, etc. have brought this picture together under a single glance, and made us see that nature is the greatest book of moral philosophy, the most moving as well as the most sublime to which we can attend. Mr. Rousseau is surprised that it is necessary to study the universe in order to admire its beauties, a proposition from such an educated man almost as surprising as the universe itself, well studied. He does not want to see that the Scripture that celebrates the Creator through the marvels of his works, that tells us to adore his power, his greatness, and his goodness in his works, thereby gives us a precept to study these marvels. He claims *that a farmer who sees the rain and the sun in turn fertilize his field* knows enough about it to *admire, praise, and bless the hand from which he receives these blessings.* [12] But if those rains rot his grain, if the sun consumes and destroys it, will he know enough to protect himself from grumbling and superstition? Does one think of that when one limits the marvels of nature to what is most common and least touching for those who see them daily; to the ways in which they are the most equivocal for the glory of nature's author? Let this ignorant farmer be taken to the celestial spheres of which Copernicus, Kepler, Descartes, and Newton have exposed for us the admirable immensity and harmony. Let him be introduced then to that other universe in miniature, to the animal economy, and develop for him that artifice beyond all expression with which the organs of the senses and movements are constructed and combined. That is where he will find himself possessed by the enthusiasm of Saint Paul, raised to the third heaven. That is where he will cry out with him: O infinite richness of the Supreme Being! O depth of his ineffable wisdom! How visible you make the existence and power of your author! How you fill me with the truths he revealed to me, with the thanks, adoration, and fidelity I owe him!

I admit, says Mr. Rousseau, *that the study of the universe ought to exalt man toward his creator. But it exalts only human vanity. . . .* It foments his *incredulity,* his impiety. *The blasphemous statement of Alphonse X will never enter the mind of a common man. That blasphemy was reserved for a learned mouth.* [13]

The statement of Alphonse X, nicknamed the Wise, only appears to be a blasphemy. It is a very misplaced joke, in truth, in its turn of phrase. But the core of the thought, which is the only thing God examines and that alone must be examined when the issue is God, is nothing but an energetic censure of the absurd system of Ptolemy, and consequently the praise of the true plan of the universe and its author, which Alphonse the Wise adored too sincerely to conceive an extravagant plan to insult it. Vast enlightenment uncovers the absurdities which men's imagination attributes to nature. But this uncovering is entirely to the shame of the men who are mistaken. It cannot reflect back on the works of the Almighty. The supreme wisdom is the guarantor of their perfection. It is proof against all examinations. Let the sciences exhaust themselves putting them in the crucible. The empty opinions of men will go up in smoke like marcasite. The divine truths will become more and more brilliant like the purest gold, because the sciences are so many rays of the divinity. Woe, therefore, to religions which cannot stand up to the test, and to which they are contrary! The true religion receives new splendor from them, and defers to them only because it surpasses them, just as the sun itself is superior to the small number of rays that emanate from it among the clouds that surround us. We will not deny, however, that they can be abused. The numberless heresies and schisms prove it well enough. These proofs have not escaped Mr. Rousseau; they offer themselves to a citizen of Geneva. And a man as well versed in literature is not less well-informed about the disorders that follow licentious writing.

But Mr. Rousseau does not want to perceive that he always returns to the abuse of the sciences, to what they sometimes do in the hands of the wicked. And not to *what they ought to do* and what they in fact do when their goal is followed, when only they participate in the action, when a depraved nature is not superimposed on them, to which equity requires these abuses to be attributed.

For the honor of humanity, let us still exert ourselves to diminish, if possible, the number of these wicked and unfortunate people, who abuse such precious talents. Let us say that the majority of those who have abused their pens ventured more into libertinage of the mind than of the heart, or at least the latter dissoluteness has not gone to the point of destroying their probity. Epicurus was the most sober and wisest philosopher of his era. Ovid and Tibullus were no less decent people for being lovers. A Spinoza and a Bayle were never accused of having infamous morals, although their religion was either monstrous or suspect. The citizen of Geneva will doubtless agree that there is a probity common to all religions, all sects. And he well understood that it is that which is at issue in the subject proposed by our academy. Without that, it would not have been proper to bring on stage the Romans and Greeks, the Scythians, Persians, and Chinese, etc. Will it be said that these licentious writings will produce more disorders in those who read them than in their own authors? This paradox is not likely. Corruption is never worse than at its source, and can only become weaker as it gets farther away. Now, if the works cited do not owe their birth to a depravity capable of destroying probity, in all likelihood it will not be taken elsewhere to any greater excesses, or else the core of those disorders will be found already in nature.

But we return willingly to a rigor that is wiser, more judicious, more suited to the healthiest doctrine. We agree it would be much better if all those authors had never been born. That true probity is inseparable from true religion and the purest morality. And finally that their works are seeds to stifle with wise precautions and by the multitude of excellent books that are the antidotes for those poisons, engendered by a depraved nature and prepared by perverted talents. Fortunately we are not lacking in antidotes, far superior in number to the poisons. Let us not lose sight of our proof of fact against the abuse Mr. Rousseau claims is *always* made of the sciences.

No one recognizes the learned man from the odious portrait Mr. Rousseau makes of him. This character of pride and vanity he confers on him reminds me of those pious people of speculative mind who—considering themselves as the elect of the most high—cast looks of scorn and indignation on all the rest of the earth, criminal to their eyes. But I do not recognize the learned man in that.

Perhaps this picture would still suit rather well those supposed philosophers of the old school, whose entire science consisted of words, most of them devoid of meaning. And who, spending their lives in the most frivolous disputes, placed their glory and pride in crushing an adversary or eluding arguments with scholastic distinctions as empty as those imagining them. But can all the disorders, all the extravagances of those ancient sects be applied to our century? Can one accuse of pride and vanity our physicists and geometers, who are occupied uniquely in penetrating the sanctuary of nature? Candor and ingenuousness of morals is a virtue that is somehow attached to them. Our physics brought back to its true principles by Descartes, supported with geometry by the same physicist, by Newton, Huyghens, Leibniz, Mairan, and a crowd of great men who followed them, has become a wise and solid science. Why throw up to us here the enumeration of ridiculous sects of the ancient philosophers? Why cite to us the proud reasoners of far distant centuries, since the issue here is the renewal of letters, since the issue is our century, ourselves really? Let this physics, this literary treasure as immense as it is irreproachable, these records of the academy of sciences and letters of Paris, and of London, be looked into. It is there we must be shown that the sciences are always abused, a proposition reserved to Mr. Rousseau and to our century, desirous of being unique. Let us examine the behavior of the learned men who have composed and compose now these famous bodies: Newton, Mariotte, de l'Hospital, Duhamel, Regis, Cassini, Morin, Malebranche, Parent, Varignon, Fontenelle, Réaumur, Despréaux, Corneille, Bossuet, Fenelon, Racine, Pelisson, La Bruyere, etc. What would happen if we added to these illustrious men the members and distinguished works of those respectable societies which produced Riccioli, Kircher, Petau, Poree, Mabillon, Dacheris, Lami, Regnault, etc.? And if we added to that the great men who, without belonging to any society, were neither less famous for their learning, nor less respectable for their probity, such as Kepler, Grotius, Gassendi, Alexander, Dupin, Pascal, Nicole, Arnauld, etc.? Let us be shown in the crowd of these learned men, and in particular in that of the academicians who followed one another over the period of nearly a century, the dissolute morals, the pride, and all the disorders Mr. Rousseau claims follow the cultivation of the sciences, and always accompany it. If his proposition is true, the volumes and men I have just cited will furnish this orator with an ample harvest of proofs and laurels. But if these books are the most precious, the most useful productions engendered by all the preceding centuries, if all these learned men are, in their respective centuries, the least proud, most virtuous, and best men, it must be acknowledged that our adversary's cause is the most absurd thing anyone ever dared to maintain.

If we were not worried that Mr. Rousseau would accuse historical citations of being displays of erudition and reserve for himself this kind of proof, as a privilege unique to him, we would in turn search through the tenth century and those following, when *the torch of the sciences stopped illuminating the earth, when the clergy remained plunged in ignorance.*[14] We would see there the dissolution of morals reaching even the clergy who ought to be the light and example of the Christian world, the virtuous universe. We would see libertinage equaling ignorance there. We would also see that the fortunate change to minds wrought by the restoration of letters bore equally on hearts, and that the reform of morals followed that of ways of thinking and writing. From this we would have the right to conclude that enlightenment and good morals go naturally together, and that every ignorant and corrupt people that receives this salutary light is restored at the same time to virtue, despite the sentence pronounced by Mr. Rousseau.

That author who, two months ago, identified only one learned man who was to his liking and who today acknowledges three or four; who made an exception for no art and no science from the anathema he cast on all of them; who defended his territory with such self-assurance, and who has today retrenched behind the bulwark of theology, morality, and the science of salvation; would this orator still find himself pressed enough to extend the favors of these exceptions even to the sciences that are the object of the labors of our academies, and to the useful arts that are under their protection, to build for himself a final wall of the arts and sciences he will call frivolous in order to attribute only to the learned men and artists of that kind all the abuses and all the disorders he says *always* accompany the cultivation of the sciences and arts?

In that case, we will ask him for the precise enumeration of these sciences and arts, the object of these imputations. We hope he will not place music on the list, which the censors of the arts count as a most futile science. We have shown that it was relaxation as charming as it is decent, that it celebrated great men, virtues, and the Author of all virtues. Mr. Rousseau knows better than anyone its usefulness and advantages, since he has made it his study and taken responsibility for that brilliant portion of the encyclopedic labors. It is not likely he will add this new contradiction between his conduct and his discourse. Music then will be one of those arts for which an exception is made, one of those arts which will not deprave morals at all . . .

> And all the commonplaces of lewd morality,
> Which Lulli stirred up with the sounds of his music.
> Boileau, *Satire*, X [15]

will be simply abuses of something good in itself, but which is *not abused much,* which is *not always abused*. For otherwise, I am sure that Mr. Rousseau would not want to be the apostle of such a doctrine.

It is my hope that our author will become more humane with regard to the other arts, in favor of the harmony he cultivates and that is so suited to softening the dispositions of the most savage. The matter is already more than half finished. We believe we have proved well that the sciences and arts have an infinity of usefulness, that they provide for thousands and thousands of needs. We have added to those essential advantages that they make men more humane, more sociable, less fierce, less wicked; that they prevent idleness, mother of all the vices. Mr. Rousseau agrees on all these points. He blames *ferocious, brutal ignorance* that makes *man like* the beasts, and he is consistent in saying that such is the ignorance of man abandoned to simple nature.[16] He admits that *the sciences and arts soften the ferocity of men*. That they create *a diversion for their passions. That the enlightenment of the wicked man is still less to be feared than his brutal stupidity. That at least it makes him more circumspect about the evil he could do, through the knowledge of the evil he himself would receive from it.*[17] Therefore, we are better in this enlightened century than in those of ignorance and barbarism. Such is the doctrine I upheld in all the preceding notes. Mr. Rousseau agrees with it finally. *Habemus confitentem reum.*[18] And the trial seems absolutely over to me. At least I hope it will be viewed as such by the equitable and knowledgeable public.

Refutation of the Discourse Which Won the Prize of the Academy of Dijon in 1750

Read at a meeting of the Royal Society of Nancy by Mr. Gautier, Canon, and Professor of mathematics and history [1]

The establishment procured by his majesty to facilitate the development of talents and genius has been indirectly attacked by a work in which one tries to prove that our souls have become corrupt as our sciences and arts have improved, and that the same phenomenon has been observed at all times and in all places. This discourse by Mr. Rousseau contains several other propositions the falseness of which it is important to show, since according to learned journalists, it appears capable of causing a revolution in the ideas of our time. I agree that it is written with unusual warmth, that it offers images painted with a vigorous and accurate touch. The more the style of this work is great and bold, the better suited it is to persuade, to accredit pernicious maxims. It is not a matter here of those literary paradoxes in which either side may be taken; of those empty topics of rhetoric, where one displays futile thoughts, ingeniously contrasted. Sirs, I am going to plead a case that concerns your happiness. I foresaw that in limiting myself to showing how defective Mr. Rousseau's arguments are,* I would fall into the aridness of the polemical genre. This drawback did not stop me, since I was convinced that the solidity of a refutation of this nature constitutes its principal merit.

If, as the author claims, the sciences deprave morals, Stanislas the beneficent will then be blamed by posterity for having created an establishment to help them flourish. And his minister, for encouraging talents and bringing forth his. If the sciences deprave morals, you ought then to detest the education you have been given, bitterly regret the time you have spent acquiring knowledge, and repent for the efforts you made to be useful to the fatherland. The author I am fighting is the apologist of ignorance. He appears to wish to have the libraries burn.

He admits that he opposes head on everything men today admire, and

---

* It would be an injustice to say that all of Mr. Rousseau's arguments are defective. This proposition ought to be modified. He deserves much praise for standing up forcefully against the misuses which slip into the arts and into the republic of the letters.

that he can expect only universal blame. But he counts on the approval of the time yet to come. He may win it, how can we be in doubt, when Europe falls back into barbarism, when ignorance and rusticity triumph insolently over the ruins of the disconsolate fine arts.

We have two questions to discuss, one of fact and the other of right. In the first part of this discourse, we will examine whether the sciences and arts have contributed to the corruption of morals. And in the second, what can result from the progress of the sciences and arts considered in themselves. That is the plan of the work I criticize.

I

Before art had molded our manners, says Mr. Rousseau, and taught our passions to speak an affected language, our morals were rustic but natural, and differences of conduct announced at first glance those of character. Human nature basically was no better, but men found their security in the ease of seeing through each other, and that advantage, which we no longer appreciate, spared them many vices. Suspicions, offenses, fears, coldness, reserve, hate, betrayal will hide constantly under that uniform and false veil of civility, that much vaunted urbanity which we owe to the enlightenment of our century. We have the semblance of all the virtues without having any of them.[2]

I reply that by examining the source of the politeness that does such honor to our era and gives such pain to Mr. Rousseau, one discovers with ease how estimable it is. It is the desire to please in society that caused the development of the mind. Men have been studied, their moods, their characters, their desires, their needs, their amour-propre. Experience showed what displeases. The amenities have been analyzed, their causes uncovered, their merit assessed, its various degrees distinguished. From an infinity of reflections about the beautiful, the honest, and the decent, a precious art has been formed, the art of living with men, of turning our needs into pleasures, of sprinkling charm into conversation, of winning over the mind by one's discourse and hearts by one's behaviors. Deference, attentions, willingness, forethoughts, and respect are so many ties that mutually bind us. The more politeness has been perfected, the more useful society has been to men. People have yielded to proprieties, often more powerful than duties. Inclinations have become gentler, characters more flexible, social virtues more common. How many people change their dispositions only because they are forced to appear to do so! The one who has vices is obliged to disguise them. It is a continual warning to him that he is not what he ought to be. His morals imperceptibly take on the shade of the accepted morals. The necessity of constantly copying virtue finally makes him virtuous, or at least his vices are not contagious, as they would be if they presented themselves directly with that rusticity my adversary laments.

He says that men found their security in the ease of seeing through each other, and that this advantage spared them many vices.[3] He did not consider that since human nature was not any better then, as he admits, rusticity did not prevent disguise. We have an irrefutable example before our eyes: we see nations whose manners are not polished, nor their language affected, use evasions, dissimulations, and artifices, cleverly deceive, without our being able to assign the blame to literature, the sciences, and the arts. Besides, if the art of veiling oneself has been perfected, that of seeing through the veils has made the same progress. Men are not judged on simple appearances. There is no waiting to test them until one is under the unavoidable obligation of having recourse to their beneficence. One is convinced that in general they must not be counted on, unless one pleases them, is useful to them, or they have some interest in doing us a favor. One knows how to evaluate specious offers of politeness, and translate its expressions to their accepted meaning. It is not that there are not an infinity of noble souls who, when they are obliging, seek only the pleasure of being so. Their politeness has a very superior tone to any that is only ceremonial; their candor, a language of its own. Their merit is their art of pleasing.

Add that just frequenting society suffices to acquire that politeness of which a gentleman boasts. There is no basis, then, for honoring the sciences for it.

To what do all Mr. Rousseau's eloquent declamations point? Who would not be indignant to hear him assert that we have the semblance of all the virtues without having any of them?[4] And why isn't anyone virtuous anymore? Because people cultivate literature, the sciences, and the arts. If one were impolite, rustic, ignorant, Goth, Hun, or Vandal, one would be worthy of Mr. Rousseau's praises. Won't we ever tire of inveighing against men? Will we always believe we are making them more virtuous by telling them they have no virtue at all? On the pretext of purifying morals, is it permitted to upset all supports? O sweet bonds of society! Charm of true philosophers, lovable virtues, it is by your own attractions that you reign over hearts. You owe your dominion neither to stoic harshness, nor to barbaric morals, nor to the counsels of a proud rusticity.

Mr. Rousseau attributes to our century faults and vices it does not have at all, or that it has in common with those nations that are not civilized. And he concludes from it that the fate of morals and of probity has regularly been subject to the progress of the sciences and arts. Let us leave these vague imputations and turn to fact.

To show that the sciences have corrupted morals in all ages, he says that several peoples came under the yoke when they were the most famous for their cultivation of the sciences. It is well known that the sciences do not bring invincibility. Does it follow that they corrupt morals? By this singular manner of reasoning, one could also conclude that ignorance leads to their depravation, since a large number of barbarous nations were subjugated by people devoted to the fine arts. Even if it could be proved by facts that the dissolution of morals has always prevailed with the sciences, it would not follow that the fate of probity was dependent on their progress. When a nation enjoys tranquil abundance, it naturally turns to pleasures and the fine arts. Wealth procures the means to satisfy one's passions. Thus, it would be wealth and not literature which could engender corruption in hearts, without mentioning several other causes, which have no less influence on this depravity than abundance does. Extreme poverty is the mother of many crimes, and it can be together with a profound ignorance. All the facts alleged by our adversary, therefore, in no way prove that the sciences corrupt morals.

He claims to show by what happened in Egypt, Greece, Rome, Constantinople, and China that the arts weaken the peoples who cultivate them. Although this assertion on which he mainly insists, appears foreign to the question that is raised, it is appropriate to show its falseness. Egypt, he says, became the mother of philosophy and fine arts, and soon after came the conquest of Cambyses. But many centuries before that era, it was made subject by Arab shepherds, during the reign of Timaeus. Their domination lasted more than five hundred years. Why didn't the Egyptians have even then the courage to defend themselves? Were they weakened by the fine arts of which they were ignorant? Is it the sciences that made the Asiatic peoples effeminate, and caused so many barbarous nations of Africa and America to be excessively cowardly?

The victories that the Athenians won over the Persians and even over the Lacedemonians show that the arts can be associated with military virtue. Their government, which had become venal under Pericles, takes on a new look. The love of pleasure stifles their bravery, the most honorable functions are degraded, impunity multiplies the bad citizens, the funds intended for war are used to nourish softness and idleness. What do all these causes of corruption have to do with the sciences?

What military glory did the Romans not earn at the time when literature held a place of honor in Rome? Were they weakened by the arts when Cicero said to Caesar: you have subdued savage and fierce nations, countless in their numbers, scattered afar in different places? Since a single one of these facts suffices to destroy the arguments of my adversary; it would be useless to emphasize this point any further. The causes of the revolutions that occur in States are known. The sciences could not contribute to their decadence except if those who are destined to defend them attend to the sciences to the point of neglecting their military functions. In this supposition, any occupation foreign to war would have the same consequences.

To show that ignorance preserves morals from corruption, Mr. Rousseau passes in review the Scythians, the first Persians, the Germans, and the Romans at the first period of their republic. And he says that these peoples, by their virtue, brought about their own happiness and an example for other nations. We admit that Justin gave a magnificent eulogy of the Scythians. But Herodotus and some authors cited by Strabo represent them as one of the most ferocious nations. They sacrificed one fifth of their prisoners to the God Mars, and put out the eyes of those who remained. On the birthday of a king, they strangled fifty of his officers. Those who lived near the Euxine Bridge fed on the flesh of foreigners who arrived there. The history of the various Scythian nations offers traits throughout which either dishonor them or horrify nature. Women were held in common among the Massagetae. The elderly were sacrificed by their relatives, who banqueted on their flesh. The Agatyrsians lived only by pillage, and held their women in common. The anthropophages, by Herodotus's report, were unjust and inhuman. Such were the peoples proposed as examples to other nations.[5]

With regard to the ancient Persians, everyone doubtless agrees with Mr. Rollin[6] that it is impossible to read without horror how far they carried disregard and scorn for the most common laws of nature. Among them, all kinds of incest were authorized. In the priestly tribe, the highest dignities were almost always conferred on those born of the marriage of a son and mother. They had to be terribly cruel to put children to death in the fire they worshipped.

The colors used by Pomponius Mela to depict the Germans will not give rise to the desire to resemble them. They were a naturally fierce people, savage to the extent of eating raw meat, among whom theft is not a shameful thing, and who recognize no other right than force.

What reproaches a philosopher enlightened by all the enlightenment of reason would rightly make to the Romans, at the time when they were not yet familiar with letters. Illustrious Barbarians, he could have said to them, all your greatness is only a huge crime. What fury animates you and makes you ravage the universe? Tigers thirsty for the blood of men, how do you dare to place your glory in being unjust, in living from pillage, in exercising the most odious tyranny? Who gave you the right to dispose of our goods and our lives, to make us slaves and wretches, to spread terror, desolation, and death everywhere? Is that the greatness of soul in which you take pride? O detestable greatness that feeds on miseries and calamaties! Do you acquire supposed virtues only to punish the earth for what they cost you? Is it force? The laws of humanity have no more of it then? Its voice does not make itself heard in your hearts? You scorn the will of the gods who destined you, like ourselves, to spend a few tranquil moments on earth. But the punishment is always close to the crime. You have had the shame of passing under the yoke, the sadness of seeing your armies cut to shreds, and soon you will have that of seeing the republic torn to pieces by its own force. Who prevents you from spending a pleasant life in the bosom of peace, the arts, the sciences, and virtue? Romans, stop being unjust. Stop carrying everywhere the horrors of war and the crimes it brings along with it.

But I would have it that there were virtuous nations in the bosom of ignorance. I ask whether it was not to wise laws, maintained with vigor and prudence, and not to the deprivation of the arts that they owed their happiness? It is claimed in vain that even Socrates and Cato disparaged letters. They were never the apologists of ignorance. The most learned of Athenians was right to say that the presumptuousness of the Statesmen, poets, and artists of Athens tarnished their learning in his eyes, and that they were wrong to believe they were the wisest of men. But in blaming their pride and discrediting the sophists, he was not singing the praises of ignorance, which he viewed as the greatest evil. He liked to make harmonious sounds on the lyre, with the hand that sculpted statues of the Graces. Rhetoric, physics, and astronomy were objects of study for him. And according to Diogenes Laertius, he worked on the tragedies of Euripides. It is true he applied himself principally to making a science of morality, and that he did not imagine he knew what he did not know. Is that favoring ignorance? Should it avail itself of the outburst by Cato the Elder against those artful speechmakers, those Greeks who taught the Romans the deadly art of casting doubt on all truths? One of the leaders of the third academy, Carneades, indicating in Cato's presence the necessity for a natural law and reversing the next day what he had established the day before, naturally had to bias the mind of this censor against the literature of the Greeks. This bias, in truth, went too far. He felt its injustice and offset it by learning the Greek language, even though he was elderly. He modeled his style on that of Thucydides and Demosthenes, and enriched his works with the maxims and facts he drew from them. Agriculture, medicine, history, and many other subjects brought him to write. These facts show that if Socrates and Cato had eulogized ignorance, they would have censured themselves. And Mr. Rousseau, who has so happily cultivated literature, shows how estimable it is by the manner in which he expresses the scorn he seems to have for it. I say seems, because it is not likely that he makes little of his knowledge. At all times, authors have been seen to decry their centuries and praise the nations of antiquity to excess. One attributes a certain glory to rejecting the common ideas, a superiority to blaming what is praised, a greatness to tearing down what men respect the most.

The best way to decide the question of fact under consideration is to examine the present state of morals of all nations. Now the outcome of this examination impartially done is that the peoples who are civilized and distinguished by the cultivation of the letters and sciences generally have fewer vices than those who are not. In Barbary and most of the oriental countries there flourish vices that are unsuitable even to mention. If you glance over the various states of Africa, you are astonished to see so many lazy, cowardly, knavish, treacherous, greedy, cruel, thieving, and debauched peoples. Here inhuman practices are established, there lewdness is authorized by the laws. There brigandage and murder are instituted as professions, here they are so barbaric that they eat human flesh. In several kingdoms, husbands sell their wives and children. In others, men are sacrificed to the Demon. Several people are killed to honor the king when he appears in public or has just died. Asia and America offer similar pictures.*

The ignorance and corrupt morals of the nations who inhabit these vast countries show how falsely this reflection of my adversary rings: "Peoples, know once and for all that nature wanted to keep you from being harmed by science just as a mother wrests a dangerous weapon from her child's hands; that all the secrets she hides from you are so many evils from which she protects you, and that the difficulty you find in educating yourselves is not the least of her benefits."[7] I would like it as well if he had said: Peoples, know once and for all that nature does not want you to nourish yourselves on the products of the earth. The difficulty she has attached to its cultivation is a warning to you to let it lie fallow. He ends the first part of his discourse with this reflection: "That probity is the daughter of ignorance; that science and virtue are incompatible."[8] This is a sentiment quite opposite to that of the Church. It

*The narrow limits I have set for myself oblige me to refer to the *History of Voyages* and to the *General History* by Abbé Lambert.

considered as the most dangerous of persecutions the emperor Julian's prohibiting the Christians to teach their children rhetoric, poetics, and philosophy.

II

Mr. Rousseau undertakes to prove in the second part of his discourse that the origin of the sciences is vicious, their objects vain, and their effects pernicious. It was, he says, an ancient tradition, passed from Egypt to Greece, that a God who was hostile to the tranquillity of mankind was the inventor of the sciences.[9] From which he infers that the Egyptians, among whom they were born, did not have a favorable opinion of them. How can his conclusion be made to agree with these words: *Remedies for the illnesses of the soul,* the inscription which, according to Diodorus of Sicily, one read on the frontispiece of the oldest of libraries, that of Ozymandias, king of Egypt.

He asserts that astronomy was born from superstition; eloquence from ambition, hate, flattery, and falsehood; geometry from avarice; physics from vain curiosity; all, even moral philosophy from human pride.[10] It suffices to relate these fine discoveries to make known their whole importance. Until now it was thought that the sciences and arts owed their birth to our needs. It had even been shown in several works.

You say that the defect of the origin of the sciences and arts is recalled to us only too clearly in their objects. You ask what we would do with arts without the luxury that nourishes them. Everyone will reply to you that the instructive and ministerial arts, independent of luxury, provide for the amenities, or conveniences, or needs of life.

You ask what purpose jurisprudence would serve without the injustices of men. We can answer that no political body could subsist without laws, even if it were composed only of just men. You want to know what would history become, if there were neither tyrants, nor wars, nor conspirators. Yet you are not unaware that universal history contains the description of countries, religion, government, morals, commerce, and the customs of peoples, the honors, magistracies, lives of peaceful princes, philosophers, and famous artists. What do all those subjects have in common with tyrants, wars, and conspirators?

Are we destined then to die fixed to the edge of the well where the truth has hidden? This truth alone should rebuff, from the outset, any man who would seriously seek to educate himself by the study of philosophy.[11] You know that the sciences with which young philosophers are kept busy in the universities are logic, metaphysics, moral philosophy, physics, and elementary mathematics. According to you, then, those are sterile speculations. The universities are greatly obliged to you for teaching them that the truth of these sciences has hidden at the bottom of a well! The great philosophers who possess them to an eminent degree are no doubt quite surprised to learn that they know nothing. Without you, they would also be unaware of the great dangers encountered in the investigation of the sciences. You say that falsity is susceptible of infinite combinations, and that the truth has only one manner of being.[12] But aren't there different routes, different methods to reach the truth? Besides, you add, who seeks it very sincerely? By what mark is one sure to recognize it? The philosophers will respond that they only learned the sciences in order to know them and make use of them. And the evidence, that is the perception of the relation between ideas, is the distinctive characteristic of the truth, and that one stays with what appears most probable in matters that are not susceptible to demonstration. Would you want to see the rebirth of the sects of Pyrrho, Arcesilaus, or Lacydes? [13]

Agree that you could have dispensed with talking about the origin of the sciences, and that you have not proved at all that their objects are vain. How could you have done so, since everything around us speaks to us in favor of the sciences and arts? Clothing, furnishings, buildings, libraries, the products of foreign countries, owed to navigation directed by astronomy. There, the mechanical arts improve our goods. The progress of anatomy assures that of surgery. Chemistry and botany prepare remedies for us; the liberal arts, instructive pleasures. They are busy transmitting to posterity the memory of noble actions, and immortalize great men and our gratitude for the services they have done for us. Here, geometry supported by algebra presides over most of the sciences. It gives lessons to astronomy, navigation, artillery, and physics. What! All these objects are vain? Yes, and according to Mr. Rousseau all those who are busy with them are useless citizens, and he concludes that every useless citizen may be considered as pernicious.[14] What do I say! According to him, we are not even citizens. Here are his own words: We have physicists, geometers, chemists, astronomers, poets, musicians, painters. We no longer have citizens; or, if a few of them are left, dispersed in our abandoned countryside, they perish there, indigent and despised.[15] Thus, sirs, stop considering yourselves citizens. Although you devote your days to serving society, although you worthily fill the jobs where your talents have called you, you are not worthy to be named citizens. That quality is the lot of peasants, and it is necessary for all of you to cultivate the soil to deserve it. How does one dare insult in this way a nation that produces so many excellent citizens of every status?

O, Louis the Great! How astonished you would be if returned to the wishes of France and those of the monarch who governs it by following in your glorious footsteps, you learned that one of our academies crowned a work in which it is upheld that the sciences are vain in their object and pernicious in their effects, and that those who cultivate them are not citizens! What! Could you say I stained my glory by giving refuge to the Muses, establishing academies, reviving the fine arts; by sending astronomers to the most distant countries, rewarding talents and discoveries, attracting learned men close to the throne! What, I tarnished my glory by giving birth to Praxiteles and Sysippus, to Appelles and Aristides, to Amphion and Orpheus! Why delay destroying those instruments of the arts and sciences, burning these precious remains of the Greeks and Romans, all the archives of mind and genius? Plunge back into the thick shadows of barbarism, into the prejudices it consecrates under the deadly auspices of ignorance and superstition. Renounce the enlightenment of your century. Let the ancient abuses usurp the rights of equity. Reestablish civil laws contrary to natural law. Let the innocent man accused by injustice be obliged, in order to justify himself, to expose himself to perish by water or by fire. Let peoples go on massacring other peoples under the cloak of religion. Let the greatest evils be done with the same tranquillity of conscience as is felt while doing the greatest good. Such, and more deplorable still, will be consequences of that ignorance to which you want to return.

No, great king, the Academy of Dijon is not presumed to adopt all the sentiments of the author it crowned. It does not think as he does that the most enlightened works of our learned men and best citizens are of almost no utility. It does not confuse as he does the discoveries truly useful for mankind with those from which no services have yet been drawn, for lack of knowing all their relations and the whole of nature's parts. But it thinks, along with all the academies of Europe, that it is important to extend the branches of our knowledge in all directions, to ferret out analogies, to follow all their ramifications. It knows that a given piece of knowledge that appears sterile for a time can cease being so when there are applications of it owed to genius, to laborious research, or even perhaps to chance. It knows that to erect an edifice, one gathers materials of all kinds. These raw materials, a formless mass, have their destination. Art smooths them out and arranges them. From them it makes masterpieces of architecture and good taste.

It can be said that certain truths detached from the body of those whose utility is recognized are, in a sense, like chunks of ice floating at the whim of chance on the surface of rivers, coming together, mutually strengthening each other, and serving as a way to get across them.

If the author asserted without foundation that the cultivation of the sciences is a waste of time, he was no less wrong to attribute luxury to letters and arts. Luxury is a sumptuousness arising from unequally shared goods. Vanity, with the help of abundance, seeks to distinguish itself and procures by some arts the means to supply it with a superfluity. But what is superfluous in relation to some conditions is necessary to others, in order to maintain the distinctions that characterize the various ranks of society. Religion itself does not condemn the expenses required by the decency of each condition. What is luxury for the artisan may not be so for men of the legal profession or military men. Will it be said that expensive furniture or dress degrade the decent man and transmit the sentiments of the vicious man to him? The great Cato, solicitor of sumptuary laws according to the remark of a political thinker, is depicted to us as greedy and intemperate, even usurious and drunken. Whereas sumptuous Lucullus, an even greater captain and as just as he, was always liberal and beneficent. Let us condemn the sumptuousness of Lucullus and his imitators. But let us not conclude that it is necessary to banish learned men and artists from our midst. The passions can abuse the arts. It is they that must be suppressed. The arts are the support of States. They continually rectify the inequality of fortunes and procure the physical necessities for most citizens. The land and war can keep only part of the nation occupied. How can the other subjects subsist, if the rich fear spending, if the circulation of specie is interrupted by an economy fatal for those who can live only by the work of their hands?

The author adds that while living conveniences multiply, arts are perfected, and luxury spreads, true courage is enervated, military virtues disappear, and this too is the work of the sciences and of all those arts which are exercised in the shade of the study.[16] Wouldn't it be said, Gentlemen, that all our soldiers are busy cultivating the sciences, and all their officers are like Maupertuis and Réaumur? Was it noticeable under the rule of Louis XIV and Louis XV that the military virtues disappeared? If one wants to talk about the sciences that have no relation to war, what the academies have in common with the troops cannot be seen. And if it is a matter of the military sciences, can they be overly perfected? With regard to abundance, it was never seen to be more prevalent in the French armies than during the course of their victories. How can it be imagined that soldiers will become more valiant because they will be badly dressed and badly nourished.

Does Mr. Rousseau have a better basis for maintaining that the cultivation of the sciences is harmful to the moral qualities? He says it is from our earliest years that a foolish education adorns our mind and corrupts our judgment. I see everywhere immense institutions where young people are brought up at great expense, learning everything except their duties.[17]

Can so many respectable bodies, devoted solely to the instruction of young people in whom they ceaselessly inculcate the principles of honor, probity, and Christianity be attacked in this way? Science, morals, and religion are the objects the University of Paris has always offered, in conformity with the regulations given to it by the kings of France. In all the institutions founded for the education of young people, all possible means are used to inspire in them the love of virtue and the horror of vice, in order to make excellent citizens of them. The maxims and examples of the great men of antiquity are continually placed before their eyes. Sacred and profane history gives them lessons supported by facts and experience, and makes an impression on their minds which one would vainly expect from the aridness of precepts.

How could the sciences harm moral qualities? One of their first effects is to draw away from idleness, and consequently from the gambling and debauchery that are its consequences. Seneca, whom Mr. Rousseau cites in support of his sentiment, agrees that literature is a preparation for virtue. (Seneca, *Letter* 88.)

What do these satirical barbs shot against our century mean? That the most evident effect of all our studies is the debasement of the virtues. That one no longer asks if a man is upright, but rather if he is talented. That virtue is left without honor. That there are a thousand prizes for fine discourses, none for fine actions.[18] How can one not know that a man who passes as lacking in probity is universally scorned? Isn't the punishment of vice already the first recompense of virtue? Respect, the friendship of one's fellow-citizens, and honorable distinctions are prizes far superior to academic laurels. Besides, will the person who is useful to his friends, who comforts poor families, go and publicize his good deeds? That would be annihilating their merit. There is nothing more beautiful than virtuous actions if not the very effort to hide them.

Mr. Rousseau speaks of our philosophers with scorn. He cites the dangerous reveries of Hobbes and Spinoza,[19] and puts them on the same level with all the products of philosophy. Why confound in this way with the works of our true philosophers, the systems we abhor? Should one attribute to the study of literature the foolish opinions of a few writers, while a large number of peoples are infatuated with absurd systems, the fruit of their ignorance and credulity? The human mind does not need to be cultivated to give birth to monstrous opinions. It is by lifting itself up with all the vigor of which it is capable that reason rises above chimeras. True philosophy teaches us to tear away the veil of prejudices and superstition. Must the cultivation of reason be proscribed because a few authors misused their enlightenment? Ah, what is not susceptible of misuse! Can't power, laws, religion, everything that is most useful be diverted to harmful uses? Such is what Mr. Rousseau did with his powerful eloquence to inspire scorn for the sciences, letters, and philosophers. To the picture he presents of those learned men, let us oppose that of the true philosopher. I shall draw it, Gentlemen, from the models I have the honor of knowing among you. What is a true philosopher? He is a very reasonable and very enlightened man. From whatever point of view one considers him, one cannot keep from according him one's full respect, and one is satisfied with oneself only when one deserves his. He knows neither the cringing pliability of flattery, nor the sly intrigues of jealousy, nor the baseness of a hatred produced by vanity, nor the unfortunate talent of obscuring the talent of others. For the envy that forgives neither successes nor its own injustices is always the lot of inferiority. He is never seen to debase his maxims by contradicting them with his actions, never accessible to the licentiousness condemned by the religion it attacks, the laws it eludes, virtue it crushes underfoot. One questions whether his character has more nobility than strength, more loftiness than truth. His mind is always the organ of his heart, and his expression the image of his sentiments. Frankness, which is a fault when it is not a merit, gives his discourses that amiable tone of sincerity, which has value only when it does not cost anything. When he obliges, you would say that it is he who is grateful, and that he receives the kindness he gives. And it always appears that he is obliging, because he always desires to oblige. He places his glory in serving his fatherland which he honors and working for the happiness of the men he enlightens. He never brings into society that sullen reason which does not know how to part with its superiority; that inflexibility of feeling which, under the name of firmness, is abrupt with attentions and condescensions; that spirit of contradiction which, shaking off the yoke of propriety, makes a game of offending the opinions he has not adopted, equally hateful whether he defends the rights of the truth or the pretentions of his pride. The true philosopher is cloaked in modesty, and to set off the qualities of others, he does not hesitate to hide the luster of his own. As safe as he is useful in his dealings, he seeks in mistakes only the way to excuse them and in conversation only the way to associate others with his own merit. He knows that one of the most solid supports of the justice we flatter ourselves that we obtain is the justice we pay to another's worth. And if he were ignorant of it, he would not base his behavior on different principles than those we have just set forth, persuaded that the heart makes the man; indulgence, true friends; modesty, likable citizens. I well know that with these strokes I am not depicting the entire worth of the philosopher, and especially of the Christian philosopher. My intention was only to give a quick sketch of him.

Letter from J. J. Rousseau of Geneva to Mr. Grimm on the refutation of his Discourse by Mr. Gautier

Professor of Mathematics and History and
member of the Royal Academy of Literature of Nancy [1]

I am returning to you, Sir, the October *Mercury*, which you had the kindness to lend me. I read with much pleasure the refutation of my Discourse that Mr. Gautier took the trouble to write; but I don't believe it is necessary, as you claim it is, for me to respond; and here are my objections.

1. I cannot persuade myself that in order to be right, one is indispensably obliged to have the final word.

2. The more I reread the refutation, the more convinced I am that I don't need to give Mr. Gautier any other rejoinder than the Discourse itself to which he responded. I ask you to read the items on luxury, war, Academies, education in each of these essays. Read the Prosopopoeia of Louis the Great and that of Fabricius. Finally, read Mr. Gautier's conclusion and mine, and you will understand what I wish to say.

3. I think so differently from Mr. Gautier about everything that if I had to pick out all the places where we don't have the same opinion, I would be obliged to dispute with him even about things I would have stated as he does; and that would give me a vexatious appearance which I would like to be able to avoid. For example, in speaking of politeness, he makes it clearly understood that to become an good man, it is good to start by being a hypocrite, and that falseness is a sure path for attaining virtue. He says further that vices adorned with politeness are not contagious as they would be if they presented themselves directly with rusticity; that the art of seeing through men has progressed as much as that of disguising oneself; that everyone is convinced that one must not count on others unless one pleases or is useful to them; that it is possible to assess the specious offers of politeness. Which is to say, no doubt, that when two men give one another compliments, and one says to the other deep in his heart: *I treat you like a fool and I laugh at you*, the other replies deep in his heart: *I know you lie shamelessly, but I return the favor as best I can*. If I had wanted to use the most bitter irony, I could well have said as much.

4. It is apparent on every page of the refutation that the Author does not understand or does not want to understand the work he refutes, which is assuredly very convenient for him. Because, since he continually replies to his own thought and never to mine, he has the finest opportunity in the world to say everything he pleases. On the other side, if this makes my rejoinder more difficult, it also makes it less necessary. For no one has ever heard it said that a Painter who exhibits a work in public is obliged to examine the eyes of the spectators and furnish glasses for all those who need them.

Besides, there is no certainty I would be understood even if I reply. For example, I know, I would say to Mr. Gautier, that our soldiers are not Réaumurs and Fontenelles, and that is unfortunate for them, for us, and above all for the enemy. I know they know nothing, that they are brutal and coarse, and yet I said, and I say again, that they are enervated by the Sciences they scorn and by the fine Arts of which they are ignorant. It is one of the great disadvantages of the cultivation of Letters that for a few men whom they enlighten, an entire nation is corrupted to no purpose. Now you can see very well, Sir, that this would only be another inexplicable paradox for Mr. Gautier, for this Mr. Gautier who proudly asks me what Troops have in common with Academies; whether the soldiers will be braver for being badly dressed and badly nourished; what I mean by proposing that by dint of honoring talents, virtues are neglected; and other questions like these, which all show that it is impossible to answer them intelligibly to the taste of the person who asks them. I believe you will agree it is useless to explain myself a second time to be no better understood than the first.

5. If I wanted to respond to the first part of the refutation, that would be the way never to finish. Mr. Gautier judges it proper to prescribe the Authors I can cite and those I must reject. His choice is completely natural: he rejects the authority of those who testify in my favor and wants me to refer to those he believes oppose me. I want in vain to make him understand that a single witness in my favor is decisive, whereas a hundred witnesses prove nothing against my sentiment, because the witnesses are parties in the trial. I would beg him in vain to make distinctions in the examples he advances. I would demonstrate to him in vain that being a barbarian and being criminal are two completely different things, and that the truly corrupt peoples are not so much those who have bad Laws as those who scorn the Laws. His rejoinder is easy to predict: how can anyone place any faith in those scandalous Writers who dare to praise barbarians who don't know how to read or write! How can anyone assume there is modesty in people who go naked, and virtue

in those who eat raw meat? We would have to argue. Herodotus, Strabo, Pomponius-Mela would be pitted against Xenophon, Justin, Quintus-Curtius, Tacitus. We would be involved in research of Critics, in Antiquarian studies, in erudition. Brochures would become Volumes, Books would multiply, and the question would be forgotten. That is the fate of Literary disputes, that after Tomes of clarifications, the result is always no longer knowing where one is. It is not worth the trouble to start.

If I wanted to reply to the second Part, it would be quick work, but I would not teach anyone anything. In it Mr. Gautier is satisfied to say yes everywhere I said no and no everywhere I said yes in order to refute me. Therefore I only have to say no again everywhere I said no before, yes everywhere I said yes, and suppress the proofs, and I will have responded very precisely. By following Mr. Gautier's method I cannot, then, respond to the two Parts of the refutation without saying both too much and too little about them. But I would prefer to do neither the one nor the other.

6. I could follow another method and examine separately Mr. Gautier's arguments and the style of the refutation.

If I examined his arguments, it would be easy for me to show that they all tend toward falsity, that the Author did not grasp the point of the question, and that he did not understand me at all.

For example, Mr. Gautier goes to the trouble of telling me that there are vicious peoples who are not learned; and I rather suspected already that the Kalmouks, the Bedouins, the Kaffirs were not prodigies of virtue or erudition. If Mr. Gautier had taken the same care to show me some learned People that was not vicious, he would have surprised me more. Everywhere he has me reason as though I had said that Science is the only source of corruption among men. If he believed that in good faith, I admire his kindness in responding to me.

He says that frequenting society is enough to acquire that politeness on which a gentleman prides himself; from which he concludes that there is no basis for honoring the sciences for it: but to what, then, will he permit us to give this honor? Ever since men have lived in society, there have been polite Peoples and those who were not. Mr. Gautier forgot to give us a reason for this difference.

Mr. Gautier everywhere admires the purity of our current morals. This good opinion he has of them assuredly does great honor to his own. But it does not indicate broad experience. From the tone with which he talks about it, one might say he has studied men the way the Peripatetics studied Physics: without leaving his study. As for myself, I closed my Books, and after listening to men speak, I watched them act. It is no wonder that having followed such different methods, we should have so little in common in our judgments. I see that people could not speak a more decent language than that of our century, and that is what strikes Mr. Gautier. But I see further that people could not have more corrupt morals, and that is what scandalizes me. Do we think we have become good people because by dint of giving decent names to our vices, we have learned not to blush for them?

He says further that even if it could be proved with facts that the dissolution of morals has always prevailed with the Sciences, it would not follow that the fate of probity was dependent on their progress. After using the first part of my Discourse to prove that those things had always gone together, I devoted the second part to showing that in fact one depended on the other. To whom can I imagine Mr. Gautier wants to respond here?

He seems to me above all very offended about the way I spoke of education at Colleges. He tells me the young people there are taught I don't know how many fine things which may be useful for their amusement when they are grown up, but whose relationship to the duties of Citizens—which should be the first things they are taught—I admit I don't see. "We will gladly inquire whether he knows Greek or Latin; whether he writes in verse or in prose. But the main thing used to be whether he has become better or more discerning, and that is what lags behind. Shout to our People about a Passerby, *Oh, the learned man!* and about another, *Oh, the good man!* They will not fail to turn their eyes and respect toward the first. There would have to be a third crier. *Oh, the blockheads!*"

I said that Nature wanted to protect us from Science just as a mother grabs a dangerous weapon from her child's hands; and that the difficulty we have in learning is not the least of its benefits. Mr. Gautier would like it just as well if I had said: Peoples, know once and for all that Nature does not want you to nourish yourself on the products of the earth. The difficulty she has attached to its cultivation is a warning to you to let it lie fallow.[2] Mr. Gautier did not consider that with a little work, one is certain to make bread; but with much study, it is very doubtful one will succeed in making a reasonable man. He did not consider, furthermore, that this is precisely only another observation in my favor. For why has Nature imposed necessary labors on us if not to keep us away from idle occupations? But by the scorn he shows for agriculture, it can easily be seen that if it were up to him alone, all Farmers would soon abandon the Countryside to go debate in the Schools, an occupation, according to Mr. Gautier and, I believe, according to many Professors, that is highly important for the happiness of the State.

Reasoning from a passage in Plato, I had supposed that perhaps the ancient Egyptians did not attach as much importance to the Sciences as might have been believed. The Author of the refutation asks me how this opinion fits with the inscription that Ozymandias placed on his library. This difficulty could have been good to raise while that Prince was alive. Now that he is dead, it is my turn to ask about the necessity for making the sentiment of King Ozymandias agree with that of the wise men of Egypt. If the votes were counted and especially weighed, who will reply to me that the word *poisons* would not have been substituted for that of *remedies*? But let us get beyond this pompous Inscription. These remedies are excellent, I agree, and I have repeated it many times. But is that a reason to administer them thoughtlessly and without regard for the temperament of the sick people? A food that is very good in itself may produce only indigestion and ill humors in a weak stomach. What would we think of a Doctor who, after praising some succulent meats, would conclude that all sick people ought to eat their fill of them?

I have shown that the Sciences and Arts enervate courage. Mr. Gautier calls that a peculiar way to reason, and he doesn't see the link that is found between courage and virtue. Yet that is not, it seems to me, such a hard thing to understand. A person who has grown accustomed once to preferring his life to his duty will scarcely delay also preferring to it those things which make life easy and pleasant.

I said that Science is suited to a few great geniuses, but that it is always harmful to the Peoples who cultivate it. Mr. Gautier says that Socrates and Cato, who blamed the Sciences, were themselves, however, very learned men. And he calls that refuting me.

I said that Socrates was the most learned of the Athenians, and I drew from that fact authority for his testimony. All that does not prevent Mr. Gautier from teaching me that Socrates was learned.

He blames me for having asserted that Cato scorned the Greek Philosophers. And he bases this on the fact that Carneades made a game of proving and disproving the same propositions, which biased Cato inappropriately against the literature of the Greeks. Mr. Gautier really should tell us what the fatherland and the profession of this Carneades were.[3]

No doubt Carneades is the only Philosopher or the only Learned man who prided himself for arguing both for and against. Otherwise everything Mr. Gautier says here would mean nothing at all. I rely on his erudition concerning this point.

If the refutation is not abundant in good reasoning, in contrast it is replete with fine declamations. The Author substitutes throughout the ornaments of art for the solidity of the proofs he promised when he began. And while lavishing oratorical pomp in a refutation he reproaches me for doing so in an Academic Discourse.

To what do Mr. Rousseau's eloquent declamations point?, asks Mr. Gautier. To abolish, if it is possible, the vain declamations of the Colleges. *Who would not be indignant to hear him assert that we have the semblance of all the virtues without having any of them.* I admit there is a little flattery in saying that we have the appearances of them. But Mr. Gautier more than anyone ought to forgive me for that. *What! Why isn't anyone virtuous anymore? Because people cultivate Literature, the Sciences, and the Arts.* Precisely right. *If one were impolite, rustic, ignorant, Goth, Hun, or Vandal, one would be worthy of Mr. Rousseau's praises.* Why not? Do any of those names exclude the possibility of virtue? *Won't we ever tire of inveighing against men?* Won't they ever stop being wicked? *Will we always believe we are making them more virtuous by telling them they have no virtue at all?* Will we believe we make men better by persuading them they are good enough? *On the pretext of purifying morals, is it permitted to upset all supports?* On the pretext of enlightening minds, is it necessary to pervert souls? *Oh, sweet bonds of society! Charm of true philosophers, lovable virtues. It is by your own attractions that you reign over hearts. You owe your dominion neither to stoic harshness, nor to barbarous outcries, nor to the advice of proud rusticity.* [4]

I will note first a rather amusing thing. It is that of all the Sects of ancient Philosophers that I attacked as useless to virtue, the Stoics are the only ones that Mr. Gautier leaves me and even seems to want to place on my side. He is right. I will hardly be prouder because of it.

But let's see whether I could render in other terms precisely the meaning of that exclamation: *Oh, lovable virtues! It is through your own charms that you prevail in people's souls. You have no need for all that great show of ignorance and rusticity. You know how to reach the heart by simpler and more natural paths. It is enough to know Rhetoric, Logic, Physics, Metaphysics, and Mathematics to acquire the right to possess you.*

Another example of Mr. Gautier's style.

You know that the Sciences with which young philosophers are kept busy in the Universities are Logic, Metaphysics, Moral philosophy, Physics, elementary Mathematics. If I knew it, I had forgotten it, as we all do when we become reasonable. *According to you, then, those are sterile speculations!* Sterile according to common opinion. But according to me very fertile in bad things. *The Universities are greatly obliged to you for teaching them that the truth of these sciences has hidden at the bottom of a well.* I don't believe I taught anyone that. I didn't invent that sentence. It is as old as Philosophy. Moreover, I know that Universities owe me no thanks, and I was not unaware when I took pen in hand that I could not both pay court to men and give homage to the truth. *The great Philosophers who possess them to an eminent degree are no doubt quite surprised to learn that they know nothing.* [5] I believe that these great Philosophers who possess all these noble sciences to an eminent degree would be very surprised indeed to learn that they know nothing. But I would be even more surprised myself if these men who know so many things ever knew that one.

I notice that Mr. Gautier, who treats me with the greatest politeness throughout, never misses any opportunity to provoke enemies for me. He extends his efforts in that respect from College Regents to the sovereign power. Mr. Gautier does very well to justify the practices of the world. One sees that they are not foreign to him. But let us come back to the refutation.

All these ways of writing and reasoning, which are not in the least suited to a man with as good a mind as Mr. Gautier seems to me to have, have led me to hazard a guess that you will find bold and that I believe is reasonable. He accuses me, most assuredly without believing it at all, of not being persuaded of the sentiment I maintain. I suspect him, with greater basis, of secretly sharing my view. The positions he occupies, the circumstances in which he finds himself, will have placed him in a kind of necessity to take a position against me. The propriety of our century is good for many things. He will have refuted me out of propriety. But he will have taken all kinds of precautions and used all possible art to do it in such a way as to persuade no one.

It is with that aim that he begins by declaring very inappropriately that the cause he is defending concerns the happiness of the assembly before which he is speaking and the glory of the great Prince under whose laws he has the pleasure to live. It is precisely as though he were saying: you cannot, Gentlemen, without ingratitude for your respectable Protector, fail to agree with me. And furthermore, it is your own cause that I am pleading before you today. Thus, however you view my proofs, I have the right to expect that you will not make difficulties about their solidity. I say that any man who talks like that is more intent on shutting people's mouths than he is desirous of convincing them.

If you read the refutation attentively, you will hardly find any line that does not seem to be there to anticipate and indicate the response. A single example will suffice to make me understood.

The victories that the Athenians won over the Persians and even over the Lacedemonians show that the Arts can be associated with military virtue. I ask whether that is not a clever way to recall what I said about the defeat of Xerxes, and to make me think about the outcome of the Peloponnesian war. *Their government, which had become venal under Pericles, takes on a new look. The love of pleasure stifles their bravery, the most honorable functions are degraded, impunity multiplies the bad Citizens, the funds intended for war are used to nourish softness and idleness. What do all these causes of corruption have to do with the Sciences?*[6]

What does Mr. Gautier do here but recall that whole Second Part of my Discourse where I showed this relationship? Notice the art with which he offers us the effects of corruption as its causes, in order to invite any man of good sense to go back on his own to the first cause of these supposed causes. Notice further how, in order to allow the Reader to make the reflection, he pretends not to know what one cannot presume he does not know in reality, and what all Historians say unanimously: that the depravation of the morals and government of the Athenians was the work of Orators. He is certain, then, that to attack me in this manner is clearly to indicate to me the responses I ought to make.

This, however, is only a conjecture that I do not claim to guarantee. Perhaps Mr. Gautier would not approve my wish to justify his knowledge at the expense of his good faith. But if in fact he spoke sincerely when he refuted my Discourse, why wasn't Mr. Gautier—Professor of History, Professor of Mathematics, Member of the Academy of Nancy—a little bit wary of all the titles he bears?

I will not reply to Mr. Gautier, therefore; that point is resolved. I could never respond seriously and follow the refutation step by step. You see the reason for that. And it would be poor acknowledgment of the praise with which Mr. Gautier honors me to use the *ridiculum acri,*[7] irony and bitter humor. I fear he may already have too much to complain about in the tone of this Letter. At least he was not unaware in writing his refutation that he was attacking a man who does not attach so much importance to politeness as to want to learn from it to disguise his feeling.

Besides, I am ready to render Mr. Gautier all the justice due to him. His work appears to me to be that of a man of wit who has much knowledge. Others perhaps will find Philosophy in it; as for myself, I find much erudition.

Sir, I am with all my heart, etc.

P.S. I have just read in the Utrecht Gazette of October 22 a pompous exposition of Mr. Gautier's Work, and this exposition seems written expressly to confirm my suspicions. An Author who has some confidence in his Work leaves to others the work of praising it, and limits himself to making a good Summary. That of the refutation is prepared with so much skill that although it focuses uniquely on trivia that I used only to serve as transitions, there is not a single one on which a judicious reader can share Mr. Gautier's opinion.

It is not true, according to him, that history derives its principal interest from men's vices.

I could leave out proofs of reasoning. And to meet Mr. Gautier on his own terms, I will cite authorities.

Happy are the peoples whose kings have made little stir in history.

If men ever become wise, their history will hardly be amusing.

Mr. Gautier says correctly that even a society entirely composed of just men could not subsist without Laws. And he concludes from it that it is not true that without the injustices of men, Jurisprudence would be useless. Would such a learned Author confuse Jurisprudence and Laws?

I could leave aside proofs of reasoning too. And to meet Mr. Gautier on his own terms, I would cite facts.

The Lacedemonians had neither Jurisconsults nor Lawyers. Their Laws were not even written. Yet they had Laws. I turn to Mr. Gautier's erudition to know whether the Laws were less well observed in Lacedemonia than in Countries that swarm with Men of the Law.

I will not stop at all the minutiae which serve as text for Mr. Gautier and which he displays in the Gazette. But I will end with this observation which I submit for your examination.

If we agree with Mr. Gautier about everything and remove from my Discourse everything he attacks, my proofs will have lost almost none of their strength. If we remove from Mr. Gautier's writing everything that does not touch on the heart of the question, nothing at all will be left.

I still conclude that it is not necessary to reply to Mr. Gautier.

Paris, November 1, 1751

Discourse on the Advantages of the Sciences and Arts

by M. Bordes[1]

It is a long time since the chimera of the golden age has been abandoned: that everywhere barbarism preceded the establishment of societies is a truth proven by the annals of all peoples. Everywhere, needs and crimes forced men to unite, to impose laws on themselves, to surround themselves with walls. The first gods, the first kings were either benefactors or tyrants; thanks and fear raised thrones and altars. Superstition and despotism then came to cover the face of the earth: new evils, new crimes followed; revolutions multiplied.

Throughout this vast spectacle of the passions and miseries of men, we hardly perceive any countries that were wiser and happier. While most of the world was unknown, while Europe was savage and Asia enslaved, Greece thought and elevated itself by the mind to all that can make a people praiseworthy. Philosophers formed its morals and gave it laws.

If one refuses to give faith to the traditions that tell us that Orpheus and Amphion drew men from the depths of the forests by the sweetness of their songs, one is forced by history to agree that this happy revolution was due to the useful arts and to the sciences. What men were these first legislators of Greece? Can one deny that they were the most virtuous and most learned of their century? They had acquired all the enlightenment that study and reflection can give to the mind, and they had joined to it the support of experience gained from voyages they had taken to Crete, to Egypt, and to all the nations where they thought they could learn something.

While they established their various political systems, by which private passions became the surest instrument of the public good, and which made virtue grow in the very bosom of amour-propre, other philosophers wrote on morality, going back to the first principles of things and observing nature and its effects. The glory of the mind and that of weapons advanced at an equal pace, wise men and heroes were born in crowds, beside Miltiades and Themistocles one found Aristides and Socrates. Haughty Asia saw its numberless forces broken by a handful of men whom philosophy led to glory. Such is the infallible effect of the mind's knowledge: morals and laws are the only source of genuine heroism. In a word, Greece owed everything to the sciences, and the rest of the world owed everything to Greece.

Will someone oppose to this brilliant picture the crude morals of the Persians and the Scythians? I will admire, if you wish, peoples who spend their life at war or in the woods, who sleep on the earth and live on vegetables. But is it among them that one will go to seek happiness? What a spectacle would the human race present if it were composed solely of farmers, soldiers, hunters, and shepherds? Is it therefore necessary to live like lions and bears to be worthy of the name of man? Will the faculties of instinct to nourish, to perpetuate, and to defend oneself be exalted as virtues? I see there only animal virtues little suited to the dignity of our being; the body is exercised, but the enslaved soul only grovels and languishes.

No sooner did the Persians conquer Asia than they lost their morals; the Scythians also degenerated, although later: such savage virtues are too contrary to humanity to be durable; to deprive oneself of everything and not desire anything is a state that is too violent, and such a crude ignorance could only be a passing state. Only stupidity and misery could subject men in this way.

Sparta, that political phenomenon, that republic of virtuous soldiers, is the only people who had the glory of being poor by institution and by choice. Its much admired laws nevertheless had great defects. The harshness of masters and fathers, the exposure of infants, theft authorized, modesty violated in education and marriage, the eternal idleness, only exercises of the body recommended while those of the mind were proscribed and scorned, the austerity and ferocity of morals that were the consequence, and which soon alienated all the allies of the republic, are already rather just reproaches: perhaps they would not be so limited if the particularities of its internal history were better known to us. It made an artificial virtue of depriving itself of the use of gold, but what became of the virtues of its citizens as soon as they left their fatherland? Lysander and Pausanias were only the easier to corrupt. This nation that only breathed war, did it achieve a greater glory in arms than its rival, which had united all kinds of glory? Athens was not less warlike than Sparta: it was in addition learned, ingenious, and magnificent; it gave birth to all the arts and all the talents, and in the very bosom of the corruption for which it is reproached, it gave birth to the wisest of the Greeks. After having been several times on the verge of winning, it was defeated, it is true, and it is surprising that it was not defeated sooner, since Attica was an entirely open country, and could only be defended by a very great superiority of dominance. The glory of the Lacedemonians was hardly solid, prosperity corrupted their institutions, which were too bizarre to be able to be preserved for long; proud Sparta lost its morals as did learned Athens. It no longer did anything worthy of its reputation, and while Athenians and several other cities struggled against Macedonia for the liberty of Greece, Sparta alone languished in rest, and saw its destruction being prepared from afar without dreaming of stopping it.

But finally, if I assume that all the States of which Greece was composed had followed the same laws as Sparta, what would remain for us of this famous country? Its name would hardly have come down to us. It would have disdained forming historians to transmit its glory to posterity; the spectacle of its fierce virtues would have been lost to us; as a result, it would be indifferent for us whether they had existed or not. The numerous systems of philosophy which have exhausted all possible combinations of our ideas, and which, if they have not extended the limits of our mind very much, have at least taught us where they are fixed: these masterpieces of eloquence and poetry which have taught us all the paths of the heart, the useful or pleasing arts which conserve or embellish life; finally, the inestimable tradition of thoughts and actions of all the great men who have caused the glory or happiness of their fellows: all these precious riches of the mind would have been lost forever. Centuries would have accumulated, generations of men would have followed each other like those of animals, without any fruit for posterity, and would only have left after them a confused memory of their existence; the world would have grown old, and men would have remained in an eternal childhood.

What, finally, do the enemies of science pretend? What? the gift of thought would be a dangerous present from the Divinity! knowledge and morals would be incompatible! Virtue would be a vain phantom produced by blind instinct, and the torch of reason would make it vanish in wishing to enlighten it! What a strange idea does one want to give us of both reason and virtue!

How are such bizarre paradoxes proven? It is objected that the sciences and arts have carried a mortal blow to ancient morals and to the primitive institutions of States; Athens and Rome are cited as examples. Euripides and Demosthenes saw Athens delivered to the Spartans and Macedonians; Horace, Virgil and Cicero were contemporaries of the ruin of Roman liberty; both the former and the latter were witnesses of the misfortunes of their countries; they were therefore the cause of them. A poorly founded conclusion, since one could say as much of Socrates and Cato.

In agreeing that the transformation of laws and the corruption of morals had a big effect on these great events, will I be forced to agree that the sciences and arts contributed to them? Corruption follows prosperity closely; sciences ordinarily make their most rapid progress at the same time; things so diverse can be born together and encounter each other, but this happens without any relationship of cause and effect between them.

Athens and Rome were small and poor in their beginnings; all their citizens were soldiers, all their virtues were necessary, the occasions to corrupt their morals didn't even exist. A little later, they acquired wealth and power. One part of the citizens was no longer used in warfare; it learned to enjoy itself and to think. In the midst of their opulence or their leisure, some perfected luxury which is the most ordinary occupation of fortunate people; others having received from nature the most favorable dispositions, extended the limits of the mind and created a new glory.

Thus, while some profaned the laws and morals by the spectacle of wealth and delights, others lit the torch of philosophy and the arts, taught or celebrated the virtues, and gave birth to these names so dear to people who know how to think: atticism and urbanity. Can occupations so opposed thus merit the same qualifications? Can they produce the same effects?

I will not deny that the general corruption sometimes spread into letters and that it produced dangerous excesses, but should one confuse the noble end of the sciences with the criminal abuses that some have been able to commit with them? Will one put in the balance a few epigrams of Catullus or Martial against the numerous philosophic, political, and moral volumes of Cicero or against the wise poem of Virgil?

Besides, licentious works are ordinarily the fruit of the imagination and not that of science and work. Men in all times and in all countries have had passions; they have sung of them. France had story-tellers and troubadors long before it had scientists[2] and philosophers. Even supposing that the sciences and arts had been stifled in their cradle, all the ideas inspired by the passions would still have been realized in prose and in verse, with this difference that we would have had less of what the philosophers, the poets, and the historians have done to please us or to instruct us.

Athens was finally forced to yield to the fortune of Macedonia, but it yielded only with the universe. It was a rapid torrent that carried everything away, and it is a waste of time to look for the specific causes when one sees such a marked superiority of force.

Rome, mistress of the world, no longer found any enemies; it formed them in its own bosom. Its greatness caused its fall. The laws of a small city were not made to govern the whole world; they had been sufficient against the factions of Manlius, Cassius and the Gracchi, but they failed under the armies of Sulla, Caesar, and Octavian. Rome lost its liberty, but it conserved its power. Oppressed by soldiers that it paid, it was still the terror of nations. Its tyrants were in turn declared fathers of the country and massacred. A monster unworthy of the name of man had himself proclaimed emperor, and the august body of the Senate had no other function than that of putting him in the rank of the gods.[3] Slavery and tyranny are strange alternatives, but such has been seen in all the States where the militia controlled the throne. Finally, numerous irruptions of barbarians came to overturn and trample on this old colossus shaken from all sides, and from its ruins were formed all the empires that have subsisted since then.

Do these bloody revolutions have something in common with the progress of letters? Everywhere I see purely political causes. If Rome still had some fine days, it was under its philosopher emperors. Was Seneca the corruptor of Nero? Is it the study of philosophy and the arts that made such monsters as Caligula, Domitian, and Heliogabalus? Didn't letters, which rose along with the glory of Rome, fall under these cruel rulers? They were thus enfeebled by degrees with this vast empire to which the destiny of the world seemed to be attached; their ruin was common, and ignorance invaded the universe a second time with barbarism and servitude, its faithful companions.

Let us say then that the muses love liberty, glory, and happiness. Everywhere I see them lavish their benefits on nations at the moment when they are the most flourishing. They have not feared the ices of Russia, as soon as they were drawn to that powerful empire by the unusual hero who was, so to speak, its creator: the legislator of Berlin, the conqueror of Silesia, establishes them today in the north of Germany where they make their songs resound.[4]

If it has happened sometimes that the glory of empires has not long survived that of letters, this is because they were at their height when letters were cultivated, and the fate of human things is not to last long in the same state. But far from the sciences contributing to it, they infallibly perish, struck by the same blows; so that one can observe that the progress of letters and their decline are ordinarily in an exact proportion with the fortune and fall of empires.

This truth is also confirmed by the experience of recent times. The human mind, after an eclipse of several centuries, seems to have awakened from a profound sleep. The ancient ashes were turned over, and the sacred fire was relit everywhere. We also owe this second generation of the sciences to the Greeks. But in what time did they take on this new life? It was when Europe, after so many violent convulsions, finally took an assured position and a happier form.

Here a new order of things is developing. It is no longer a question of those small domestic kingdoms enclosed in the walls of a city; of those peoples condemned to fight for their inheritances and their houses, endlessly trembling for a fatherland that is always in danger of escaping: it is a vast and powerful monarchy, integrated in all its parts by strong legislation. While a hundred thousand soldiers fight gaily for the State's security, twenty million happy and tranquil citizens, occupied with its internal prosperity, cultivate the immense countryside without alarm, make laws, commerce, arts, and letters flourish within the walls of cities. All the diverse professions, applied uniquely to their own object, are maintained in a just equilibrium and directed to the general good by the powerful hand that leads and animates them. Such is the weak image of the noble reign of Louis XIV and of that under which we have the happiness to live: France, rich, warlike and scientific, has become the model and the arbiter of Europe; she knows how to conquer and to sing of her victories, her philosophers measure the earth and her king pacifies it.

Who will dare assert that the courage of the French has degenerated since they have cultivated letters? In what century has it shined more gloriously than at Montalban, Lawfelt, and in so many other occasions that I could cite? Have they ever shown more constancy than in the retreats from Prague and from Bavaria? What is there in Antiquity superior to the siege of Berg-op-Zoom and to those brave grenadiers renewed so many times, who ran with alacrity to the same positions where they had just seen shot and swallowed up the heroes who preceded them?[5]

It is useless to try to persuade us that the reestablishment of the sciences has spoiled morals. One is first obliged to agree that the gross vices of our ancestors are almost entirely forbidden among us.

This admission, which one is forced to make, is already a great advantage for the cause of letters. In fact, the debaucheries, the quarrels and the combats which were their consequence, the violences of the great, the tyranny of fathers, the peculiarity of the aged, the impetuous aberrations of the young, all these excesses which were so common in the past, fatal effects of ignorance and idleness, no longer exist since our morals have been softened by the knowledge with which all minds have been occupied or amused.

We are reproached for refined and delicate vices; it is because everywhere where there are men, there will be vices. But the veils or the dress with which they are covered are at least an admission of their shame and a testimony of the public's respect for virtue.

If there are styles of madness, ridiculousness, and corruption, they are only found in the capital and there only in a whirl of men ruined by wealth and idleness. Entire provinces and the largest part of Paris are unaware of these excesses or only know of them by name. Will the entire nation be judged for the failings of a small number of men? Ingenious writings declaim however against these abuses: corruption only enjoys its pretended successes in ignorant heads; sciences and letters do not cease to take a position against it; morality unmasks it, philosophy humiliates its little triumphs; comedy, satire, epigram pierce it with a thousand arrows.

Good books are the only defense of weak minds, that is to say, of three-quarters of men, against contamination by examples. They alone can faithfully preserve the trust of morals. Our excellent works of morality will survive forever those licentious brochures that disappear quickly with the fashionable taste that gave birth to them. It is an unjust insult to the sciences and arts to impute to them these shameful productions. The mind alone, warmed by passions, is enough to give birth to them. Far from being their authors, the scientists, philosophers, great orators, and great poets scorn them or even are unaware of their existence. Moreover, in the infinite number of great writers of all kinds who have made the last reign illustrious, barely can two or three be found who have abused their talent. What is the proportion between the reproach that can be made against them and the immortal advantages that humankind has gained from the cultivation of the sciences? Writers, mostly obscure, have thrown themselves in our own day into the greatest excesses; happily, this corruption hasn't lasted; it seems almost completely extinguished or worn out. But this was a specific consequence of the light and frivolous taste of our country: England and Italy do not have similar reproaches to make toward letters.

I could dispense myself from speaking of luxury because it is born immediately from wealth and not from the sciences and arts. And what relation can there be between letters, and the luxury of display and softness which alone can be condemned or restrained by morality?

There is, in truth, a kind of ingenious and learned luxury that animates the arts and raises them to perfection. This one multiplies the productions of painting, sculpture, and music. The things that are most praiseworthy in themselves should have their limits; and a nation would be justly scorned which, in order to increase the number of painters and musicians, allowed itself to lack farmers and soldiers. But when the armies are full and the earth cultivated, how should the leisure of the rest of the citizens be used? I do not see why they could not give themselves paintings, statues and spectacles.

To wish to bring large States back to the small virtues of small republics is to wish to constrain a strong and robust man to babble in his crib. This was the madness of Cato: with the temperament and hereditary prejudices of his family, he declaimed all his life, fought, and finally died without ever having done anything useful for his fatherland. The ancient Romans plowed with one hand and fought with the other. They were great men, I believe, although they did only small things. They devoted themselves entirely to their fatherland because it was eternally in danger. In these first times nothing was known except how to exist; temperance and courage could not be true virtues because they were only forced qualities; it was then a physical impossibility to be voluptuous, and whoever wanted to be a coward had to resolve to be a slave. States developed; inequality of goods necessarily was introduced: could a proconsul of Asia be as poor as the ancient consuls, half-bourgeois and half-peasant, who one day ravaged the fields of the Fidenates and the next day came home to cultivate their own? Only circumstances made these differences: neither poverty nor wealth make virtue; it is solely in the good or bad use of the good or the ill that we have received from nature and from chance.

After having justified letters on the question of luxury, it remains for me to show that the politeness that they have introduced into our morals is one of the most useful presents that they can make to men. Let us assume that politeness is only a deceptive mask that veils all vices: this is to present the exception in place of the rule, and the abuse of the thing in the place of the thing itself.

But what will become of these accusations if politeness is only the expression of a soft and beneficent soul? The habit of such a praiseworthy imitation alone would be capable of raising us to virtue itself; such is the scorn of custom. We become finally what we pretend to be. More philosophy enters in the politeness of morals than one thinks; it respects the name and quality of being a man; it alone conserves between them a kind of fictive equality; a weak but precious remainder of their ancient natural right. Among equals, it becomes the mediator of their amour-propre; it is the perpetual sacrifice of the temper and the spirit of singularity.

Will it be said that a whole people that habitually shows these demonstrations of softness, of beneficence, is composed only of liars and dupes? Will it be believed that all are at the same time deceivers and deceived?

Our hearts are not perfect enough to show themselves without a veil: politeness is a varnish that softens the glaring hues of personalities; it brings men together and engages them to love each other by the general resemblances that it spreads among them; without it, society would only offer disparities and clashes; we would hate each other for little things, and with this disposition it would be difficult to love each other even for the greatest qualities. One needs tolerance more often than services; the most generous friend will perhaps oblige me at most once in his life, but a soft and polite society embellishes all the moments of the day. Finally, politeness puts virtues in their place; it alone teaches them the delicate combinations that subordinate some to others in admirable proportions such as the golden mean, beyond or short of which they lose infinitely their value.

One is not content to attack sciences in the effects attributed to them; one poisons them even in their source; one paints for us curiosity as a fatal inclination; one burdens its portrait with the most odious colors. I will admit that the allegory of Pandora can have a good side in the moral system, but it is not less true that we owe to our knowledge and consequently to our curiosity all the good things which we enjoy. Without it, reduced to the condition of the beasts, our life would be passed in crawling on the small portion of land destined to nourish us, and one day to swallow us. The state of ignorance is a state of fear and of need; everything is then a danger to our fragility; death grumbles over our heads, it is hidden in the grass on which we tread. When one fears everything, and needs everything, what is more reasonable than the disposition to want to know everything?

Such is the noble distinction of a thinking being: would it therefore be in vain that we alone should have been endowed with this divine faculty? It is to make oneself worthy of it that one uses it.

The first men were content to cultivate the land in order to get wheat from it; then they dug in its bowels, they extracted metals from it. The same progress has been made in the sciences: they were not content with the most necessary discoveries, they eagerly took hold of those which would only seem difficult and glorious. What was the point where they should have stopped? What we call genius is nothing else but a sublime and courageous reason; it alone ought to judge itself.

These luminous globes placed at such enormous distances from us are our guides in navigation, and the study of their respective positions, which perhaps could have been considered at first only as the object of the most vain curiosity, has become one of the most useful sciences. The peculiar property of magnets, which was only a frivolous engima of nature to our fathers, has led us, as if by the hand, across the immensity of the seas.

Two glasses placed and shaped in a certain manner have shown us a new scene of marvels that the eyes did not suspect.

The experiments with the electrified tube only seem to be a game: perhaps knowledge of the universal reign of nature will one day be due to them.

After the discovery of these completely unforeseen and majestic relationships between the smallest and the largest things, what kinds of knowledge would we dare disdain? Do we know enough to scorn what we don't know? Far from stifling curiosity, doesn't it seem on the contrary that the Supreme Being had wished to reawaken it by these peculiar discoveries that no analogy had announced?

But how many errors have assailed the study of the truth? Isn't it daring, we are told, or rather isn't it foolhardy to embark on the deceptive route where so many others have gotten lost? On these principles there would not be anything further that we should dare undertake; eternal fear of evils would deprive us of all the goods to which we could have aspired since there is none that is without mixture. Genuine wisdom, on the contrary, consists only in purifying them as much as our condition allows.

All the reproaches made against philosophy attack the human mind, or rather the author of nature who has made us what we are. Philosophers were men; they made mistakes. Should this be astonishing? Let's pity them, profit from their mistakes, and correct ourselves; remember that it is to their multiple errors that we owe the possession of the truths we enjoy. It was necessary to exhaust the combinations of all the varied systems, most of which are so reprehensible and so outrageous, to arrive at something reasonable. A thousand paths lead to error, only one leads to the truth. Must we be surprised that people have been mistaken about it so often, and that it was discovered so late?

The human mind was too limited to embrace the totality of things at first. Each of these philosophers only saw one face of it; some brought together reasons for doubt, others reduced everything to dogmas: each of them had his favorite principle, his dominant object, to which he related all his ideas. Some made virtue into a component of happiness, which was the goal of their research; others proposed virtue itself as their sole object and flattered themselves at finding happiness within it. There were some who considered solitude and poverty as the refuge of morals;

others used wealth as an instrument of their own happiness and that of others; some frequented courts and public assemblies in order to make their wisdom useful to kings and peoples. A single man is not all; a single mind, a single system, does not comprise all science; it is by comparing the extremes that one finally takes hold of the golden mean. It is by the conflict between errors that destroy each other that the truth triumphs; the different parties change themselves, raise themselves, perfect each other mutually, and finally come together to form the chain of truth; the clouds clear; and the light of evidence arises.

I will, nevertheless, not hide that the sciences have rarely gained the objective which they proposed for themselves. Metaphysics wanted to know the nature of minds and, perhaps no less useful, it only developed their operations; the physicist undertook the history of nature and only imagined novels, but in pursuing a chimerical objective, how many admirable discoveries did he make? Chemistry has not been able to give us gold, and its madness has gained us other miracles in its analyses and its mixtures. The sciences are therefore useful even in their mistakes and their confusions; it is only ignorance that is never good for anything. Perhaps they raised their pretensions too high. The ancients, in this respect, seemed wiser than we: we have the mania of wanting to proceed always by demonstrations; there isn't a little professor who doesn't have his arguments and his dogmas and, as a result, his errors and his absurdities. Cicero and Plato presented philosophy in dialogues: each one of the interlocutors made a case for his opinion; they disputed, they sought, and they did not make a point of deciding. We have perhaps written all too much about evident truth; it is more appropriate to be felt than to be defined; but we have almost lost the art of comparing probabilities and likelihoods and of calculating the degree of agreement they are owed. How few things are demonstrated! And how many are there which are nothing but probable! It would be rendering men a great service to give them a method for opinion.

The systematic spirit which has long been attached to objects where it could do almost nothing but confuse us should rule the acquisition, the linking, and the progress of our ideas; we need an order among the diverse sciences to lead us from the simplest to the most complex, and to come thus to build a kind of spiritual observatory from which we can contemplate all our knowledge; which is the highest degree of the mind.

Most of the sciences have been made by accident; each author has followed the idea that controlled him, often without knowing where it should lead him: a day will come when all the books will be edited and refounded according to a certain system that will have been formed; then minds will not make useless steps outside the road and often backward. But who is the genius in condition to embrace all human knowledge and to choose the best order to present them to the mind. Are we advanced enough for that? It is at least glorious to try: the new Encyclopedia ought to form a memorable epoch in the history of letters.[6]

The temple of the sciences is an immense edifice which can only be finished over a period of centuries. The work of each man is a little thing in such a vast work, but the work of each man is necessary for it. Should the brook that sends its waters to the sea stop in its course by considering the smallness of its flow? What praises are owed to those generous men who have foreseen and written for posterity? Let us not limit our ideas to our own life; extend them to the total life of the human species, let us merit participation in it so that the short instant in which we will have lived may be worthy of being marked in its history.

To judge properly how far a philosopher or a man of letters is raised above the common level of men, it is only necessary to consider the outcome of their thoughts; those of some, useful for the general society, are immortal and consecrated to the admiration of all centuries; while others see their ideas disappear with the day, the circumstance, the moment that saw them born; for three quarters of men, each new day erases the last without leaving the slightest trace.

I will not speak of judiciary astrology, of Kaballa, and of all the sciences that are called occult: they have only served to prove that curiosity is an invincible tendency, and that even if the true sciences had only delivered us from those that so shamefully usurped the name, we would already owe them a great deal.

A judgment by Socrates that pertains not to the learned but to the sophists, not to the sciences but to the abuse that can be made of them, is raised in opposition to us: Socrates was the head of a sect that taught doubt, and he justly censured the pride of those who claimed to know everything. True science is very far from this affectation. Socrates is a witness against himself here: the most learned of the Greeks was not ashamed of his ignorance. The sciences therefore do not have their sources in our vices; they are therefore not all born in human pride; a vain declamation that could deceive only predisposed minds.

One asks, for example, what will become of history if there were neither warriors, nor tyrants, nor conspirators. I reply that it would be the history of the virtues of men. I will say more: if men were all virtuous, there would no longer be need of judges, magistrates, or soldiers. What would they do? All that would be left for them would be the sciences and the arts. The contemplation of natural things, the exercise of the mind, are thus the noblest and the purest function of man.

To say that the sciences are born of idleness is manifestly to abuse terms. They are born from leisure, it is true; but they protect from idleness. The citizen whose needs keep him at the plow is not more occupied than the geometer or the anatomist: I admit that his labor is of the first necessity, but under the pretext that bread is necessary, is it necessary that everyone begin to plow the land? And because it is more necessary than the laws, will the farmer be raised above the magistrate or the minister? There are no absurdities to which such principles could not lead us.

It seems, we are told, that we have too many farmers and that we fear a lack of philosophers. I will ask in turn if we fear that the lucrative professions will lack subjects on which to work. This is to understand the power of greed poorly: from infancy everything directs us to useful conditions, and what prejudices had to be conquered, what courage wasn't needed, to dare to be a Descartes, a Newton, a Locke?

On what basis can one reproach the sciences for being harmful to moral qualities? What! The exercise of reason, which has been given to us as a guide; the mathematical sciences, which by including so many things useful for our present needs, keep the mind so far from the ideas inspired by the senses and by greed; the study of Antiquity, which makes the first science of man into a part of experience; the observation of nature, so necessary to the conservation of our being, and which raises us to its author: all this knowledge would contribute to destroying morals! By what trick would they produce an effect so contrary to the objectives that they give themselves? And one dares to treat as senseless education that which occupies the young with all that has ever been noble and useful in the mind of men! What, the ministers of a pure and holy religion, to whom youth is ordinarily confided among us, would let it be ignorant of the duties of man and of citizen! Is it enough to advance such an unjust imputation to persuade us of it? One claims to make us regret the education of the Persians, that education based on barbarous principles which gave one preceptor to teach to fear nothing, another for temperance, another finally for teaching not to lie, as if the virtues were divided and should each form a separate art. Virtue is a single and indivisible being. The issue is to inspire us with it, not to teach it; to make its practice loved, and not to demonstrate its theory.

Then new declamations are delivered against the arts and sciences under the pretext that luxury is rarely found without them, and that they are never found without it. If I would accept this proposition, what could be concluded from it? Most of the sciences seem to me at first perfectly unrelated to this pretended objection: the geometer, astronomer, physicist, are assuredly not suspect. With regard to the arts, if they have in fact some relationship with luxury, it is a praiseworthy side of this luxury itself against which one declaims so much without knowing it well. Even though this question should be considered foreign to my subject, I cannot forbear to say that as long as one would only want to reason on this subject by a comparison of the past with the present, one will derive the worst conclusions in the world. When men went about completely naked, the one who first decided to wear clogs was considered a voluptuary. From century to century, people have never ceased crying against corruption without understanding what they meant to say: the prejudice that has always been overcome has been faithfully reborn along with each novelty.

Commerce and luxury have become the bonds of nations. Before them, land was only a field of battle, war a plunder, and men barbarians who thought they were only born to enslave, to pillage, and to massacre each other. Such were the ancient centuries that one wants to make us regret.

The land sufficed neither for the nourishment nor the labor of its inhabitants: subjects became a burden on the State; as soon as they were disarmed, it was necessary to get them back to war to be relieved of an inconvenient burden. Those frightful emigrations of the Northern people, the shame of humanity which destroyed the Roman empire and which desolated the ninth century, did not have other sources than the misery of an idle people. Lacking the equality of goods, which has long been the chimera of politics, and which is impossible in large States, only luxury can nourish and occupy the subjects. They do not become less useful in peace than in war; their industry is as useful as their courage. The labor of the poor is paid from the excess of the rich. All orders of citizens are attached to the government by the advantages that they gain from it.

While a small number of men enjoys with moderation what is called luxury, and an infinitely smaller number abuses it because men necessarily abuse everything, it produces the hope, the emulation, and the subsistence of a million citizens who would languish in the horrors of beggary without it. Such is, in France, the condition of the capital. Travel in the provinces: the proportions there are even more favorable. There you will find little excess; the commodious necessities are rare; the artisan, the laborer, that is to say, the body of the nation, is limited to simple existence, so that one can consider luxury as a humor discharged on a very small part of the body politic which makes the force and the health of the rest.

But, we are told, the arts weaken courage. Several peoples with letters are cited who have been little warlike, such as ancient Egypt, the Chinese, and the modern Italians. What an injustice to accuse the sciences of it! It would take too long to search out the causes here. It will be enough to cite, for the honor of letters, the example of the Greeks and the Romans, of Spain, of England, and of France, that is, of the most warlike and the most learned nations.

If barbarians have made great conquests it is because they were very unjust. They have sometimes conquered civilized peoples: I will conclude, if it is wished, that a people is not invincible because it is learned. To all these revolutions, I will only oppose the most extensive and the easiest conquest that has ever been made, that of America, which the arts and the sciences of Europe have subjugated with a handful of soldiers, proof without answer of the difference that they can make among men.

I will add that it is a barbarism that has finally passed out of style to suppose that men are born only to destroy each other. Talents and military virtues merit without doubt a distinguished rank in the order of necessity, but philosophy has purified our ideas on glory, the ambition of kings is only in its eyes the most monstrous of crimes. Thanks to the virtues of the prince who governs us, we dare celebrate moderation and humanity.

That some nations in the midst of ignorance have had ideas of glory and of virtue are exceptions so singular that they cannot form any prejudice against the sciences. To convince ourselves of this, let us cast our eyes upon the immense continent of Africa, where no mortal is bold enough to penetrate or lucky enough to have tried to do so with impunity. An arm of the sea barely separates the learned and happy countries of Europe from these deadly regions where man is the born enemy of man, where sovereigns are only the privileged assassins of an enslaved people. What is the source of such prodigious differences among such neighboring climates, and where are those beautiful shores that one paints for us as adorned by the hand of nature? America does not offer to us spectacles less shameful for the human species. For one virtuous people in ignorance will be counted one hundred that are barbarous or savage. Everywhere I see ignorance give birth to error, prejudices, violences, passions, and crimes. The land, left uncultivated, is not idle: it produces thorns and poisons, it nourishes monsters.

I admire Brutus, Decius, Lucretia, Virginius, Scaevola,[7] but I will admire even more a powerful and well-governed State where the citizens would not be condemned to such cruel virtues.

Victorious Cincinnatus returned to his plow: in a happier century, triumphant Scipio came back to taste the charms of philosophy and letters, and those of an even more precious friendship, with Laelius and Terence.[8] We celebrate Fabricius, who, with his turnips cooked under the ashes, scorns the gold of Pyrrhus; but Titus, in the sumptuousness of his palace, measuring his own happiness with that which he provides the world by his beneficence and his laws, becomes the hero of my heart. Instead of that antique heroism which is superstitious, rustic, or barbaric that I admire while shuddering, I adore an enlightened, happy, and beneficent virtue; the idea of my own existence is embellished, I learn to honor and to cherish humanity.

Who could be so blind, or so unjust as not to be struck by these differences? The most beautiful spectacle of nature is the union of virtue and of happiness; the sciences and the arts alone can elevate reason to this sublime harmony. It is from their help that it borrows the strength to defeat the passions, the enlightenment to dissipate their illusions, and the elevation to appreciate their pettiness, finally the attractions and the compensations to distract from their seductions.

It has been said that crime was only a false judgment. The sciences, whose first object is the exercise and the perfection of reasoning, are therefore the most assured guides of morals. Innocence without principles and enlightenment is only a quality of temperament that is as fragile as it is. Enlightened wisdom knows it enemies and its strengths. By means of its fixed point of view, it purifies material goods and takes happiness from them; it knows how to abstain and to enjoy in turn within the limits that it prescribes for itself.

It is not more difficult to show the utility of the arts for the perfection of morals. One will count the abuses that passions have sometimes made of them, but who can count the goods that they have produced?

Remove the arts from the world. What remains? The exercises of the body and the passions. The mind is no longer anything but a material agent or the instrument of vice. One is only delivered from his passions by his tastes: the arts are necessary for a happy nation; if they are the occasion of some disorders, let us only accuse the very imperfection of our nature: what does it not abuse? They have given being to the pleasures of the soul, the only ones worthy of us; we owe to their useful seductions the love of truth and of the virtues which most men would have hated and feared if they had not been adorned with their hands.

It is wrongly that one pretends to consider their productions as frivolous. Sculpture and painting flatter tenderness, console regrets, immortalize virtues and talents, they are the living sources of emulation. Caesar shed tears in contemplating the statue of Alexander.

Harmony has natural rights upon us that we would disdain in vain:

the Fable said that she stopped the breaking of the waves. She does more: she suspends thought, she calms our agitations and our cruelest troubles; she animates valor and presides over the pleasures.

Does it not seem that divine poetry has stolen the fire from heaven to animate all of nature? What soul can be inaccessible to its touching magic? It softens the severe demeanor of truth, it makes wisdom smile, the masterpieces of the theatre should be considered as the learned experiences of the human heart.

It is to the arts, finally, that we owe the fine choice of ideas, the graces of the mind, and the ingenious playfulness which make the charms of society. They have gilded the bonds that unite us, ornamented the stage of the world, and multiplied the benefits of nature.

Final Reply [1]

J. J. Rousseau
Of Geneva [2]

Ne, dum tacemus, non verecundiae sed diffidentiae causa tacere videamur. [3]
Cyprian, *Against Demetrianus*

It is with extreme reluctance that I amuse idle Readers who care very little about the truth with my disputes. But the manner in which it has just been attacked forces me to spring to its defense once again, so that my silence is not taken by the multitude as consent, nor by Philosophers as disdain.

I must be repetitious. I know that very well, and the public will not forgive me for it. But the wise will say: this man does not need to seek new reasons continually. That is a proof of the solidity of his own.*

Since those who attack me never fail to stray from the question and leave out the essential distinctions I included, I must always begin by taking them back to them. Here, then, is a summary of the propositions I affirmed and will continue to affirm as long as I consult no other interest than that of the truth.

The Sciences are the masterpiece of genius and reason. The spirit of imitation produced the fine Arts and experience has perfected them. We are indebted to the mechanical arts for a great number of useful inventions which have added to the pleasures and conveniences of life. These

---

*There are very reliable truths that appear at first glance to be absurdities, and that will always be viewed as such by most people. Go say to a man of the People that the sun is closer to us in winter than in summer, or that it has set before we stop seeing it, and he will laugh at you. The same is true of the sentiment I hold. The most superficial men have always been the the quickest to oppose me. The true Philosophers are in less of a hurry. And if I have the honor of having made some proselytes, it is only among the latter. Before explaining myself, I meditated on my subject at length and deeply, and I tried to consider all aspects of it. I doubt that any of my adversaries can say as much. At least I don't perceive in their writings any of those luminous truths that are no less striking in their obviousness than in their novelty, and that are always the fruit and proof of an adequate meditation. I dare say that they have never raised a reasonable objection that I did not anticipate and to which I did not reply in advance. That is why I am always compelled to restate the same things.

are truths about which I surely agree wholeheartedly. But now let's consider all this knowledge in relation to morals.*

If celestial intellects cultivated the sciences, only good would result. I say the same of great men, who are destined to guide others. A learned and virtuous Socrates was the pride of humanity. But the vices of ordinary men poison the most sublime knowledge and make it pernicious for Nations. The wicked derive many harmful things from it. The good derive little more. If no one other than Socrates had prided himself on Philosophy in Athens, the blood of a just man would not have cried out for revenge against the fatherland of the Sciences and Arts.**

One question to examine is whether it would be advantageous for men to have Science, assuming that what they call by that name in fact deserves it. But it is folly to pretend that the chimeras of Philosophy, the errors and lies of Philosophers can ever be good for anything. Will we always be the dupe of words? And won't we ever understand that study, knowledge, learning, and Philosophy are only vain semblances constructed by human pride and very unworthy of the pompous names it gives them?

To the extent that the taste for these foolish things spreads in a nation, it loses the taste for solid virtues. For it costs less to distinguish oneself by babble than by good morals, as soon as one is dispensed from being a good man provided one is a pleasant man.

The more the interior is corrupted, the more the exterior is com-

---

* *Knowledge makes men gentle,* says that famous philosopher whose work—always profound and sometimes sublime—exudes everywhere love of humanity.[4] In these few words and, which is rare, without declamation, he wrote the most solid statement ever made in favor of letters. It is true, knowledge does make men gentle. But gentleness, which is the most appealing of the virtues, is sometimes also a weakness of the soul. Virtue is not always gentle. It knows how to arm itself appropriately with severity against vice; it is inflamed with indignation against crime.

And the just knows no way to pardon the wicked.

A King of Lacedemonia gave a very wise reply to those who praised in his presence the extreme goodness of his Colleague Charillus. *And how can he be good,* he said to them, *if he doesn't know how to be terrible to the wicked?*[5] Brutus was not a gentle man. Who would have the impudence to say that he was not virtuous? On the contrary, there are cowardly and pusillanimous souls that have neither fire nor warmth, and that are gentle only through indifference about good and evil. Such is the gentleness that is inspired in Peoples by the taste for Letters.

** It cost Socrates his life to say precisely the same things I am saying. In the proceedings that were instituted against him, one of his accusers pleaded for Artists, another for Orators, the third for Poets, all for the supposed cause of the Gods. The Poets, the Artists,[6] the Fanatics, the Rhetoricians triumphed; and Socrates perished. I am very afraid I have given my century too much credit in asserting that Socrates would not have drunk the Hemlock now.[7]

posed.* In this way the cultivation of Letters imperceptibly engenders politeness. Taste is also born from the same source. Public approbation being the first reward for literary works, it is natural for those preoccupied by them to reflect on the ways to please. And it is these reflections which, in the long run, form style, purify taste, and spread the graces and urbanity everywhere. All these things will be, if you will, the supplement of virtue. But it will never be possible to say that they are virtue, and they will rarely be associated with it. There will always be this difference, that the person who makes himself useful labors for others, and the one who thinks only of making himself pleasing labors only for himself. The flatterer, for example, spares no effort to please, and yet he does only evil.

The vanity and idleness that have engendered our sciences have also engendered luxury. The taste for luxury always accompanies that of Letters, and the taste for Letters often accompanies that for luxury.** All these things are rather faithful companions, because they are all the work of the same vices.

If experience were not in accord with these demonstrated propositions, it would be necessary to seek the particular causes of that contrary result. But the first idea of these propositions is itself born from a long meditation about experience. And to see to what extent it confirms them, it is necessary only to open the annals of the world.

The first men were very ignorant. How would anyone dare to say they were corrupt in times when the sources of corruption were not yet open?

Across the obscurity of ancient times and the rusticity of ancient Peoples, one perceives very great virtues in several of them, especially a severity of morals that is an infallible mark of their purity, good faith, hospitality, justice, and—what is very important—great horror for de-

---

*I never attend a presentation of a Comedy by Molière without admiring the delicacy of the spectators. A word that is a little loose, an expression that is coarse rather than obscene, everything wounds their chaste ears. And I have no doubt whatever that the most corrupt are always the most scandalized. Yet if the morals of Molière's century were compared with those of ours, is there anyone who believes that the result will be in favor of ours? Once the imagination has been sullied, everything becomes a subject of scandal for it. When nothing good is left but the exterior, all efforts are redoubled to preserve it.

**Somewhere the luxury of Asiatic peoples has been used to contradict me, by the same manner of reasoning which uses the vices of ignorant peoples to contradict me. But through a misfortune that pursues my adversaries, they are mistaken even about facts that prove nothing against me. I know that the peoples of the Orient are not less ignorant than we are. But that doesn't prevent them from being as vain and from writing almost as many books. The Turks, those who cultivate Letters the least of them all, counted five hundred eighty classical Poets among them toward the middle of the last century.

bauchery,* the fertile mother of all the other vices. Virtue is therefore not incompatible with ignorance.

It is not always its companion, either, for several very ignorant peoples were very vicious. Ignorance is an obstacle to neither good nor evil. It is only the natural state of man.**

One cannot say as much about science. All learned Peoples have been corrupt, and that is already a terrible prejudice against it. But since comparisons from People to People are difficult, since a great number of objects must be taken into consideration, and since they always lack exactness in some respect, it is much more certain to follow the history of the same People and compare the progress of its knowledge with the revolutions of its morals. Now the result of this examination is that the beautiful time, the time of virtue for each People was that of its ignorance. And to the extent to which it has become learned, Artistic, and Philosophical, it has lost its morals and its probity. It has redescended in this respect to the rank of ignorant and vicious Nations which are the

---

*I have no scheme to pay court to women. I consent to their honoring me with the epithet Pedant, so dreaded by all our gallant Philosophers. I am coarse, sullen, impolite on principle, and want no supporters. Therefore I am going to speak the truth just as I please.

Man and woman are made to love one another and unite. But beyond this legitimate union, all commerce of love between them is a dreadful source of disorders in society and morals. It is certain that women alone could restore honor and probity among us. But they disdain to take from the hands of virtue an empire they wish to owe only to their charms. Thus, they do only evil, and often receive themselves the punishment for this preference. It is hard to conceive how, in such a pure Religion, chastity could have become a base and monkish virtue, capable of making ridiculous any man and I daresay almost any woman who would dare to pride themselves on it. Whereas among the Pagans, this same virtue was universally honored, regarded as suited to great men, and admired in their most illustrious heroes. I can name three of them who will not be inferior to any other and who—without Religion being involved—all gave memorable examples of continence: Cyrus, Alexander, and Scipio the Younger.[8] Of all the rare objects in the King's Collection, I would like to see only the silver shield that was given to the latter by the Peoples of Spain, on which they engraved the triumph of his virtue. This was the Romans' way of subjugating Peoples, as much by the veneration due to their morals as by the effort of their arms. This was how the city of the Falisci was subjugated and Pyrrhus the victor chased out of Italy.

I remember having read somewhere a rather good reply by the Poet Dryden to some young English Lord, who reproached him because in one of his Tragedies, Cleomenes enjoyed chatting tête-à-tête with his love rather than formulating some enterprise worthy of his love. When I am near a beautiful woman, the young Lord said to him, I make better use of my time. I believe it, replied Dryden, but you also have to admit that you aren't a Hero.

**I can't help laughing when I see I don't know how many very learned men who honor me with their criticism always raising in objection the vices of a multitude of ignorant Peoples, as though that had something to do with the question. Does it follow from the fact that science necessarily engenders vice that ignorance necessarily engenders virtue? This manner of arguing may be good for Rhetoricians or for the children by whom I was refuted in my country.[9] But Philosophers ought to reason in another way.

shame of humanity. If one wishes to persist stubbornly in seeking out
the differences, I can recognize one, and this is it: It is that all barbarous
Peoples, even those who are without virtue, nonetheless always honor
virtue, whereas by dint of progress, learned and Philosophical Peoples
finally come to ridicule and scorn it. It is when a nation has once reached
this point that corruption can be said to be at its peak and there is no
hope for remedies.

That is the summary of the things I asserted, and for which I believe
I gave proofs. Let us look now at the summary of the Doctrine opposed
to me.

"Men are naturally evil. They were that way before the formation of
societies. And every place where the sciences have not carried their flame,
peoples—abandoned to the *faculties of instinct*[10] alone, reduced with the
lions and bears to a purely animal life—have remained immersed in barbarity and wretchedness.

"Greece alone in ancient times thought and *elevated itself by the mind*
to all that can make a People praiseworthy.[11] Philosophers formed its
morals and gave it laws.

"Sparta, it's true, was poor and ignorant by institution and by choice.
But its laws had great defects, its Citizens a great tendency to allow themselves to be corrupted. Its glory had little solidity, and it soon lost its
institutions, its laws, and its morals.

"Athens and Rome degenerated too. One yielded to the success of
Macedonia. The other succumbed under the weight of its own greatness,
because the laws of a small city were not made to govern the whole
world. If it has happened sometimes that the glory of great Empires has
not long survived that of letters, it is because the Empire was at its peak
when letters were cultivated there, and it is the fate of human things not
to last long in the same state. By granting, then, that the alteration of
laws and morals influenced these great events, one is not forced to agree
that the Sciences and Arts contributed to it. And on the contrary, it can
be observed that the progress of letters and their decline is always in exact
proportion with the success and fall of empires.[12]

"This truth is confirmed by the experience of recent times, when one
sees in a vast and powerful Monarchy the prosperity of the State, the
cultivation of the Sciences and Arts, and warlike virtue cooperating simultaneously for the glory and greatness of the Empire.

"Our morals are the best there can be. Several vices have been proscribed among us. Those that remain belong to humanity, and the sciences have no part in them.

"Luxury has nothing in common with them either. Thus the disorders it can cause must not be attributed to them. Besides, luxury is necessary in large States. It does more good than harm. It is useful in occupying idle Citizens and providing bread for the poor.

"Politeness ought to be counted among the virtues rather than among the vices. It prevents men from showing themselves as they are, a very necessary precaution to make them tolerable to one another.

"The Sciences have rarely attained the goal they set, but at least they aim for it. We progress by slow steps in knowledge of the truth, which doesn't prevent us from making some progress.

"Finally, even if it were true that the Sciences and Arts enfeeble courage, aren't the infinite goods they procure for us still preferable to the barbarous and fierce virtue that makes humanity tremble?" I skip the useless and pompous review of these goods. And to start on this last point with an admission suited to forestall much verbiage, I declare once and for all that if something can compensate for the ruin of morals, I am ready to concede that the Sciences do more good than harm. Let us turn now to the rest.

I could without much risk assume all this as proven, since in so many boldly advanced assertions, there are very few that touch on the heart of the question, fewer still from which one can draw any valid conclusion against my sentiment, and since most of them even provide new arguments in my favor if my cause needed some.

Indeed, 1. If men are wicked by nature, it can happen, if you will, that the sciences will produce some good in their hands. But it is very certain that they will do much more harm. Madmen should not be given weapons.

2. If the sciences rarely attain their goal, there will always be much more time lost than time well used. And if it were true that we had found the best methods, most of our labors would still be as ridiculous as those of a man who, very sure he follows the plumb line precisely, would like to drive a well to the center of the earth.

3. We must not be so afraid of the purely animal life, nor consider it as the worst state into which we can fall. For it is still better to resemble a sheep than a fallen Angel.

4. Greece owed its morals and its laws to Philosophers and Legislators. I acknowledge that. I have already said a hundred times that it is good for there to be Philosophers provided that the People doesn't get mixed up in being Philosophers.

5. Not daring to assert that Sparta didn't have good laws, one blames the laws of Sparta for having had great defects. So that in order to twist around my reproaches to learned peoples for having always been corrupt,

ignorant Peoples are reproached for not having attained perfection.

6. The progress of letters is always proportional to the greatness of Empires. So be it. I see that one always speaks to me of success and greatness. I was talking about morals and virtue.

7. Our morals are the best that wicked men like ourselves can have. That may be. We have proscribed several vices. I don't disagree about that. I don't accuse the men of this century of having all the vices. They have only those of cowardly souls. They are merely imposters and rascals. As for the vices that presuppose courage and firmness, I think they are incapable of them.

8. Luxury may be necessary to provide bread for the poor. But if there were no luxury, there would not be any poor people.* It keeps idle Citizens occupied. And why are there idle Citizens? When agriculture held a place of honor, there was neither misery nor idleness, and there were many fewer vices.

9. I see they take very much to heart this issue of luxury, which they pretend, however, to want to separate from that of the Sciences and Arts. I will agree, then, since they wish for it so absolutely, that luxury serves to support States as Caryatids serve to hold up the palaces they decorate, or rather like those beams with which rotted buildings are supported and which often end up toppling them. Wise and prudent men, get out of any house that is propped up.

This may show how easy it would be for me to turn around in my favor most of the things with which people claim to oppose me. But to speak frankly, I don't find them well enough proved to have the courage to take advantage of them.

It is asserted that the first men were wicked, from which it follows that man is naturally wicked.** This is not an assertion of slight importance. It seems to me it was worth the trouble of being proved. The Annals of all the peoples one dares to cite as proof are much more favorable to the opposite assumption. And there would have to be much testimony to oblige me to believe an absurdity. Before those dreadful words

---

*Luxury feeds a hundred poor people in our cities and causes a hundred thousand to die in our countryside. The money that circulates between the hands of the rich and the Artists in order to provide for their superfluities is lost for the subsistence of the Farmer. And the latter has no clothes precisely because the former have braid on theirs. The waste of materials that go into food for people alone suffices to make luxury odious to humanity. My adversaries are most fortunate that the culpable delicacy of our language prevents me from offering details about this that would make them blush for the cause that they dare defend. Gravy is necessary for our cooking; that is why so many sick people lack broth. We must have liquors on our table; that is why the peasant drinks only water. We must powder our wigs; that is why so many poor people have no bread.

**This note is for Philosophers. I advise others to skip over it.

If man is wicked by his nature, it is clear that the Sciences will only make him worse.

thine and *mine* were invented, before there were any of that cruel and brutal species of man called masters and of that other species of roguish and lying men called slaves; before there were men abominable enough to dare have superfluities while other men die of hunger; before mutual dependance forced them all to become imposters, jealous, and traitors; I very much wish someone would explain to me what those vices, those crimes could have been with which they are reproached so emphatically. I am assured that people have long since been disabused of the chimera of the golden Age. Why not add that people have long since been disabused of the chimera of virtue?

I said that the first Greeks were virtuous before science corrupted them, and I don't want to recant on that point, although in taking a closer look, I am not without distrust about the solidity of the virtues of such a garrulous people, nor about the justness of the praises it so loved to lavish on itself and which I don't see confirmed by any other testimony. What is proposed in opposition to that? That the first Greeks whose virtue I praised were enlightened and learned, since Philosophers formed their morals and gave them laws. But with that manner of reasoning, what prevents me from saying as much about all the other Nations? Didn't the Persians have their Magi, the Assyrians their Chaldeans, the Indians their Gymnosophists, the Celts their Druids? Didn't Ochus shine among the Phoenicians, Atlas among the Libyans, Zoroaster among the Persians, Zamolxis among the Thracians? [14] And haven't some even asserted that Philosophy was born among the Barbarians? By this calculation were all those peoples learned then? *Besides Miltiades and Themistocles, one found,* I am told, *Aristides and Socrates.* [15] Besides them if you will, for what does that matter to me? However, Miltiades, Aristides, Themistocles—who were Heroes—lived at one time; Socrates and Plato—who were Philosophers—lived at another. [16] And when public schools of Philosophy began to open, a debased and degenerate Greece had already renounced its virtue and sold its freedom.

Haughty Asia saw its numberless forces broken by a handful of men whom Philosophy led to glory. It is true: the Philosophy of the soul leads to true glory, but it is not learned from books. *Such is the infallible effect of the*

Thus their cause is lost by this assumption alone. But it is necessary to note well that although man is naturally good, as I believe and as I have the happiness to feel, it does not follow from this that the sciences are salutary for him. For every situation that places a people in the position to cultivate them necessarily announces the beginning of corruption which the sciences quickly accelerate. Then the vice of the constitution does all the harm that nature could have done, and bad prejudices take the place of bad inclinations. [13]

mind's knowledge. I beg the Reader to be attentive to this conclusion. *Morals and laws are the only source of genuine heroism.* The Sciences have nothing to do with it then. *In a word, Greece owed everything to the Sciences, and the rest of the world owed everything to Greece.* Neither Greece nor the world owed anything, then, to laws or morals. I beg the pardon of my adversaries, but there is no way to overlook these sophisms.

Let us examine for one more moment this preference that is claimed for Greece over all other peoples, and that seems to have become a capital point. *I will admire, if you wish, peoples who spend their life at war or in the woods, who sleep on the earth and live on vegetables.* [17] This admiration is indeed very worthy of a true Philosopher. Only a blind and stupid people would admire those who spend their life not in defending their freedom but in robbing and betraying each other to satisfy their indolence or their ambition, and who dare feed their idleness with the sweat, blood, and labor of a million unhappy men. *But is it among these coarse men that one would go to seek happiness?* It is much more reasonable to seek it there than to seek virtue among the others. *What a spectacle would the Human Race present if it were composed solely of farmers, soldiers, hunters, and shepherds?* A sight infinitely more beautiful than that of the Human Race composed of Cooks, Poets, Printers, Silversmiths, Painters, and Musicians. It is only the word *soldier* that must be erased from the first picture. War is sometimes a duty, and is not at all made to be a profession. Every man must be a soldier for the defense of his freedom; nobody should be one to invade that of another. And to die in the service of one's fatherland is too noble a task to be confided to mercenaries. *Is it therefore necessary to live like lions and bears to be worthy of the name of men?* If I have the luck to find a single Reader who is impartial and a friend of the truth, I beg him to cast a glance at contemporary society, and to notice who lives in it like lions and bears, like tigers and crocodiles. *Will the faculties of instinct to nourish, to perpetuate, and to defend oneself be exalted as virtues?* They are virtues, let us not doubt it, when they are guided by reason and wisely managed. And they are, above all, virtues when they are used to help our fellows. *I see there only animal virtues, little suited to the dignity of our being. The body is exercised, but the enslaved soul only grovels and languishes.* I would willingly say in looking through the ostentatious research of all our Academies: "I see in them only ingenious subtleties, little suited to the dignity of our being. The mind is exercised, but the enslaved soul only grovels and languishes." *Remove the arts from the world,* we are told elsewhere, *and what remains? The exercises of the body and the passions.* [18] I beg you to see how reason and virtue are always forgotten! *The arts have given being to the pleasures of the soul, the only ones worthy of us.* That is to say, they substituted others for that of doing good, far more worthy of us still. By following the spirit of all this, one will see in it—as in the reasonings of most of my adversaries—such pronounced enthusiasm for the marvels of understanding that this other faculty, infinitely more sublime and more able to uplift and ennoble the soul, never figures in it for anything. This is the effect that is always certain from the cultivation of letters. I am sure that there is not now one learned man who does not have far more esteem for Cicero's eloquence than his zeal, and who would not have vastly preferred to have written the *Catiline orations* than to have saved his country.[19]

The embarrassment of my adversaries is visible every time Sparta must be mentioned. What wouldn't they give for this deadly Sparta never to have existed; and they who claim that great actions are good only for being celebrated, what price would they pay for Sparta never to have been celebrated! It is a terrible thing that in the middle of famous Greece which owed its virtue only to Philosophy, the State where virtue was purest and lasted longest was precisely that one where there were no Philosophers. The morals of Sparta were always proposed as an example for all Greece. All Greece was corrupt, and there was still virtue in Sparta. All Greece was enslaved; Sparta alone was still free. That is devastating. But finally proud Sparta lost its morals and its freedom, as they had been lost by learned Athens. Sparta ended. What can I reply to that?

Two more observations about Sparta, and then I will move on to something else. Here is the first. *After having been several times on the verge of winning, Athens was defeated, it is true, and it is surprising that it was not defeated sooner, since Attica was an entirely open country, and could only be defended by a very great superiority of dominance.*[20] Athens ought to have won for all sorts of reasons. It was larger and much more populated than Lacedemonia.[21] It had large revenues and several peoples were its tributaries. Sparta had nothing of all that. In its location above all, Athens had an advantage of which Sparta was deprived, which put it in a position to devastate the Peloponnesus several times, and which alone should have assured it of Empire over Greece. It was a vast and convenient port. It had a formidable Navy which it owed to the foresight of that bumpkin Themistocles who didn't know how to play the flute. It could be surprising, then, that Athens with so many advantages still succumbed at last. But although the Peloponnesian War, which ruined Greece, brought honor to neither one of the Republics and was, especially on the part of the Lacedemonians, an infraction of the maxims of their wise Legislator, it must not come as a surprise that in the long run true courage won out over resources, nor even that Sparta's reputation gave it some which facilitated its victory. In truth, I am very ashamed to know those things and to have to say them.

The other observation will be no less remarkable. Here is the text I believe I ought to place before the reader's eyes.

I assume that all the States of which Greece was composed had followed the same laws as Sparta. What would remain for us of this famous country? Its name would hardly have come down to us. It would have disdained forming historians to transmit its glory to posterity; the spectacle of its fierce virtues would have been lost to us; as a result it would be indifferent for us whether they had existed or not. The numerous systems of Philosophy which have exhausted all possible combinations of our ideas, and which, if they have not extended the limits of our minds very much, have at least taught us where they are fixed; these masterpieces of eloquence and poetry which have taught us all the paths of the heart; the useful or pleasing arts which conserve or embellish life; finally, the inestimable tradition of thoughts and actions of all the great men who have caused the glory or happiness of their fellows: all these precious riches of the mind would have been lost forever. Centuries would have accumulated, generations of men would have followed each other like those of animals, without any fruit for posterity and would only have left after them a confused memory of their existence; the world would have grown old, and men would have remained in an eternal childhood.[22]

Let's assume in our turn that a Lacedemonian impressed with the strength of these reasons had wanted to expose them to his compatriots. And let's try to imagine the discourse he might have made in the public square of Sparta.

"Citizens, open your eyes to your blindness.[23] I see with sadness that you are laboring only to acquire virtue, to exercise your courage and maintain your freedom. And yet you forget the more important duty of amusing the idle people of future races. Tell me, what good is virtue if it doesn't cause a stir in the world? What good will it do you to be good people if no one talks about you? What difference will it make to centuries to come that you sacrificed your life at Thermopylae for the safety of the Athenians if you don't leave behind as they do either systems of Philosophy, poems, comedies, or statues?"* "Hasten then to abandon laws

---

*Pericles had great talents, much eloquence, magnificence, and taste. He embellished Athens with excellent works of sculpture, sumptuous buildings, and masterpieces of all the arts. And God knows how he was extolled by the crowd of writers! Yet it still remains to be seen whether Pericles was a good Magistrate. For in leading States, the point is not to erect statues but to govern men well. I will not amuse myself by developing the secret motives for the Peloponnesian war which was the ruin of the Republic. I will not seek to know whether Alcibiades' counsel was well or badly founded, whether Pericles was justly or unjustly accused of embezzlement. I will ask only whether the Athenians became better

that are only good for making you happy. Think only of making yourselves much talked about when you are no longer alive. And never forget
that if great men were not celebrated, it would be useless to be one."

That, I think, is approximately what this man would have said if the
Ephors had allowed him to finish.

It is not in this passage alone that we are warned that virtue is good
only for making people talk about us. Elsewhere, the thoughts of the
Philosopher are also vaunted because they are immortal and consecrated
to the admiration of all centuries, *while others see their ideas disappear with
the day, the circumstance, the moment that saw them born. For three-quarters
of men, each new day erases the last, without leaving the slightest trace.*[25] Ah!
Some trace of it remains at least in the testimony of a good conscience,
in the wretches one has comforted, in the good deeds one has done, and
in the memory of that beneficent God whom one has served in silence.
Dead or alive, said the good Socrates, the good man is never forgotten
by the Gods.[26] I will be answered, perhaps, that it is not about those
kinds of thoughts that one wished to speak, and I say that all others don't
deserve to be talked about.

It is easy to imagine that making so little of Sparta, they show scarcely
more esteem for the ancient Romans. *One consents to believe that they were
great men, although they did only small things.*[27] On that basis, I admit that
for a long time only great things have been done. Their temperance and
courage are reproached for being not true virtues but forced qualities.*
However, a few pages after that, it is admitted that Fabricius scorned
Pyrrhus's gold, and one cannot be unaware that Roman history is full of
examples of the ease with which those Magistrates, those venerable war-

---

or worse under his government. I will beg them to name for me someone among the
Citizens, among the Slaves, even among his own children whom his efforts made a worthy
man. That however, it seems to me, is the first function of the Magistrate and the Sovereign.
For the quickest and surest way to make men happy is not to decorate their cities nor even
to make them rich, but to make them good.[24]

*I see most of the minds of my time being ingenious about obscuring the glory of the
fine and generous actions of antiquity, giving them some base interpretation and inventing
vain causes and occasions for them. Such subtlety! Give me the most excellent and pure
action and I will plausibly furnish fifty vicious intentions for it. For whoever wants to
extend them, God knows what a diversity of images is tolerated by our inner will. The
ingenious ones do not make their slander so much maliciously as heavily and coarsely. I
would gladly give the same effort and the same license they use to detract from these great
names to uplift them! I will not hide the fact that I am reinstating in honor by interpretation and favorable circumstances, to the extent my inventiveness allows, those rare figures
who have been selected as examples for the world by the consent of the wise. And it must
be believed that the efforts of our invention are far beneath their worth. It is the duty of
worthy men to depict virtue as beautifully as is possible. And we would not behave badly
if passion were to carry us away for the benefit of such sacred matters. It is not Rousseau
who says all this, it is Montaigne.[28]

riors who made so much of their poverty, could have made themselves rich.* As for courage, isn't it known that cowardice cannot listen to reason? And that a coward still flees even though he is sure to be killed as he does so? *To wish,* they say, *to bring large States back to the small virtues of small Republics is to wish to constrain a strong and robust man to babble in his crib.* That is an expression which should not be new at courts. It would have been worthy of Tiberius or Catherine de Medicis, and I don't doubt that each of them often used ones like it.

It would be difficult to imagine that morality had to be measured with a surveyor's instrument. However, it cannot be said that the size of States is altogether indifferent to the morals of Citizens. There is surely some proportion between those things; I don't know whether it might not be an inverse proportion.** That is an important question on which to meditate. And I believe it can still be considered undecided, despite the tone which is more scornful than philosophic with which it is disposed of here in two words.

This was, they continue, *the madness of Cato: with the temperament and hereditary prejudices of his family, he declaimed all his life, fought and finally died without ever having done anything useful for his Fatherland.* I don't know whether he did nothing for his Fatherland, but I do know that he did a great deal for the human race, by giving it the spectacle and model of the purest virtue that ever existed. He taught those who sincerely love genuine honor to know how to resist the vices of their century and to detest that horrible maxim of fashionable people that one must do what others do, a maxim that would no doubt take them far if they had the misfortune to fall in with some band of Highwaymen. Our descendants will learn someday that in this century of wise men and Philosophers, the most virtuous of men was ridiculed and called a madman for not wanting to stain his great soul with the crimes of his contemporaries, for not having wanted to be a scoundrel with Caesar and the other brigands of his time.

We have just seen how our Philosophers speak of Cato. We will see now how the ancient Philosophers spoke of him. *Ecce spectaculum dig-*

---

*In refusing the gifts of the Samnites, Curius said he preferred to be in command of those who had money than to have money himself.[29] Curius was right. Those who love riches are made to serve, and those who scorn them to command. It is not the strength of gold that enslaves the poor to the rich, but that they want to become rich in turn. Were it not for that, they would necessarily be the masters.

**The arrogance of my adversaries would finally make me indiscreet, if I were to continue arguing against them. They think they impress me with their scorn for small States. Don't they have any fear that I will ask them sometime whether it is good that there are large states?[30]

num ad quod respiciat, intentus operi suo, Deus. Ecce par Deo dignum, vir fortis cum mala fortuna compositus. Non video, inquam, quid habeat in terris Jupiter pulchris, si convertere animum velit, quam ut spectet Catonem, jam partibus non semel fractis, nihilominus inter ruinas publicas erectum.[31]

Here is what we are told elsewhere about the first Romans. *I admire Brutus, Decius, Lucretia, Virginius, Scaevola.* That is something in our century. *But I would admire even more a powerful and well governed state.* A powerful and well governed state! And truly so would I. *Where the citizens would not be condemned to such cruel virtues.*[32] I understand. It is more convenient to live in a constitution of things where everyone is excused from being a good man. But if the Citizens of that state they admire found themselves reduced by some misfortune either to renounce virtue or to practice those cruel virtues, and if they had the strength to do their duty, would that then be a reason to admire them less?

Let's take the example that revolts our century the most and examine the conduct of Brutus as sovereign Magistrate having his children killed for having conspired against the State at a critical moment when almost nothing was needed to topple it.[33] It is certain that if he had pardoned them, his colleague would inevitably have saved all the other accomplices, and the Republic was lost. What difference does it make, I will be asked. Since it matters so little, let's assume then that it did survive, and that when Brutus condemned some evil-doer to death, the guilty person had spoken to him like this: "Consul, why do you put me to death? Have I done something worse than to betray my fatherland? And am not I, too, your child?" I would really like someone to take the trouble to tell me what Brutus could have replied.

Brutus, I will be told in addition, should have abdicated the Consulate rather than put his children to death. And I say that any Magistrate who, in such a perilous circumstance, abandons care of the fatherland and abdicates the Magistracy is a traitor who deserves death.

There is no middle ground. Either Brutus had to be an infamous person or the heads of Titus and Tiberinus had to fall by his order to the axe of the Lictors. I don't mean by this that many people would have chosen as he did.

Although people don't openly favor the last days of Rome, they nonetheless let it be understood well enough that they prefer them to the earlier ones. And they have as much difficulty perceiving great men in the simplicity of the former as I myself have in perceiving decent men in the pomp of the latter. They compare Titus[34] to Fabricius. But they have omitted the difference that in Pyrrhus's time, all Romans were like Fabricius, whereas during the reign of Titus, he alone was a good man.* I will forget, if desired, the heroic actions of the first Romans and the crimes of the last. But what I cannot forget is that virtue was honored by the former and scorned by the latter, and that when there were crowns for the victors of the games at the Circus, there was no longer one for the person who saved a Citizen's life. It should not be believed, moreover, that this was peculiar to Rome. There was a time when the Republic of Athens was rich enough to spend immense sums for its spectacles, and to pay the Authors, the Actors, and even the Spectators a very high price. It was at this same time that no money was found to defend the State against Philip's ventures.

We finally come to modern peoples, and I am careful not to follow the reasonings that are judged to be appropriate on this subject. I will only note that it is not a very honorable advantage that is procured by not refuting the reasons of one's adversary, but by preventing him from stating them.

I will not pursue, either, all the reflections they take the trouble to make about luxury, about politeness, about the admirable education of our children,** about the best methods to expand our knowledge, about the utility of the Sciences and the pleasure of the fine Arts, and about other things of which several have no relation to me, several others refute themselves, and the rest have already been refuted. I will be content to cite further a few fragments selected randomly and which seem to me to need clarification. I must limit myself to sentences, since I find it impossible to follow reasonings whose thread I cannot grasp.

It is asserted that the ignorant Nations which have had *ideas of glory and virtue, are exceptions so singular that they cannot form any prejudice against the sciences.*[37] Very well. But all the learned Nations, with their fine ideas about glory and virtue, have always lost the love and practice of them. This is without exception. Let's move to the proof. *To convince ourselves of this, let's cast our eyes upon the immense continent of Africa, where*

---

*If Titus had not been Emperor, we would never have heard of him. For he would have continued to live like others. And he did not become a good man until, ceasing to take his example from his century, he was allowed to give it a better one. *Privatus atque etiam sub patre principe, ne odio quidem, nedum vituperatione publica caruit. At illi ea fama pro bono cessit, conversaque est in maximas laudes.*[35]

**It is not necessary to ask whether fathers and teachers will be careful to keep my dangerous writings away from the eyes of their children and pupils. Indeed, what dreadful disorder, what indecency would ensue if these well-brought-up children came to disdain so many pretty things and roundly to prefer virtue to learning. This reminds me of the reply of a Lacedemonian tutor who was mockingly asked what he would teach his pupil. *I will teach him,* he said, *to love decent things.*[36] If I encountered such a man in our midst, I would whisper to him: Be very careful not to talk like that, for you will never have disciples. But say that you will teach them to babble pleasantly and I can guarantee your success.

no mortal is bold enough to penetrate or lucky enough to have tried to do so with impunity. Thus from the fact that we have been unable to penetrate the continent of Africa, that we don't know about what happens there, we are made to conclude that its peoples are full of vices. It would have been necessary to draw that conclusion if we had found the way to bring our own vices there. If I were the leader of one of the peoples of Niger, I declare that I would have a gallows built at the frontier of the country where I would hang without pardon the first European who would dare enter it, and the first Citizen who would try to leave.* *America does not offer us spectacles less shameful for the human species.* Especially since the Europeans have been there. *For one virtuous people in ignorance will be counted one hundred that are barbarous and savage.* So be it; at least one will be counted. But a virtuous people cultivating the sciences has never been seen. *Land left uncultivated is not idle: it produces poisons, it feeds monsters.* That is what it begins to do in places where the taste for the frivolous Arts has caused the taste for agriculture to be abandoned. *Our soul,* it can also be said, *is not idle when virtue leaves it. It produces fictions, Novels, Satires, Poetry. It nurtures vices.*

If barbarians have made conquests it is because they were very unjust. What were we, then, I ask you, when we made the conquest of America that is so greatly admired? But how can people who have cannons, maritime maps, and compasses be able to commit injustices! Will I be told that the event indicates the valor of the Conquerors? It indicates only their ruse and their skill. It indicates that an adroit and subtle man can obtain by his industry the success that a brave man expects only from his valor. Let's talk without partiality. Whom shall we judge to be more courageous: odious Cortez subjugating Mexico by means of gunpowder, perfidy, and betrayals, or unfortunate Guatimozin stretched out on burning coals by decent Europeans for his treasures, scolding one of his Officers from whom the same treatment evoked some moans, and saying to him proudly: and I, am I on roses? [38]

To say that the sciences are born of idleness is manifestly to abuse terms. They are born from leisure, but they protect against idleness. [39] I don't understand this distinction between idleness and leisure. But I am perfectly sure that no decent man can ever boast of having any leisure as long as there is some good to be done, a fatherland to serve, unhappy people to comfort. And I defy anyone to show me in my principles any decent

---

* I may perhaps be asked what harm can be done to a state by a Citizen who leaves and does not return. He does harm to others by the bad example he gives, he does harm to himself by the vices he seeks. In any case, it is the law that has to forestall him, and it is better for him to be hanged than to be wicked.

meaning of which this word leisure can be susceptible. *The Citizen whose needs keep him at the plow is not more occupied than the Geometer or the Anatomist.* Nor than the child who builds a castle of cards, but more usefully. *Under the pretext that bread is necessary, is it necessary that everyone begin to plow the land?* Why not? Let them graze even, if necessary. I prefer to see men graze on grass in the fields than devour one another in cities. It is true that as I ask them to be, they would greatly resemble animals; and as they are, they greatly resemble men.

The state of ignorance is a state of fear and of need; everything is then a danger to our fragility; death grumbles over our heads, it is hidden in the grass on which we tread. When one fears everything and needs everything, what is more reasonable than the disposition to want to know everything?[40] It is necessary to consider only the continual worries of Doctors and Anatomists about their life and health to know whether knowledge serves to reassure us about our dangers. Since it always reveals to us many more of them than it does means to protect ourselves from them, it is no wonder if it only increases our fears and makes us fainthearted. Animals live in profound security with respect to all that, and are no worse off for it. A Heifer has no need to study botany to learn to sort through its hay, and the wolf devours its prey without thinking about indigestion. To respond to that, does one dare take the side of instinct against reason? That is precisely what I ask.[41]

It seems, we are told[42], *that we have too many farmers, and we fear a lack of Philosophers. I will ask in turn if we fear that the lucrative professions will lack subjects on which to work. This is to understand the power of greed poorly; from infancy, everything directs us to useful conditions, and what prejudices had to be conquered, what courage wasn't needed to dare to be a Descartes, a Newton, a Locke?*

Leibnitz and Newton died covered with goods and honors, and they deserved even more of them. Will we say it is through moderation that they did not rise to the plow? I am familiar enough with the power of greed to know that everything moves us toward the lucrative professions. That is why I say that everything moves us away from the useful professions. An Hebert, a Lafrenaye, a Dulac, a Martin[43] earn more money in one day than all the farmers in a Province can earn in a month. I could suggest a rather peculiar problem about the passage I am addressing now. It would be to guess, removing the first two lines and reading it by itself, whether it is taken from my writings or those of my adversaries.

Good books are the sole defense of weak minds, that is to say of three quarters of men, against contamination by examples.[44] First, the Learned will never write as many good books as they give bad examples. Second, there will always be more bad books than good. In the third place, the best guides decent people can have are reason and conscience: *Paucis est opus litteris ad mentem bonam.*[45] As for those who have a suspicious mind or a hardened conscience, reading can never be good at all for them. Finally, for any man whatever, the only necessary books are those of Religion, the only ones I have never condemned.

One claims to make us regret the education of the Persians.[46] Note that it is Plato who claims that.[47] I believed I had safeguarded myself with the authority of that Philosopher, but I see that nothing can protect me from the animosity of my adversaries: *Tros Rutulusve fuat.*[48] They prefer to wound one another rather than to give me the least quarter, and hurt one another more than me.* *That education was based on barbarous principles*, it is said, *because a teacher was given for the exercise of each virtue, although virtue is indivisible. The issue is to inspire us with it, not to teach it; to make its practice loved, and not to demonstrate its theory.* How much I would have to say in reply, but I must not insult the Reader by telling him everything. I will be satisfied with these two remarks. The first is that a person who wants to raise a child doesn't start by telling him he has to practice virtue, for he wouldn't be understood. Rather he must first teach him to be truthful, and then to be temperate, and then courageous, etc., and finally he teaches him that the collection of all these things is called virtue. The second is that it is we who are satisfied to demonstrate the Theory of virtue, but the Persians taught its practice. See my Discourse, page 52.[50]

All reproaches made against Philosophy attack the human mind.[51] I agree. *Or rather, the author of nature, who has made us what we are.* If he made us Philosophers, what good is it to give us so much difficulty to become one? *The Philosophers were men. They made mistakes. Should this be astonishing?* It is when they are no longer wrong that we should be astonished. *Let's pity them, profit from their mistakes, and correct ourselves.* Yes, let's correct ourselves and philosophize no more. . . . *A thousand paths lead to error, only one leads to the truth?* That is precisely what I said. *Must we be surprised that people have been mistaken about it so often, and that it was discovered so late?* Ah! Have we finally found it then!

A judgment by Socrates that pertains not to the Learned but to the Sophists, not to the sciences but to the abuse that can be made of them, is raised in

---

*A new plan of defense has come into my head, and I don't guarantee that I will not have the weakness to execute it some day.[49] This defense will be composed solely of reasons taken from the Philosophers. From which it will follow that they have all been prattling as I claim, if their grounds are found to be bad; or that I have won my cause, if they are found good.

opposition to us.[52] What more can the person ask who asserts that all our sciences are only abuses and all our Learned only true Sophists? *Socrates was the head of a sect which taught doubt.* I would gladly diminish my veneration for Socrates if I believed he had the foolish vanity to want to be the leader of a sect. *And he justly censured the pride of those who claimed to know everything.* That is, the pride of all the Learned. *True science is very far from this affectation.* That is true, but I am talking about our own. *Socrates is a witness against himself here.* To me, that seems hard to understand. *The most learned of the Greeks was not ashamed of his ignorance.* The most learned of the Greeks knew nothing, by his own admission. Draw the conclusion about everyone else. *The sciences therefore do not have their sources in our vices.* Our sciences therefore do have their sources in our vices. *They are therefore not all born of human pride.* I have already expressed my sentiment about that. *A vain declamation that could deceive only predisposed minds.* I don't know how to reply to that.

In speaking of the limits of luxury, they claim that on this matter one must not reason from the past to the present. *When men walked about completely naked, the one who first decided to wear clogs was considered a voluptuary. From century to century, people have never ceased crying against corruption, without understanding what they meant to say.*[53]

It is true that until the present time, luxury—although often prevailing—had at least been regarded in all ages as the deadly source of an infinity of evils. It remained for Mr. Melon[54] to be the first to publish this poisonous doctrine, whose novelty gave him more sectarians than did the solidity of his reasons. I am not afraid to be the only one in my century to combat these odious maxims, which tend only to destroy and debase virtue, and to make the rich and the wretched, that is to say always the wicked.

It is believed I am much embarrassed by being asked to what point it is necessary to limit luxury. My sentiment is that there must be no luxury at all. Everything beyond physical necessity is a source of evil. Nature gives us only too many needs. And it is at least a very great imprudence to multiply them unnecessarily, and to thus place one's soul in a greater dependency. It is not without reason that Socrates, looking at a shop display, congratulated himself for having nothing at all to do with all that. The odds are a hundred to one that the first person to wear clogs was a man who deserved punishment, unless he had sore feet. As for us, we are too in need of having shoes to be excused from having virtue.

I have already said elsewhere that I was not proposing to overthrow contemporary society, burn the Libraries and all the books, destroy the Colleges and Academies. And I should add here that I don't propose either to reduce men to being satisfied with bare necessities. I feel very well that one must not form the chimerical project of making them decent men. But I believed I was obligated to state without disguise the truth for which I was asked. I saw the evil, and tried to find its causes. Others who are bolder or more senseless can seek the remedy.

I am weary and I put down my pen for the last time in this overly long dispute. I learn that a very large number of Authors* have made the effort to refute me. I am very sorry that I cannot answer them all. But I believe I have shown, in those I have chosen to answer, that it isn't fear that holds me back with regard to the others.

I have tried to erect a monument that did not owe its strength and solidity to Art. Truth alone, to which I have consecrated it, has the right to make it unshakeable. And if I ward off one more time the blows they give it, it is more in order to honor myself by defending it than to give it a support which it does not need.

Let me be permitted to proclaim in concluding that only love of humanity and virtue has made me break my silence; and that the bitterness of my invectives against the vices of which I am the witness is born only of the sadness they inspire in me and of my ardent desire to see men happier and above all more worthy of being so.

* Even in little pages of criticism written to amuse young people they have done me the honor of remembering me. I have not read them and most assuredly will not read them. But nothing prevents me from giving them the attention they deserve, and I don't doubt that all that is very amusing.

I am assured that Mr. Gautier did me the honor of responding, although I did not reply to him and I even set forth my reasons for not doing so. Apparently, Mr. Gautier does not find these reasons good, since he takes the trouble to refute them. I can see that I must yield to Mr. Gautier. And I wholeheartedly concur about the wrong I did in not responding to him. Thus, we are in agreement. My regret is that I cannot make amends for my mistake. For unfortunately it is no longer timely, and no one would understand what I want to talk about.

Refutation of the Discourse which Won the Prize of the Academy of Dijon in the Year 1750, by an Academician of Dijon Who Denied It His Vote[1]

Preface of the Editor of the Discourse
with Critical Remarks

Literature has its comets as does the sky. The Discourse of the citizen of Geneva ought to be put in the rank of these singular phenomena, which are even sinister for credulous observers. I have read, as has the whole world, this celebrated work. As the whole world has, I have been charmed by the style and the eloquence of the author; but in this piece I believed I found more art than naturalness, more likelihood than reality, more attractiveness than solidity. In a word, I suspected that this Discourse was itself a proof that talents can be abused, and that the art of exposing the truth and rendering it lovable can be made to degenerate into that of seducing and making the most paradoxical and even the most false propositions pass for true.

> There is no serpent nor odious monster,
> Which cannot please the eyes through the art of embellishing.
> Boileau, *Art poetique*, 3

But at the same time I believed that I perceived that this abuse of art did not have all the success promised it by appearances. Error becomes visible to the attentive mind under the sophisms by which one attempted to cloak it with the mask of truth, just as crafty morals betray themselves in the countenance and discourses of the hypocrites whom one suspects and studies. Nevertheless the great diffidence that I have for my own enlightenment caused my reading of the eloquent Discourse to put me into a sort of perplexity. "What side to take?" I said to myself. The hope of contributing to the general happiness of society, as to my own, to be more useful and more pleasing to others and to myself, finally to be better than nature alone had formed me is the motive that has sustained me up to now in the study of the sciences and the arts. Could such a praiseworthy project have deceived me? With the plan of seeking improvement, could I have taken exactly the opposite route? Could so many labors lead me to degrade the talents and inclinations that simple nature had given me? If this is so, I learn every day, and by doing so every day I work to make myself worse than I was. If this is so, I propose to give education to my children, and by doing so I weave a conspiracy against society, against the fatherland, by forming a project that tends toward the corruption of its subjects. Great God! What have I done, and in what abyss was I going to throw my own. Woe to those *who have broken down the door of the sciences*![2] Let's go, burn the books, forget even the art of reading and beware of teaching it to others.

This new plan deserves some reflections. It has all the appearance of an extravagance. What! we would deliberately plunge again into darkness and barbarism? This action alone would be, it seems to me, the master-piece of blindness and even barbarism.

> Barbarus hic ego sum,

But the author crowned by the respectable Academy of Dijon, assures me that this barbarism is only apparent; that I only believe it is so because I do not understand the question . . .

> quia non intelligor illis[3]

I admit that I had already been very surprised that this celebrated body had proposed this question: for every question that is proposed is pre-sumed to be problematic; but the homage rendered today to the Dis-course by the same society adds the finishing touch to my astonishment, and impresses me. I hardly dare examine. There is a way of clarifying my doubts, more decent, more certain, more in conformity with the diffi-dence that I have in my enlightenment. I have the honor of being linked in friendship with one of the members of the learned Areopagus of Di-jon, with one of the judges who must have concurred in the triumph of the Genevan orator. Let's consult him. He is a man who does nothing lightly. He will share with us the reasons that won his vote, and they will doubtless decide mine. I followed this project, and I received from my illustrious correspondent the following letter.

"Yes, Sir, I was one of the judges of the Discourse that won the prize in 1750; but not one of those who gave it his vote. Far from having taken that side, I was the zealous defender of the contrary opinion, because I think that the latter has the truth on its side, and that the true alone has the right to aspire to our laurels. I even pushed my zeal to the point of annotating the Discourse with critical notes, the collection of which is more substantial than the text itself. I believed that the honor of the truth, that of all the academies, and particularly of ours, required this of me. These same motives bound me to send you the copy of them, and to permit you to make them public. With this aim, I have read the edition that the author has made of it, and I have added some new remarks to which his additions have given rise.

"Do not lose sight of the fact, if you please Sir, that these are only annotations, notes that I send to you, and not a florid discourse; that my plan has never been to oppose eloquence to eloquence, paradox to paradox: I would possibly have attempted the former in vain, and the latter would not have been to my taste. I naturally expose to my colleagues what I think of a piece of which I am examiner; in opposing, according to my weak enlightenment, exact reasoning to oratorical figures, clear truth to paradox. Along with the public I applaud the genius and talents of our author; but I dare to think that his piece is only an elegant badinage, a witticism, and that his thesis is false. If I can convince you of this I have won my case. I will always prefer the art of enlightening and instructing to that of amusing and pleasing, when it will not be possible for me to unite them. I have the honor of being etc."

From Dijon, August 15, 1751

The generosity of Mr.*** fulfilled my wishes; I applauded the decision I had made: I devoured his notes; I found myself again, so to speak, throughout. To feel how much this conformity flattered me, it would be necessary to know all that Mr.*** is worth. I am persuaded that all lovers of the sciences and the arts will find themselves as flattered as I am, and for the same reasons, by reading his reflections. Thus I will use to its full extent the power that he gives me to publish them. His motives seem as just to me as his remarks. They conserve for us the right so sweet, so flattering, of thinking with Horace, that . . . *in all of nature the philosopher has only the Gods above him . . .*

> *Ad summam*, sapiens uno minor est Jove, *dives,*
> *Liber, honoratus, pulcher, rex denique regum.*[4]

> Decipimur specie recti.[5]
> . . . Sunt certi denique fines
> Quos ultra citraque nequit consistere rectum (*1).[6]

*1. The epigraph, *Decipimur specie recti* . . . chosen by the author of this discourse, to announce to us that our bias in favor of the sciences is an error; this epigraph, I say, is the only excuse that one can grant him for himself. Still it is not very good: for one can sometimes be fooled by the appearances, and go astray; but one must nevertheless agree that the road to the true has distinctive marks, limits, boundaries, *certi denique fines*; that there are rules for finding one's way there: and in truth they seem to me so evident in the contrary opinion to that of the author, that I suspect that he has been less seduced by the simple appearances of the true, than by the hope of bringing them about in our eyes by the force of genius.

Has the restoration . . . yet does not think any the less of himself.[7] The author is very learned, and consequently plays here a character that is feigned and convenient for the scene. But in general, on what foundation would an honest man who knew nothing not think any the less of himself? Who can disagree that if this honest man were learned, he would always have an additional talent, and that thus he would be even more estimable? But is it really true that one can be a perfectly honest man and perfectly ignorant both at the same time? Isn't it at least necessary to know one's duties to fulfill them? Isn't it necessary to have learned them by an education which has inculcated in us the principles of a sound morality? A science as essential as that is worth enough, it seems to me, not to be counted for *nothing*, and the one who possesses it, does not look at himself as a *man who knows nothing*. If the author understands by to *know nothing*, not to be geometer, astronomer, physicist, doctor, jurist, etc., I will agree that one can be an honest man without all these talents: but is one pledged in society only to be an honest man? And what is an honest man who is ignorant and without talents? a useless weight, a burden even to the earth, whose productions he consumes without deserving them, one of those men whom Horace makes say . . .

> Nos numerus sumus, et fruges consumere nati.[8]

It is very far from this honest man to the good man, true citizen, who imbued with his duties with regard to other men, with regard to the State, cultivates, from childhood, all the sciences, all the arts by which he can serve them, and by which he does in fact serve them, as much as it is possible for him to do so.

> . . . Quod si
> Frigida curarum fomenta relinquere posses,
> Quo te coelestis sapientia duceret, ires.
> Hoc opus, hoc studium, parvi properemus et ampli,
> Si partriae volumus, si nobis vivere cari,
> > Horat, Epist. 3.1.3, v.25.[9]

It will be difficult, . . . have not rebuffed me.[10] The solution of this problem is rendered very curious and very interesting by the superior genius and seductive style of the author; but he did not at all reconcile the contradictions that he himself feels.

I am not abusing Science . . . before virtuous men.[11] To defend virtue against science that one regards as incompatible with the former, is this not to ill-use this science? And if the whole discourse of the author tends to prove the incompatibility of these two qualities, virtue and science, how can he compose each academician of Dijon of two men, the one *virtuous* and the other *learned*? Isn't this subtle distinction, by which he believed he escaped the contradictions that he himself remarked in his proceeding, one of the most frivolous contradictions?

Integrity is . . . the sentiment of the orator.[12] The sentiment of the orator, if I am not mistaken, makes up the principal part of the constitution of the discourse. If the former is not sound, the latter cannot be solid; and a discourse without soundness and without solidity may well be seductive, it will not have my vote.

Equitable sovereigns . . . judge of his own case.[13] The author agrees then that he attacks the sciences, and that because of this we become his opponents. He regards us here only as learned; but we will remember one thing that he has already forgotten, which is that we are good men, and because of this we will be his partisans against science and the first to renounce it, if he proves well that it is contrary to virtue.

I

It is a grand and beautiful sight . . . in recent generations.[14] Without a doubt this is what the author calls the renewal of the sciences and the arts. He is right to find this sight grand, beautiful, marvelous. One can boldly add, upon this description alone, that this admirable revolution, the triumph, the apotheosis of the human mind, is even more of the greatest utility for morals, for the good of society, since our orator himself recognizes that a part of these sciences includes the knowledge *of man, his nature, his duties and his end.*

Europe . . . worse than ignorance.[15] Ignorance thus is already a very pitiable state; it is nevertheless the subject of the praises of this discourse, the basis of integrity and the great spur of felicity, according to our author.

A nondescript scientific jargon . . . to common sense.[16] Barbarism, the savage state, the deprivation of the sciences and the arts thus places men outside of common sense since this marvelous revolution has returned them to it.

It finally came from the least expected quarter . . . natural.[17] There is nothing strange here other than a little enigmatic turn of phrase in the style; a fault which is perhaps also only too natural to the writers of our century. *The Sciences followed Letters*: this is very natural it seems to me; one learns languages; one learns to speak them, to write them, to politely, before penetrating into the sciences. *The art of writing was joined by the art of thinking.* What! would one think only of the Academy of Sciences? and would that of Belles-Lettres be composed of *automatic writers*? The author is too closely concerned not to have this opinion. He wishes to say only that the science of belles-lettres which demands only an application of a mediocre mind, only superficial and trivial reflections, had been followed by the study of abstract profound sciences in which the most transcendent geniuses find something to exhaust their efforts; and he preferred to express this difference between belles-lettres and sciences in a manner as pointed as it is accurate.

And people began . . . their mutual approval.[18] This advantage of commerce with the muses is very real and very important. To inspire the pleasure of pleasing men is to cooperate in the great work of the common felicity; for with these dispositions not only does one beware of doing anything that would be opposed to them, but one also uses all of one's talents to be useful and pleasant to them. Consider all the resources that a lover puts into play to please his mistress and remember that in the continuation of this discourse, the author agrees that, by the commerce of the muses, man becomes the lover of society and it becomes his mistress. I believe that he will have trouble reconciling his thesis with these principles which are very good.

The mind has its needs . . . with which men are burdened.[19] These portraits are prettier than they are accurate. It would have to be the case that the sciences and the arts were simply *pleasant*. Their uses are numberless. It is not at all true that they only cause our iron chains to be covered with flowers: everywhere such chains are found they place shackles on genius and extinguish the sciences and the arts.

Stifle in them . . . civilized peoples.[20] Far from the sciences stifling in us the sentiment of original liberty, on the contrary they teach us that nature has made all men equal and that slavery is the fruit of a tyranny established by violence, *by the reason of the stronger*, inevitable consequence of barbarism. But it is to dishonor the true idea of a *civilized people*, to represent it to us as a half-tamed ferocious beast, as a slave without feelings for his *original liberty*, and subjected to a shameful yoke that he still cherishes, so extreme is his stupidity. The civilized man is the one that the enlightenment of reason and of morality have convinced that the laws and established subordination in a State have equity as their principle and his own felicity and that of his fellows as their goal. Persuaded of these truths, he is the first to execute, to love, to defend these laws which have won his vote, and which bring about his safety and his happiness. A society of men who think and who act in this way form what is truly called *a civilized people*.

In societies there are always *perverse individuals* who have neither the enlightenment, nor the reason, nor the education necessary to resemble the sociable man whom I have just described. These are the ones who are held in the order of a civilized people only by chains, only under a yoke: but one sees that these ferocious men are the members of our species who cannot be tamed. This is the uncivilized part of the people and the one that the rest of society is concerned to hold back in a sort of slavery. It is this slave whom the orator gives us here as a civilized people; a slave which is precisely that shameful portion of humanity without any of the social virtues, without any of the qualities of a civilized people.

Need . . . the Arts have strengthened them.[21] Need and reason have raised the thrones of true kings. The sciences and the arts, which are in their turn the throne of reason, thereby become the firmest support of legitimate sovereigns, through the happy effects of reason and justice as much upon the sovereign as upon the subjects.

Earthly Powers . . . Happy slaves.[22] The author always sacrifices accuracy to pleasantness and novelty. The throne of a civilized people does not at all make slaves, but happy wards under the tutelage of a tender father.

You owe to them . . . of all the virtues without the possession of any.[23] It is here that our Orator begins to lift the mask. He wants softness of character, urbanity of morals, the amiable and easy relations to be merely charms to fool men. He depicted us occupied with the desire to please these same men. Here our unique care is to fool them. There we were the lovers of society; here we are among those suborning and perfidious lovers, who have no lover but appearances, and whose wicked heart has no other goal than to dishonor the unfortunate one who is weak enough to be their dupe. The portrait is not flattering, but is it true? This is what we are going to examine in following the author.

By this sort of civility . . . social intercourse.[24] Decency is already a sort of virtue, or at least an ornament of genuine virtue when one possesses it, and a great step toward it if one has not yet attained its perfection.

If our maxims served as our rules.[25] One wishes to say if our conduct was in conformity with our maxims and our rules. Doubtless it often happens that it is not in conformity with them; but how much more often will this disorder happen to those who have neither rule nor maxim, to ignorant people, to rustics, to barbarians?

If true Philosophy . . . from the title of philosopher![26] By the same reason there are many philosophers who have only the name; but there would be still fewer philosophers if there were no philosophy at all!

But so many qualities . . . in such great pomp.[27] If there is pomp here, it is in the discourse of our orator, and not in decency and in the *title of philosopher*, which decorates the man who is wise, virtuous and simple all together. Moreover

> . . . aut virtus nomen inane est,
> Aut decus et pretium recte petit experiens vir.
>   Horat. *Epist.*[28]

Does the author of the discourse want us to believe that he renounces virtue because he aspires to the title of great orator, and to the pomp of a victory over all his competitors?

Richness of attire . . . is known by other signs.[29] The wise man, like the robust man, is known by his actions, but both the one and the other can be adorned and elegant without this circumstance degrading their merit: on the contrary this increases it if decency presides in their attire.

It is in the rustic clothes . . . vigor of the body will be found.[30] This is not always true to the letter. M. le Marechal de Saxe, and so many others would have passed their time badly with the most rustic farmers: the gilt of clothes removes neither health nor strength, it can only increase their brightness.

Ornamentation . . . likes to compete in the nude.[31] The good man is a brave man ready to combat under all the forms that accident or chance will force him to take: nude, well-attired, poorly equipped; all these accessaries are indifferent to him.

He disdains all those vile ornaments . . . some deformity.[32] It is ornaments and arms that tend to render victory both more certain and more brilliant. The wise man does not neglect them against vice and error. He yields to circumstances, to times, to tolerate them or rectify their outcomes. He accommodates himself to what is decent in the morals of his century to succeed better in correcting what is defective. He makes himself the friend of men to make them friends of virtue.

Omnis Aristippum decuit color, et status et res.[33]

Before Art had . . . spared them many vices.[34] Never have men been less vicious than they are now for the reason that never have the sciences and the arts been so much cultivated. Abandoned to itself nature makes man an assemblage of so many vices that the feeble germ of virtue put in him by his author is soon found to be stifled. The earth no sooner saw two men on its surface and even two brothers, alone masters of the universe, than it also saw one of the two massacre the other out of a principle of jealousy. In vain does a God preside over the first small tribe, instruct it, exhort it, menace it, it continues as it began. Crime is multiplied with men. They carry it to such a peak of horror that the sovereignly good, infinitely wise being repented of having created such a perverse race and knew no better remedy for the abominations that he saw it commit than to exterminate it. In the entire world there was only a single family that was virtuous and exempted from the punishment. This is a sample of what human nature is capable of when abandoned to itself, to its passions, without the bridle of the laws, without the enlightenment of letters, sciences, and arts.

Let us return to the history of this race. Several centuries after this terrible chastisement, we will soon find it as criminal as before. We will find it scaling heaven itself, and revolting as it were against its author. Finally, dispersed into all the parts of the earth by a second punishment, they carry there all their vices. Soon the skillful and robust Nimrod[35] raises the standard of tyranny and makes all his brothers who are neither as strong nor as evil as he so many slaves and ministers of his passions and of his violence. Under this troop, assembled by crime and for crime, succumb entire nations, which were taught by these misfortunes only to carry crime in their turn into other climates. I see the entire earth delivered to these lessons of barbarism: each individual becomes a Nimrod if he can; nations having conspired against nations cutting each other's throats or loading themselves down with chains. Today they form empires which collapse by themselves the next day. They yield to the fiery tumult and torrent of the same passions which have raised them. What that is durable can be expected from a principle more disordered and more impetuous than a sea in fury? All powerful God, when will you grow weary of seeing all nature victim of so many horrors? I see your mercy moved by the unfortunate state of the weakest and least guilty part of humankind, the plaything and slave of the other. What does your infinite wisdom do to give a new aspect to the universe. It causes rare men to be born with whom it seems to share its ineffable essence. Source of light, you open your treasures to these chosen souls. The sciences, the arts, urbanity, reason, and justice, come forth from the bosom of these creative geniuses and spread themselves over the earth. Men love each other, unite, and make laws to restrain those whom chance deprived of this enlightenment and whom the passions still govern. The earth enjoys a felicity that it did not know at all. The earth itself is astonished by this prodigy. It deifies the authors of it, and attributes to a miracle the natural effect of the culture of the sciences and arts. Apollo is adored as a god. Orpheus is a divine man whose chords inspire lions and tigers with the gentleness of the lamb, whose enchanting art animates and gives feelings of admiration and concord to the trees and even to the rocks. Amphion is no longer a learned orator and profound political thinker, who by the force of his eloquence transforms the ferocious and barbarous Thebans into a gentle, sociable, and civilized people; he is a *demi-God*, who by the magic accents of his lyre gives even to the rocks the movement and intelligence necessary for arranging themselves and for forming the walls of a city. What the first geniuses of Arabia, of Egypt, and of Greece have done formerly, those born in the reigns of Augustus, the Medicis, François I, Louis XIV have repeated in subsequent centuries. From this have come those great resources of wise policy, those reasoned and salutary alliances, that balance of Europe, the support of the States that compose it. Finally the wise men of the Orient had been only the legislators of peoples; those of the Occident have pushed the progress of wisdom to the point of becoming the legislators even of sovereigns, because no century has pushed the sciences and the arts and consequently reason and wisdom so far.

Nevertheless in all centuries these bonds that are so salutary, so reasonable, established between kings, between peoples are often found to be broken. These misfortunes would never happen at all if a whole people were learned, if all kings were philosophers. However enlightened, however civilized a State might be, the philosopher is much rarer there than are the pilings of those bulwarks in a dam that oppose the overflowing of a rapid stream, the furies of an agitated sea. The peoples are those impetuous waves that sometimes knock over the pilings and the dam that they sustain; and unfortunately kings themselves are sometimes people in this way.

But do we need to go back to the first centuries of the world and go over all its ages to prove that educated, civilized men are better? Do we not have at present on the earth, even in our regions, samples of men of all types. Tell me, I beg you, illustrious orator, is it in the kingdoms where universities and academies flourish that one encounters the gallant nations of anthropophagi;[36] this people full of humanity and feeling, among whom children are honored for having beaten their mothers well, and where it is regarded as a law of the State and a duty toward one's parents burdened with years to let them die of hunger.(*2) Let us not go so far to seek examples of barbarism and vice attached to the darkness of

*2. We do not see the gallant nation of the anthropophagi, it will be said, but we have that of Cartouche, Nivet, Raffiat, etc.[37] Let us speak more nobly, we see that of the brave men who cut each others' throats for a slight affront, in spite of the law and religion.

The law and religion are thus opposed to these crimes, and doubtless prevent a great number of them; whereas to massacre and eat men is a custom, a law of the nation about which I just spoke. There are some Cartouches among us. Ferocity is a vice in unison among all the anthropophagi: our scoundrels are abhorred; they are seized as soon as they are known, and they expire under torture. The anthropophagi engage in the horrible commerce whose name they carry for their whole lives and are applauded by their compatriots.

Dueling in particular is an accident depending on warlike ferocity; and it would not remain any more than its principle does, if the empire of letters and fine arts were more extended, if all men were philosophers. But in the presupposition that this ferocity is a necessary evil, however fatal, however blameworthy dueling might be, it can in some way be excused by the delicacy of feelings that it presupposes and that it maintains in our warlike youth, by the decency and reciprocal respect that it inspires in them. Thus even from this disorder there results a sort of order and harmony. Nothing like it can be alleged in favor of the anthropophagi and the Hottentots, people cruel without necessity, by habit, and by the sole pleasure of being cruel.

ignorance. Let us look over only the country regions of France that are least cultivated by the arts, least civilized and compare their morals with those of the inhabitants of the large cities. Let thirty young peasants of different villages of Thiérache or of Brittany etc. be found assembled to dance at a village festival, you will have more fights, more injuries, more murders from the passionate and fierce grossness of these thirty rustics than you will have in a hundred balls at the opera which assemble five hundred persons, than you will have in three months in a city peopled with a million inhabitants. Do you have a farm, land in these civilized cantons? Your farmer is as much the proprietor of it as you yourself. He pays you, it is true, the contents of your lease, but he does not leave you the liberty of being still better paid by another. Your goods pass from father to son to the descendants of the farmer as to those of the proprietor, and if you take it into your head to prove that you are the master of disposing of it in favor of another line, either the latter will not be bold enough to accept it, or you will soon see your land reduced to ashes and your new farmer assassinated. You are in France, the laws will avenge you; they will prove to you as to me that virtue resides and finds protection only in a well-civilized State, and that you would be lost without resources, if your land had been placed in regions where laws are unknown, except those of the passions and of violence; if finally you were in those first centuries when nature alone governed men: true centuries of iron whatever the fable and its ministers the poets say about it.

Such is the very succinct brief of the proofs that the history of past centuries and even of our own furnish us about the intimate union of crime with barbarism, with ignorance and, on the contrary, of the necessary link of virtue, of reason, with the sciences, the arts, urbanity. But if history would not say a word about it, do we not have in the physical principles of these things themselves, in their nature, something to prove what these events have just taught us?

The particular constitution of man renders him subject to a thousand needs. He has senses that inform him about them, and each of his sensations of needs is accompanied by an action of the will, with a desire all the more violent as its need is greater, or the organ instructed by it is more sensitive. This same act of the will causes to act all the springs of the motion of the machine appropriate for satisfying the needs, for fulfilling the desires. This is the natural progress of human nature, and a sequence of effects which are as attached to its mechanism as the separation of the day into 24 hours is to a clock. By himself the well-being of the individual is his unique object, the unique end to which this individual relates all his actions. If there were only one man in the universe he would be able to satisfy himself without doing so at the expense of any being who could oppose it or complain about it; but as soon as the object of his desires is found divided among several men, it often happens that he must learn to do without or steal it from the one who possesses it. What does nature say to him in such a case? It does not waver; it has nothing more dear than itself, and more urgent than to satisfy itself. It says to him very positively that if the possessor of the desired object is weaker, one must steal it from him without ceremony; and that if he is capable of a resistance that renders the acquisition doubtful, one must make up for this with art, lay an ambush for him, or imagine a bow and arrow which strikes him from afar, and which rids us from the restlessness into which desire puts us, or the fear of being troubled in the possession of the object when we have acquired it. Thus speaks nature; thus has it led the first men; thus has it produced those centuries of horrors that we have run through above.

What has the culture of the sciences and the arts done? What has nature perfected by reflection done? Finally what has reason done to rescue totally brute human nature from the dishonor into which it has plunged? Listen, she has said to this individual, you want to take away from your neighbor something that belongs to him: but what would you think if he stole something of yours? Why do you believe yourself authorized to do against him what you would be very angry to have him do against you? And who told you that your other neighbor will not join him to punish you for your violence? Then repress an unjust desire which can have deadly consequences for you. Desire only what belongs to you, or what you can obtain legitimately. You are skillful and vigorous, use your talents to defend yourself and not to attack. Employ them to defend your neighbors. They will love you; they will regard you as their protector, their leader; and by this generous route you will have from them both their friendship and all that you would have been able to steal from them only with injustice, and by undergoing dangers. Answer me, it says to a second, you who join an industrious character to genius, I have seen you construct your hut with more skill and more art than anyone else. Why not make a similar or even finer one for your neighbor who does not have the skill to make one for himself? He is a better hunter than you, he will provide abundantly for needs that you are barely able to satisfy, and he will also pay you with both his gratitude and his friendship. You sleep, it says to a third, and you imitate your herd which is sated and tired out by the pastures where you have driven them all day. I know you are capable of more vast reflections. Can't you lift your eyes to those shining stars with which the sky is adorned this beautiful night.

Identify them, observe their paths, draw from them the means to know the regions of the earth, the plan of the universe, and to determine the year, its seasons. You will become the admiration of other men and the object of their praises and their tributes. What are you doing, lazy one? it says to a fourth. You are ingenious, and you pass entire days in idleness and reverie. Take this reed from me, empty its pith, bore holes in it, breathe against the first, and move your fingers artfully upon the others. You are going to produce sounds which will make all the humans of the country hasten around you. Entranced by hearing you, they will esteem you above the others, and there are no presents that they will not give you to hire you to procure this pleasure for them. Look, it says to a fifth, at what your neighbors have just done for the general good of the dwelling place? What emulation and what reciprocal esteem has placed inventive genius among them? What union results from the mutual services that they render each other or pleasures that they bring about thereby? What safety is produced in this union by this esteem, this reciprocal friendship, and the equity with which most of its members pride themselves? You who feel better than any other the utility and happiness of such a state, and who is one of the wisest and most eloquent of the dwelling place, persuade them all to make a law for themselves always to live as the best among them do, to punish those who swerve from it, and to excite by your praises and rewards virtuous and clever men, to whom they owe these precious advantages, to carry them to a still greater perfection.

Thus spoke reason; thus genius, by taking flight, developed the seed of equity and urbanity which had been stifled by barbarism. But without this reason, first effort of genius, what might have become of virtue? Without education, without the cultivation of the sciences and arts, what might become of morals? What are the essential objects of this education? Let my orator follow me here and not elude the question by the brilliance of his sophisms: are they not our duties with regard to the Supreme Being and with regard to our neighbor? It is to children that one inculcates these duties, it is on the soft wax that one impresses this obligation. Then they grow not only well-educated but also convinced of the necessity of these duties. How would they not fulfill them as soon as they are well convinced of them? How would they fail virtue, integrity, which they esteem, which they love and which they revere? And if there are still some of them whose perverse nature urges them to degrade themselves, to give themselves up to vice, in spite of so many circumstances fit for setting them under the standard of honor; what might they not have done, and how much larger a number of them might there not have been, if they lacked all these helps from education and letters?(*3)

Today . . . cast in the same mold.[39] So much the better if the form is good.

Incessantly politeness demands . . . own genius.[40] One does very well not to follow one's own genius if it is in conformity with a perverse nature. So one should take as a rule the reforms that have been made in it by the reflections of the wise: but if one possesses a good genius, one can boldly let oneself go. One will make oneself admired and loved at the same time.

One no longer dares to appear as he is.[41] Oh! Here we are: one is naturally evil; education has taught us that it is necessary not to be so. We are ashamed to feel in ourselves that this education has not yet uprooted these vices; we make efforts at least to appear virtuous. This effort is a first step toward virtue, *initium sapientiae timor Domini,*[42] and the proof of the good that education has done among us. Without it, this very man

*3. Someone will say, you make the sciences, the arts, reason do what the natural law has always done, since you attribute to them even this first very simple principle, *alteri ne feceris quod tibi fieri non vis.*[38]

What is understood by the natural law? Is it the instincts, the motions that all men receive from completely brute nature? In this case, I say that the natural law dictates to us only to satisfy our desires, however unrestrained they might be, that it is the principle of barbarism, and that it does nothing that we have just seen done by reason, the sciences, and the arts, as I have just proven. Does one wish to call natural law that which commands men to cherish each other reciprocally? Then I maintain that this law is a consequence of reflection and experience; that it is a natural law reduced into art, into science, by reasonings that make us see that empire over our passions, privation of several of our desires, are often more advantageous to us than the illegitimate enjoyment of desired goods; and that even if we would not find our own advantage in this, justice requires of us that we act in this way. Now, these improvements of reason toward equity are the first foundations that it lays for morality, they are already a beginning of the great art of behaving among other men; but this science, which tends to the good of society, at the same time opposes the natural movements of the private individual.

How does it happen, I beg you, that one accords so much esteem to virtue, so much admiration to generous actions by which private individuals have sacrificed themselves for their friends, for their fellow citizens? It is because all these fine actions are not in simple nature; it is because to form the project, the system, of performing them, there must have been efforts of genius, and to execute them, in addition still greater efforts on the part of the soul, possibly even a bit of a certain enthusiasm, to renounce one's own interests and to prefer to them that of one's friends, one's fellow citizens, one's fatherland. What is generosity, if not this sacrifice of one's private good to that of others? Now all these proceedings are superior to the purely natural law, superior to those instincts of which we were just speaking. It is even because of this reason and because of the private interest we have that when other men do so many similar actions we grant them so many praises. Thus, when it is commonly said that this principle, *do to another only what you would want him to do to you,* is a natural law, it is understood that this is the first consequence that reason has drawn from its reflections and experience, the first principle finally of the science of natural morality, of the morality established independently of the enlightenment of revelation; but this morality is truly one of those arts, one of those sciences to which I have attributed the fortunate revolution achieved in humankind.

would have been evil without shame and very openly. The more ashamed he will be of being vicious, the less he will succumb; and, all other things being equal, the more education he will have had, the greater this shame will be and the less he will dare to be vicious. With this, the author agrees, in spite of himself, about the usefulness of the sciences, the arts, education.

To this same principle can be related what we call honor, the point of honor, that magnanimous tyrant whose despotic and often salutary power governs all civilized people, this great motive of the actions of all men, even of those who have neither religion nor real virtues. Now where does this most powerful, most universal bridle against base, shameful, vicious actions come from if not from education? Why a does Savage woman prostitute herself publicly and off-handedly, whereas what we call a woman of honor would lose her life rather than the reputation which causes her to be given that epithet; and those who have lost it, still hide their weaknesses with care? It is because the savage follows the instinct of nature alone, and she has never been told that it was wrong to let oneself go in the torrent of one's passions. Instead of which the rules of divine and human morality about this point have been inculcated in our women since birth, and they have been persuaded that it is shameful to abandon themselves to vices, against the enlightenment and precepts of this morality.

This point of honor, this bridle more general than religion itself, and which is often very useful to it, will thus be all the more powerful, as these truths, these precepts of morality will have been better inculcated, and more education will have been given. Men will thus be all the less vicious as they will be less ignorant, better educated.

And in this perpetual constraint . . . that it would have been essential to know him.[43] Who is the dupe of the courtesies that usage has established and who will confound them with the sincere offers of services that a friend makes to you? Simple urbanity and urbanity warmed by a lively and sincere friendship have such different tones that the person least versed in the commerce of the world is not mistaken about them. It is hardly more difficult to penetrate even the cheat who studies to play the character of the latter than it is bothersome to distinguish a coquette from a genuine lover. For the rest, if men betray each other in a century in which education, honor, and feelings reign more than ever, what ought to be expected in the centuries of ignorance and barbarism? Do you believe that the more vicious of that time were less cunning, less deceivers because they were less learned? It is a very glaring error to believe that the sciences and the arts render men more shrewd, more crafty. I could cite a hundred strokes of the most naive simplicity taken in great men, from La Fontaine to Newton. The one who relates with so much art the cheating of the fox and the wolf kept for himself only the simplicity of the lamb. The one whose sagacity astonished the universe when it was a question of sounding the depths of nature, when it was a question of putting light to the torture, of extorting all of its secrets from it by physical ruses as fine as that matter is subtle; in the presence of a woman or a man of the world, the very same one had nothing but a timidity, a rustic ingenuity that is found surpassed even by frivolity. The eagle of the academies becomes the oaf of social circles. It will be even worse if it is a question of the art of penetrating the little details of interest, business affairs, the subtleties, the stratagems that form a part of this art so well known by ordinary men. I dare to advance, without fear of being contradicted by any reasonable man, that in this part a dozen of these transcendent men will be the playing of a Low Norman or Manceau peasant, and the reason for this is as simple as they are: their sublime genius is entirely occupied with the subjects that are proportionate to them. It never descends into those little details of usages and affairs of ordinary life. They are ignorant about all the recesses, all those little detours which the peasant has made his unique study.

If there are large numbers of these crafty men in the polite world, it is because the greatest number of members of society prefer the science of the world, of its manners, its ruses, its interests, to the science of nature and the fine arts. And why does the most lovable and the most to be feared, the weakest and the most seductive part in this society pass for the craftiest? It is because through its sort of life it is the least educated, the least learned. Today let us get over the warning against learned women, let us recognize them to be as much and even more fit than we are for beautiful knowledge, let them apply themselves to it. What is at the same time more lovable and more certain than their commerce? If then you seek artifice, address yourself in the two sexes to that frivolous part, whose education as futile as it is, admits no science, no solid art whatsoever, which knows only the name of these torches of truth, these ramparts of virtue. You will not find the crafty man among the learned, among the people completely given over to the fine arts; or, if it is possible that he is found there, he will be one in ten thousand, whom the art most capable of doing so will not have preserved from this too natural inclination.

What a procession of vices . . . to the enlightenment of our century.[44] We have just responded to this declamation.

The name of the Master of the Universe will no longer be profaned . . . he will be cleverly slandered.[45] Our Author agrees that our educated people, that our polite, lettered people are not capable *of grossly insulting their enemies*, but that, in return, clever dissimulation, slander, cheating, make up the portion of this civilized part.

It is already a great advantage for society that letters have extirpated the coarse vices. But if the author believes that less important faults have been multiplied and have made a compensation, it is an error which no one will grant. Who could be persuaded that a man wild enough to execute theft, murder, such as is found in the dregs of the people and country folk, etc., will have any scruple about being dissembling, a cheat? These are fine bagatelles for scoundrels capable of dipping their hands in human blood! Let us agree then that the coarse part of the men even of this century, the least civilized part, half barbaric, is the most wicked; and we will conceive that when all the human race was savage, barbaric, still worse than the coarse type of which we just spoke, all men were much more wicked than they are today.

National hatreds will die out . . . as their cunning simplicity.[46] Our Orator here copies the Misanthrope of Molière. He only misses saying with him . . .

> I enter into a black humor, and a profound chagrin
> When I see men live as they do among themselves
> Everywhere I find only cowardly flattery,
> Only injustice, interest, treachery, cheating;
> I can no longer hold back, I am enraged, and my plan
> Is to quarrel openly with the human race.[47]

We will answer him with *Ariste*[48] . . .

> This philosophic chagrin is a little too wild;
> I laugh at the black fits in which I envisage you.

Such is the purity . . . would guess our morals to be exactly the opposite of what they are.[49] A savage, doubtless, who would take all our courtesies at the letter, and who would believe naively that all the world is his *servant*, because all the world says this to him, would be very surprised not to find a single lackey in his hire among his honest *servants*. But if he would subsequently compare the basis of the life and morals of our peoples with what happens in his barbaric nation; if he would be in a condition to compare the prodigies that the sciences and the arts have invented for the safety, the needs and the commodities of life, for the amusement and the happiness of men, with the poverty and the shocking misery of his compatriots, exposed to the injuries of all the seasons, living by hunting, fishing, and by what the earth gives by itself, and dying of hunger, of cold, or the most easily cured illnesses, when accident and nature, their only resources fail them in their need; if he would be educated enough to compare our jurisprudence, that admirable police who shelter the weak and the orphan from the violence of the stronger and the more wicked, who make millions of men live together with mildness, politeness, consideration, reciprocal services, as our orator says so elegantly if he would be, I say, in a condition to compare that admirable harmony with the shocking disorders attached to barbarism, to savage morals, then he would believe himself transported into the abode of the gods, and in fact in comparison with his first condition he would be there.

When there is no effect . . . advancement of our sciences and arts to perfection.[50] One says go to perfection, and not *to advance to perfection*, but indeed to advance *toward* perfection: as one says *to go to Paris*, and not *to advance to Paris*, but indeed to advance *toward* Paris; and the reason for this is simple. It is that the one who goes to a place is presumed to arrive there, to go as far as there; instead of which the one who advances toward something can very well make only several steps toward it, and stay there. As regards Sciences, I would not look so closely, I willingly sacrifice purity of language to a plainer and stronger expression; but an orator ought to be scrupulous about language.

Can it be said that this is a misfortune . . . and in all places.[51] Here is a very explicit declaration of the paradox that the author dares to support; let us follow him through the alleged proofs he is going to give of propositions which are both revolting and false.

Consider Egypt . . . and finally the Turks.[52] Do these historical facts prove in the least that Egypt, being polished by the sciences and the arts, became less virtuous from them in order to have become weaker? On the contrary, when reduced to the truth, this proof teaches us that the conquering Egypt is the barbaric and ferocious Egypt; that the conquered Egypt is the learned, civilized, virtuous, Egypt, assailed by peoples as barbaric and ferocious as she herself used to be. What is there in this that does not conform to nature and to our thesis? Isn't it in the ordinary course of this nature, all things being equal moreover,

That ferocity overwhelm virtue.

Consider Greece . . . enervated by luxury and the Arts.[53]

Enervated we will pass, but corrupted morals, this is a question that our orator has not even skimmed, and that I dare to defy him to prove.

It is in the time of Ennius . . . the title arbiter of good taste.[54] The whole world knows that Rome owes its origin to a band of brigands gathered together by the privilege of impunity, within the walls built by its foun-

der. Here is the germ of the conquerors of the world, object of the praises
of this discourse, and here is the pattern of scoundrels brought together
by crime and for crime. I advise our orator to place these heros that today
we would see expiring by diverse well-deserved tortures, to place them,
I say, face to face with Ovid, Catullus, etc.

*What shall I say about that Capital . . . perhaps more through wisdom
than barbarism.*[55] Here is a *perhaps* that is very prudent and very necessary
in this sentence; for how can it be believed that the peoples of Europe
being still barbarians, refused on good grounds to admit the sciences
among them? They had not read the discourse of our orator.

*All that is most shameful in debauchery . . . the enlightenment of which
our century boasts.*[56] All these horrors prove that in the best civilized, the
most learned empire there were ignorant people, there were barbarians.
Can the entire people be learned in the kingdom in which the sciences
are the most cultivated? Do all men have morals in the States in which
the purest morality reigns with the greatest vigor? The most numerous
part of the subjects of such a State is always deprived of fine education
and there are doubtless among the other still some natures rebellious
enough to conserve their passions, their wickedness, in spite of the power
of the sciences and the arts. An enlightened civilized century is more
struck than another by those anecdotes that are shameful to the human
race. It is fertile in historians who do not fail to transmit them to posterity: but how many thousand volumes against one would not have
been filled with the foul deeds that happened in the barbaric centuries,
in the centuries of iron, if they had not been too common to deserve
attention, or if there were found spectators, people of integrity, and in a
condition to write?

But why seek . . . free and invincible.[57] *To purify morals*, and to give what
the author understands here by *courage*, are two completely different, and
perhaps even opposite things.

Warlike valor is of two sorts; the one that I will call *courage* along with
the author, has its principle in the lively passions of the soul, and a little
in the strength of the body. This one is given to us by nature, it is this
one which distinguishes the English mastiff from the poodle and spaniel.
The proper name of this courage is *ferocity*, and it is consequently a vice.
The warlike valor of the second sort, and that which truly deserves the
name of *valor*, is the virtue of a soul that is great and enlightened both
together, which impressed by the justice of a case, by the necessity and
the possibility of defending it, and believing it superior to the advantages
of its particular life, exposes the latter to obtain the former, while making
all its enlightenment serve for the choice of prudent means that lead to

its goal. Ferocious courage is the ordinary valor of the soldier; it is an impetuous and blind movement given by nature, and which will be all the more violent, all the more powerful, as the passions will be more lively, more mutinous, as they will have been less mastered. In a word the less education the individual will have had, the more he will be barbaric. This is why the peasants of the provinces far from the center of a civilized State, and the mountaineers are more courageous than the artisans of large cities. It is beyond doubt that the cultivation of the sciences and the arts extinguishes this sort of courage, this ferocity; because the submission, the perpetual subordination imposed by education, the morality which masters the passions, the habituation to the yoke stifles its fire, its conflagrations. From this is born gentleness of morals, equity, virtue; but at the expense of ferocity which makes the good soldier. The art of reasoning can become a very great evil in the one who ought to have only the talent of acting. What would become of the majority of warlike expeditions if the soldier in them reasoned as accurately as the ass in the fable . . .

> And what does it matter to me to whom I belong?
> Strike, and let me graze:
> Our enemy is our master;
> I tell you this in good French.
> La Fontaine, Fable 8.1.VI.

Kings of the earth, whose wisdom ought to employ even vices usefully, do not labor at preserving ferocity for your peoples, but chose the arms of your armies in the least polished, the most barbaric, the least virtuous part of your subjects. You will still have only too many to choose from whatever protection you accord to the sciences and arts. But seek the head which should guide these arms, seek it in the temple of Minerva, goddess of weapons and of wisdom together; among those subjects whose soul—as enlightened as it is strong—no longer knows the great passions except to transform them into great virtues, no longer feels those impetuous movements of nature except to employ them to undertake and to execute the greatest things.

From the concepts that I have just given of courage (and I believe them to be very sound, and taken from nature) it follows that an army made up completely of civilized people, an army composed completely of bourgeois, artisans, grammarians, rhetoricians, musicians, painters, sculptors, academicians even of the highest merit and of the purest virtue would not be a very formidable army. Apparently such was in part the one that the Chinese, the Egyptians, very learned and very civilized, opposed to the incursions of the Barbarians; but this army, completely pitiful though it was, was so only because it was composed of too great a number of honest people, of too great a number of humane and reasonable people, of people who said . . .

> He is a great fool who
> Makes life the smallest of his cares;
> As soon as it is stolen from us,
> We are worth half as much.
> . . . .
> By my faith, when he is dead
> A demi-God is a very small matter.
> From the moment that the proud Parca[58]
> Makes us enter the barque
> Into which the body is not received,
> Both glory and renown
> Are only dream and smoke,
> And do not go all the way to the dead.
>   Voiture, tome 2.[59]

At least we will be correct to believe that these warriors having become cowardly by virtue of learning and politeness, were not less filled with reason, humanity and virtue, until the author of the Discourse has well proven to us that one cannot be an honest man and a poltroon at the same time.

But if there is no vice . . . for its fidelity, which could not be corrupted by bad example.*[60] Everywhere the author confuses the warlike virtue of the soldier, ferocity, with true virtue, integrity, justice. Following his principles, one would believe that soldiers were more virtuous than their officers, country folk better people than their lords, and one would decry it as an injustice to see that our tribunals are occupied only with the punishment of these same more honest people. I do not presume that the discourse of our orator will cause the reform of these universally received, and apparently well-founded names by which the men of society are commonly distinguished into two classes: one without birth, without education, which consequently is designated by some epithets that mark that it has few feelings, little honor and integrity; the other well-born and educated in all the parts of the sciences and arts which enter into fine education, and which for this reason is regarded as the class of *honest people*.

> With a delicate brush pleasant artifice,
> Makes a lovable object out of the most shocking object.
>   Boileau, *Art poetique*

**I dare not speak of those happy nations . . . they don't wear pants!*[61] When one has seen the portrait that our orator makes of the disorders caused by the art of civilizing nations and establishing harmony in them, one knows what one ought to think of the flattering portraits that Montaigne has left us of the Barbarians.

But all these reasonings evaporate as soon as they are examined thoroughly. The words of *pure nature*, of *simple nature*, of *Savages governed* solely by it; the reign of Astraea,[62] the morals of the golden age, are expressions that present to the imagination the most beautiful ideas. It is a great pity that there is nothing but imagination in all of these flowery turns of phrase. It is not in true nature that the entirely brutish human race is better than when it is cultivated. I have already proven it, I am going to confirm this truth by a new proof which would have overburdened the already very ample passage given about this topic. The whole question of the preeminence between the ancients and the moderns, being once and for all well understood, says Mr. de Fontenelle, comes down to knowing whether the trees which formerly were in our countryside are bigger than those of today.[63] I dare to believe the application of this analogy to our question to be even more accurate, and one can guarantee that it is reduced to knowing if the productions of the uncultivated earth are preferable to those that it furnishes when it is well cultivated? What is pure nature, simple nature, I ask you, in trees, in plants in general? What are they in this state? Unworthy wildlings, incapable even of furnishing our food, and it was necessary for the genius of man to invent agriculture, gardening, to render these productions of the earth fit to serve as fodder for men. It was necessary to graft onto these wildlings some of those fortunate species which were doubtless the rarest, and which can be compared to those great geniuses, to those very uncommon souls who have invented the sciences and the arts. It was necessary to put them in certain terrains, at certain exposures, to prune them, to lop off certain superfluities, certain harmful parts; to give a certain preparation in a certain way during certain seasons to the earth which surrounded them. I do not believe that any mortal is found who dares to say that all these parts of agriculture are not useful, necessary to the production and to the perfection of the fruits of the earth. How then could there be found someone so little reasonable as to advance that this art, far from being useful to these fruits, tends on the contrary to render them less abundant and less good? Nevertheless this is exactly the case of those who maintain that the sciences and the arts, the cultivation of the mind and heart, introduce depravation of morals among us.

One can think that there are some men born with so much enlightenment, so many talents, such a beautiful soul, that cultivation becomes useless to them. If you reflect about it, you will agree that the most fortunate natures, even those men who ought to be chosen to graft onto the others, so to speak, those, I say, still need cultivation, or at least one cannot deny that they become still more virtuous, more capable, more useful, if they are cultivated by the sciences and the arts; as the tree of the best species becomes still more fertile and more excellent, if it is placed in the ground most fitting for it, in the best exposed espalier, and if it is, so to speak, handled by the most skillful gardener.

> Fortes creantur fortibus et bonis.
> . . . .
> Doctrina sed vim promovet insitam,
> Rectique cultus pectora roborant.
> Horace, *Ode* IV. l. IV.[64]

Let us stress these reasonings of approbation of a man whose enlightenment and judgment deserve consideration. "I admit, says Cicero, that there have been several men of a superior merit, without science, and by the sole strength of their almost divine nature; I will even add that a good nature without science, has more often succeeded than science without a good nature; but I also maintain that when one joins science, cultivation, to an excellent nature, there ordinarily results from it a man of a completely superior merit. Such have been, he adds, Scipio Africanus, Laelius, the very learned Cato the Elder etc. who would never have ventured to develop their virtues by the cultivation of the sciences, if they had not been very persuaded that it would lead them to that praiseworthy end."[65]

> . . . Alterius sic
> Altera poscit opem res, et conjurat amice.
> Horace, *The Art of Poetry*, V, 409.[66]

It is not through stupidity . . . to disdain their doctrine.[67] One is tempted to believe that the author is joking when he gives these historical anecdotes as strokes of wisdom. The one about the Romans, who drive out the doctors, is good to join to the *Doctor in Spite of Himself*, and to the other banter of Moliére against the faculty. If the gods themselves did not appeal from the upright tribunal of the Athenians; it was thus in its accesses of madness that this people departed from them. The outbursts and insults of a people more tumultuous and more stormy than the sea have never been referred to in order to disparage things regarded as excellent, divine. Would one pass for reasonable, if one wished to prove that Alcibiades and Themistocles, the greatest men of Greece, were cowards and traitors, because the Athenians exiled and condemned them to death? That Aristides, surnamed *the Just, the best man that the Republic had ever had*, says Valerius Maximus, was an infamous man because that same republic banished him? These seditious intrigues, these squalls of the people whose jealousy, inconstancy, and stupidity are their only motive power, don't they prove rather the superior merit and excellence of the object of their rage? What has Aristides done to you, said this wise man himself to an Athenian of the assembly who condemned him? Nothing, the conspirator responded to him, I do not even know him; but I am bored with always hearing him called the just.[68] Here is one of those reasonable people on whom our orator founds his proofs.

Could I forget that . . . artists, the sciences and scientists away from your walls.[69] The goal of Lycurgus was less to make honest men than soldiers in a country which had a great need of them, because it was not extensive, scarcely peopled. For this reason all the laws of Sparta aimed at barbarism, at ferocity rather than at virtue. It is to arrive at this goal that they extinguished in fathers and mothers the seeds of natural tenderness, by accustoming them to make their own children perish, if they had the misfortune of being born deformed, feeble, or weak. How many great men we would have lost if we were as barbaric as the Spartans! It is for the same plan that they took the children away from their parents and caused them to be raised in public schools where they instructed them to be thieves and to expire under the blows of whips without giving the least sign of repenting, of fear, or of pain. Wouldn't one believe one sees the illustrious Cartouche, that Lycurgus of the scoundrels of Paris, giving his subjects some lessons of skill in his art, and of patience in the tortures that await them? *Oh Sparta, oh eternal disgrace* of humanity! Why occupy yourself with transforming men into Tigers? Your policy worthy of the Titans, your founders gives you soldiers! How does it happen then that the Athenians your neighbors who are so humane, so civilized, have beaten you so many times. How does it happen that you had recourse to them in the invasions of the Persians? How does it happen that the oracles force you to ask them for a general? Madmen, you put the whole body of your republic into arms and give it no head. You would not be able to put your leaders in parallel with the two Aristomenes, Alcibiades, Themistocles, Cimon, etc., children of Athens, children of the fine arts, and the principal authors of the most dazzling victories ever won by Greece. You do not know then that the exploits of an army depend principally on its leader, that the general makes the soldier, and that chance alone can sometimes render barbaric generals lucky against nations that are surprised and without discipline.(*4) But this immortal hero who completely effaced all of you, who subjugated all of you, and with you those Persians, those peoples of the Orient who had made you tremble so many times, even those whom you did not know, and even those Scythians so renowned for their ignorance, their rusticity and their bravado; this conqueror who was as magnanimous as he was

*4. Czar Peter I is a recent proof of this truth.

courageous, was he a barbarian like you? was he a disciple of Lycurgus? Certainly not, ferocity is not capable of such a great elevation of soul: it is reserved to the student of Homer and Aristotle,[70] to the patron of Appelles and Phidias; as one sees in our century that it is still appended to the princes who are students of Descartes, of Newton, of Volf;[71] to the princes who are founders and patrons of academies; to the princes who are friends of the learned and learned themselves. All Europe hears me and I do not fear that it disavows these recent, even present, proofs of the intimate and natural union of knowledge, true valor and equity.

The outcome showed this difference . . . Athens has left us?[72] It is becoming of Socrates, the son of a sculptor, great sculptor himself, and even greater philosopher, to say that no one knows the arts less than he does, to eulogize ignorance, to complain that all those talented people are nothing less than they are wise men. Is he not himself a proof of the opposite? Would he preach virtue so well, would he have been the father of philosophy and one of the wisest among men in the judgment of the oracle itself, if he had been an ignoramus? Socrates here plays the part of our preachers who find their century the most corrupt of all those which have preceded it, *o tempora, o mores!*[73] and who out of zeal for the progress of virtue exaggerate both the vices of the time, and the modest opinion they have of themselves.

Can it be believed that if he were reborn . . . Thus is it noble to teach men![74] We agree that the Fine Arts enervate that type of courage that depends on ferocity; but they render us proportionally more virtuous, proportionally more humane.

But the sciences . . . and the fatherland forgotten.[75] Rome is mistaken to neglect military discipline and to despise agriculture, and our orator is mistaken to attribute this misfortune to the sciences and the arts. Ignorance and sloth are the very natural causes of this.

Cato was right to inveigh against the cunning, subtle, Greeks, corrupters of good morals; but the sciences and the arts had no part whatsoever either in this corruption or in the anger of Cato who himself was very learned and as distinguished by his ardor for letters and the sciences as for his austere virtue, according to the testimony of Cicero cited above.

The sacred names of liberty . . . of conquering the world and making virtue reign in it.[76] In the beginnings the talent of Rome was to assemble people without morals, scoundrels, to set traps for neighboring peoples by means of festivals and religious ceremonies that all these honest people always made to serve their purposes, and to perpetuate in this way the breed and the maxims of these brigands. Having become more famous and better known in the world, it had to show itself in this theatre with more seductive colors, under at least the appearances of honor and virtue.

The Roman people passed itself off as the protector of all the peoples who sought its alliance and begged for help; but the traitor soon made itself the master of those who had only wished it for a friend. That is the virtue of Rome and of Cato. He who says conqueror, ordinarily says unjust and barbarian; this maxim is true above all for Rome; and if this famous city produced some great men, showed some rare virtues, it degraded them by employing them by committing injustices and cruelties without number, by which it desolated and invaded the universe.

When Cineas took our senate . . . of commanding Rome and governing the earth.[77] It has just been seen what sort this virtue was. As for the particular case, if there were virtuous men there, it has been seen, on the report of Cicero even, that this virtue was due, at least in part, to the culture of letters and sciences, because he gives the name of very learned to Cato the Elder, and he cites Scipio Africanus, Laelius, Furius, etc., the wise men of Rome, as people distinguished in the sciences.

But let us leap over the interval of space . . . and scorn a hundred times worse than death.[78] This is good for the discourse. There is nothing worse than hemlock except to live. One writes the eulogy of our century by believing it humane enough not to force Socrates to swallow that fatal beverage; but one does not render it justice by not believing it reasonable enough not to scorn Socrates. At least one can be certain that the scorn would not have been general.

Behold how luxury . . . if they had the misfortune to be born learned.[79] They would have been born as they have made themselves by dint of labor; they would have been born at the same time humane, compassionate, polite, and virtuous.

How humiliating for humanity are these reflections! How mortified our pride must be![80] I do not see what ought to humiliate us or mortify our pride, by thinking, according to the principles of the Author that we are born in a happy and innocent ignorance, by which alone we are able to be virtuous; that it is up to us only to remain in that fortunate state, and that nature itself has taken measures to preserve us in it. It seems to me on the contrary that such a fine prerogative as that of being naturally virtuous, that such a great attention on the part of nature to preserve us in virtue ought to flatter our pride extremely; but if we think that we are born brutes, that we are born barbaric, evil, unjust, guilty, and that we need a study and labor of several years, even of our whole life, to make ourselves good, just, humane: Oh! it is thus that we ought to be humiliated to see that by ourselves we are so perverse, and not to be able to succeed at being men, except by an always irksome and often doubtful labor.

What! could probity . . . from these prejudices?[81] Conclusions very disadvantageous to the author himself and to all our academies; but fortunately the premises of the reasoning are very false.

But to reconcile these apparent contradictions . . . with historical inductions.[82] Thus, to reconcile apparent contradictions between science and virtue, the author is going to prove that the contradiction is real, or that these two qualities are incompatible. This is a singular reconciliation.

II

It was an ancient . . . the inventor of the sciences*[83] Science is *hostile to tranquillity*, without a doubt; it is thereby that it is the *friend of man* who is corrupted by tranquillity; it is thereby that it is the source of virtue, because *idleness* is the mother of all the vices.

The allegory in the fable of Prometheus is easily seen; . . . This is the subject of the frontispiece.[84] In the fable of which the author speaks, Jupiter, jealous of the enlightenment and the talents of Prometheus, fastened him on the Caucasus. Far from designating the horror of the Greeks for knowledge, this allegorical deed is on the contrary a proof of the infinite esteem in which they held the sciences and inventive genius because they made Prometheus equal in some measure to Jupiter, by rendering the latter jealous of this divine man, apparently author of the first arts, of the rough outline of the sciences, the effect of genius, of that fire that it seems that man has stolen from the Gods. Even the Romans, those children of Mars, were not able to refrain from rendering to the fine arts the homages owed to them; and the prince of their poets accedes to the men who have distinguished themselves in them the first honors in the Elysium Fields.

> Quique pii vates et Phaebo digna locuti,
> Inventas aut qui vitam excoluere per artes,
> Omnibus his nivea cinguntur tempora vitta.
> Virgil. *Aeneid* L. VI. v. 662.[85]

With regard to the frontispiece.[86] I do not see the subtlety of this allegory. It is very simple that fire burns the beard. Does the author want to say that man is no more to be trusted than fire? But he presents him naked and leaving the hands of Prometheus, of nature; and this is, according to him, the only condition in which he can be trusted. Does he wish to say that all the subtlety of his thesis, of his discourse is not known, that it must be respected like fire? Would it not be possible through a much more natural allegory to make the celestial man who with a lighted torch comes near the head of the statue-man say: satyr, you admire it, you are infatuated by it, because you do not know it; learn imbecile, that the object of your transports is only a vain idol that this torch is going to reduce into ashes.

What must the Egyptians themselves, in whose country the sciences were born, have thought of them? . . . the idea we like to have of it.[87] I would have advised the orator to substitute another term for that of *leafs through*.[88]

Astronomy was born from superstition.[89] Astronomy is the daughter of idleness and of the desire to know the thing in the universe most worthy of our curiosity. This simple curiosity, already very noble by itself and capable of preserving man from all the vices attached to idleness, has already produced a thousand advantages in society that our calenders, our geographic maps and the art of navigating attest to whoever does not wish to close his eyes. On the usefulness of all the sciences see the famous preface that Mr. de Fontenelle has put at the head of the history of the Academy.

Eloquence . . . falsehood.[90] Was it to support all these vices that Demosthenes and Cicero employed their eloquence? Is it for this detestable use that our orators, our preachers employ it? There are some who abuse it, I believe the author of the discourse on his word; but how many more are found who make it serve to enlighten the mind and to direct the movements of the heart to virtue? At least, the Roman orator thought this way about it. He knew a little about it. Let us listen to him for a moment on this subject. He thoroughly examined the question that is stirred up in this discourse, in relation to eloquence. He also recognized that one can make a very bad use of it; but, everything well taken into consideration, he concluded that, from whatever side one considers the principle of eloquence, one will find that it owes its origin to the most honest motives, to the wisest reasonings. "As for its effects; what is more noble, he says, more generous, greater than to aid the innocent, than to lift up the oppressed, than to be the salvation, the liberator of honest people, to rescue them from exile? What other power than eloquence has been able to assemble men formerly dispersed in the forests, and to recall them from their kind of ferocious and savage life to these humane and civilized morals that they have today? For there was a time when the men were as dispersed and vagabonds in the fields, and lived there like wild beasts. Then it was not *reason* that ruled their conduct, but almost always force, violence. There was no question of religion, nor of duties with regard to other men: the usefulness of justice, of equity was not known at all there. Thus *by error and ignorance the blind and reckless passions were dominant by themselves, and in order to satiate themselves abused the strength of the body, dangerous minister of their violence.* Finally wise, great men rose up whose eloquence won over these savage men, and from being ferocious and cruel though they were, rendered them gentle and truly humane." This is a very different origin and end of eloquence than the ones given to it by our French orator.

Geometry from avarice.[91] To fix the limits of one's field, to distinguish it from that of one's neighbor; to make, in a word, an exact distribution of the earth for those to whom it belongs; these are the functions and the origin of ordinary and practical geometry, and there is nothing there but what is very just and what our tribunals direct every day to remedy avarice and usurpation. Thus it is from equity and rectitude that geometry is born.

Physics from vain curiosity.[92] Physics is born from curiosity, so be it; but that this curiosity is vain, is what I do not believe that the author thinks. Society is indebted to this science for the invention and perfection of almost all the arts which provide for its needs and its conveniences; and what ought not to be forgotten, by displaying the marvels of nature to the eyes of men, it raises their soul up to its author.

All, even moral philosophy, from human pride.[93] Was it then out of pride that the wise men of Greece; the Catos, and those I should have named before them all, the divine missionaries of Christian morality, preached humility, virtue?

Thus the sciences and arts . . . owed it to our virtues.[94] As there is no doubt at all about the origin of the sciences and arts the majority of which are acts either of virtue or tending toward virtue, their advantages are also evident.

The defect of their origin . . . without the luxury that nourishes them?[95] Luxury is an abuse of the arts, as a discourse made to persuade us of what is false is an abuse of eloquence, as drunkenness is an abuse of wine. These defects are not in the thing, but in those who use it badly.

Without the injustices of men, what purpose would Jurisprudence serve?[96] That is to say, if men were born just, laws would have been useless; if they were born virtuous, rules of morality would not have been needed. The author agrees then that all these sciences had been imagined to correct man born perverse, to render him better.

What would History become . . . nor conspirators?[97] It would be much more beautiful and much more honorable to humanity, it would be filled with the wisdom of kings, and the virtues of subjects; with great and beautiful actions of both, and containing only deeds worthy of being admired and imitated by readers, never crimes, never horrors, it could never do anything but please and lead to virtue, the genuine goal of history.

In a word, who would want . . . the unfortunate and his friends.[98] There is no science of sterile speculation; all of them have their utility, either in relation to those who cultivate them, or with regard to society.

Are we destined then . . . by the study of Philosophy.[99] It is not necessary to remain on the edge of the well where the truth has hidden, it is necessary to descend it and pull it out, as so many great men have done; what they have done another can do. This reflection ought to encourage whoever seriously desires it.

What dangers there are! . . . investigating the Sciences.[100] *Investigating.* In an Orator as pure in style and polished as ours, I cannot let pass a frenchified Latin term from Clenard *Investigatio thematis.*[101]

How many errors, . . . who among us will know how to make good use of the truth.[102] If so many difficulties and errors surround those who seek the truth with the aids given to them by the sciences and the arts, what will become of those who do not seek it at all? Will the author persuade us that it is going to seek whoever flees it, and that it flees whoever seeks it? That is all that could be believed about blind fortune. With regard to good use of the truth, it is not, it seems to me much more perplexing than the good use of virtue; but a thing that seems to me more perplexing is the means of making a good use of the error and the vice into which we are plunged without the enlightenment of the sciences and the instructions of morality.

If our Sciences are vain . . . a pernicious man.[103] What is more laborious than a learned man. The first utility of the sciences is thus to avoid idleness, boredom and the vices that are inseparable from them. If they had only that use, they would become necessary, because they are the source of the virtues and happiness of the one who practices them. "If the sciences were not as useful as they are, says Cicero, and if one applied oneself to them only for one's pleasure; you will think, I believe, that there is no relaxation more noble and more worthy of man; for the other pleasures are not for all times, for all ages, for all places; that of study makes food for youth, joy for the old, the ornament of those who are in prosperity, the resource and consolation of those who are in adversity; it gives us delight at home, does not encumber us at all when we are outside, passes the night with us and does not leave us when traveling to the country."

Here is the first and nevertheless the least usefulness of the sciences; no idleness, nor boredom, a sweet and tranquil but perpetual pleasure. I say that this is their least usefulness, for this one concerns only the one who applies himself to them, and we have shown that the sciences are the soul of all the arts that are useful to society, and that in this way the learned man who is in appearance the most contemplative is occupied with the public good.

Answer me then . . . less flourishing or more perverse?[104] Yes without a doubt. Astronomy cultivated by geometers renders geography and navigation more certain; from the insects are drawn secrets for the arts, for our needs. The anatomy of animals leads us to a more perfect knowledge of the human body, and consequently to more certain principles for heal-ing it or for preserving it in health. The science of physics and of morality causes us to be better governed and less perverse; and the harmony of a government in which all these sciences, all these arts shine is what renders it flourishing and formidable.

Reconsider, then, the importance . . . the substance of the State. [105] It is natural that we think still less badly of them than of those who occupy their leisure by disparaging the enlightenment and the talents to which France possibly has more obligation than to its arms.

Did I say idle? . . . O passion to gain distinction, of what are you not capable? [106] Here again the author sticks to the abuse that perverse sub-jects make of an excellent thing. But if there are some of these unfortun-ates, what a crowd of divine works does one not have to oppose to them, by which the idols of the pagans have been reversed, the true God and the purity of Christian morality proven, the sophisms of the depraved geniuses of which the orator speaks annihilated? Can the extravagances of some scatterbrains who abuse the sciences be cited seriously against their utility? And will it be necessary to renounce building houses be-cause there are people mad enough to throw themselves out of windows.

The misuse of time is a great evil . . . they never develop without it. [107] Luxury and science do not at all develop together. It is always the igno-rant part of a State which affects luxury; the latter is the child of riches and its corrective is knowledge, philosophy which shows the nothingness of these bagatelles.

I know that our Philosophy . . . those of our time talk only of business and money. [108] Luxury is an abuse of riches corrected by the sciences and rea-son; but this abuse must not be confounded, as the author does, with commerce, the part of the arts the most fit for making a State powerful and flourishing, and which does not necessarily carry luxury along with it as the author believes. We have the proof of this in our illustrious neighbors. England and Holland have a much more extended and richer commerce than ours; do they carry luxury as far as we do? This is because commerce, far from favoring luxury, as our orator believes, on the con-trary represses it. Whoever is devoted to the art of enriching himself and increasing his fortune keeps himself very well from losing it by mad ex-penses. Moreover, this passion for enriching oneself through commerce is not incompatible with virtue. What integrity, what admirable fidelity reigns among the merchants who, without ever seeing each other, and who being situated sometimes at the extremities of the universe, keep such an inviolable faith in their engagements! Compare this conduct with the ruses, the deceits, the villainies of the savages into whose hands they sometimes fall in their voyages.

One will tell you that in a given country a man . . . made Asia tremble.[109] We agree with the author that riches whose use is perverted by luxury and softness corrupt courage. But all these faults have no relation to the sciences and the arts; they are not their consequences, as we have shown above. Alexander who subjugated the whole Orient with thirty thousand men was the Prince who was most learned and best educated in the fine arts in his whole century; and it is with this superior knowledge that he vanquished these so vaunted Scythians who had so many times resisted the incursions of the Persians even though their armies were as numerous as they were ferocious, even though they where commanded by this Cyrus the hero of this monarchy.

The Roman Empire . . . except morals and citizens.[110] Everywhere the author confounds barbarism, ferocity with valor and virtue; it was apparently such very honest people as these Goths, these Vandals, these Normans, etc., who desolated all of Europe which did not say a word in their favor? Here we would be made to understand it is by their good morals and by their virtues that these peoples vanquished civilized peoples; but all the histories attest that they were brigands, scoundrels, who made a game, a glory of crime, for whom nothing was sacred, and who profited from the divisions, the revolts raised in the center of those civilized kingdoms, which would have crushed those wretches if they had been the least united and forewarned.

Precisely what, then, is at issue . . . with the taste for honesty.[111] Is it not possible to be an honest man under braided clothes? and is it necessary to wear sackcloth to obtain this qualification? Have no fear then in our forests, except when you meet a well-gilded, well-mounted man provided with brilliant arms and followed by a domestic in as good attire. Then tremble for your life; you are in the power of a man of the most corrupt sort, abandoned to luxury, to all sorts of vices. But if you find yourself alone with a peasant clothed in homespun, weighed down with a bad gun and leaving the undergrowth where he seemed to hide his misery: then fear nothing; this evident poverty is a sure sign that you are meeting virtue itself.

No, it is not possible . . . the courage would be lacking.[112] Is it the learned that occupy themselves with *futile concerns*? Are these the people occupied with the arts? Certainly not, it is the rich ignoramuses. Thus this argument proves against its author.

Every artist wants to be applauded. . . . leads in turn to the corruption of taste.[113] I know an infinite number of people who are passionately fond of baroque drawings, of difficult Italian music which is of the same type; of works known by the name of curiosities, and who are nonetheless the most honest people in the world. Don't their morals feel the effects of their bad taste at all? It even seems to me that I do not see any connection between taste and morals because their objects are completely different.

Since there is only one good manner of thinking and writing, painting, singing, etc., and the preceding century so to speak exhausted it, taste is corrupted because one does not wish to either copy or imitate it; and out of the rage to gain distinction, one swerves from beautiful nature,[114] one falls into the ridiculous and the baroque.

> The wit one wishes to have spoils the wit one has.
> One loses the happy language of the heart, of nature.
> For the absurd talent of a sad banter.
>
> Gresset[115]

In a more serious genre, the transcendent geniuses of the last century having begotten and executed the sublime, bold project of demolishing the mad imaginings of the Peripatetics[116] their faculties, their occult virtues of all species, it has taken a half century to establish the knowledge of physical effects upon the known and evident properties of matter, upon their mechanical causes. How can one gain distinction for novelty after the establishment of such solid, such universal principles? One must say that they are too simple and absolutely insufficient; that these great men were good people, a little touched in the head, and as mechanical as their principles are; and that our spiritual century sees, or at least suspects new properties in matter that must always be set as the basis of physics, while waiting for them to be conceived: properties that do not depend on extension, impenetrability, shape, movement or any other old modification of matter; properties, not occult but hidden, which raise this matter to something a little above matter, that one does not dare to say aloud, and which, in truth, lowers the physicist much beneath this quality. Finally, our ancestors were gothic, our fathers friends of nature, we are singular and baroque, we have only this path to take not to resemble either of the two.

But morality has no part whatsoever in this disorder. To copy, to imitate the virtues of great men of all centuries is made a pleasure and an honor. The more centuries pass by the more examples of them we have; and as long as the art of inculcating them, that is to say as long as the sciences and the fine arts are in vigor, the centuries farthest along will always be the most virtuous.

I am very far from thinking . . . and defending so great a cause.[117] The author strangely contradicts himself. He wants women to be given education, he wants them to be removed from ignorance. Doubtless he is right; but it is against his principles, according to which to teach someone and to render them more wicked are synonymous expressions.

And if, by chance . . . or it must stay idle.[118] The admirable works of Le Moine, Bouchardon, the Adams, Slodtz,[119] to perpetuate the memory of the greatest men, to decorate public squares, palaces and the gardens that accompany them, are monuments that set our minds at rest against the vain declamations of our orator.

One cannot reflect . . . in order to live in the temples themselves.[120] This golden age and this mixing of gods and men is a pretty fairy tale; but hardly anyone is amused by it but children and rhetoricians who are more florid than solid.

Or at least the temples of the gods . . . Corinthian capitals at the entry of great men's palaces.[121] The Ancients hardly thought that the cultivation of the sciences and the arts depraved morals, that the talent of building cities, raising temples and palaces, added the finishing touch to vices; when they represented to us Amphion building the walls of Thebes by the concord of his lyre alone; when they speak to us with so much veneration of the peoples who raised temples to the immortals, and palaces to the majesty of legitimate sovereigns.

While living conveniences . . . in the shade of the study.[122] We agree with the author that the sciences and the arts enervate ferocious courage, and this is so much gained for humanity and virtue. But that true valor is extinguished by the enlightenment of the sciences and the cultivation of the arts is what has been amply refuted.

When the Goths . . . than to strengthen and animate it.[123] That is to say to render them less ferocious, well done, but at the same time more humane and more virtuous.

The Romans admitted . . . a few centuries ago.[124] Here the author puts back on the table precisely the same proofs related in the first part. Thus we direct the reader back to the refutation that we placed there. We will add only that in the recent war the Genoans have shown very well that valor was not so extinguished in Italy as the orator imagines, and that these peoples only need occasions and great captains to show to all of Europe that they are still capable of the greatest things.

The ancient Greek Republics . . . the vigor of the soul[125] That is to say, ferocity.

What view . . . the strength to travel on horseback?[126] And what relation does this vigor of body have to virtue? Can one not be weak, delicate, ill fit for fatigue, for war, and at the very same time be virtuous?

Let no one raise as an objection . . . the best of our armies in a few days.[127] Everything that our author says here is very true, aside from a little exaggeration which is a license in eloquence as it is in poetry. It is certain that the exercise of the body is too neglected in France, and that comforts are too much loved there. Horse races are no longer seen there, prizes are no longer given to the most skillful in different exercises; all the tennis courts are destroyed; and there it is the epoch in which the vapors have reached the men and put them on a level with women, because they have begun to put themselves there by the nature of their occupations. Oh let our orator strike our manner of living on this point and I will support him with my vote; but to let him claim to conclude from it that these men, for being as weak, as prone to vapors as women are more depraved, more vicious because of it is what I will not grant him; and if they were completely women, as long is it were of the good sort, which is most common, without a doubt I would have only a better opinion of their virtue. Who does not know that this sex is the devout and virtuous one par excellence?

Intrepid warriors . . . the latter conquered your ancestors.[128] Unfortunately for our orator this little exaggeration comes a little too close to our last war in Italy in which the whole world knows that our troops under the Prince de Conti crossed the Alps, after having forced a powerful enemy commanded by one of the bravest Kings of the world onto the summit of those mountains; and it is more than likely that the Alps, at the time of Hannibal, were not any more steep than they are today.

Fighting does not always . . . by the enemy's sword.[129] Oh! The author is right; we are not robust enough. Let the Olympic games of all sorts be renewed, let the horse races, foot races, fights of a bit more humane contest than the ancient one, tennis matches, archery, cross-bow, harquebus, gun contests be renewed; let them be protected, let them be organized, let there be privileges, awards attached to them; let laws for sobriety be attached to this; we will have citizens, soldiers, as robust as they are courageous; and if the cultivation of the sciences and the arts—all things very compatible—are continued with these reforms, we will have officers capable of commanding good soldiers, the two essential parts of a good army.

If cultivating the sciences . . . at least his body would be more fit.[130] Very good. I applaud the orator's censure against the majority of ill-directed educations. But let us beware of regarding a particular abuse as a general depravation which is appended to the sciences. *Cultivation of the sciences is harmful to moral qualities?* What an absurdity! I have demonstrated in several passages placed above that the perfection of morals was the principal effect of this cultivation of the sciences; woe to the directors of the education of the young who lose sight of this object; I believe that this disorder is very rare: but even if it were more common, it is not the fault of the sciences, but that of the persons destined to teach them. Even languages, the least useful part of education, ought never to draw us away from this goal. The foreign words that we learn doubtless express things; these things ought to be solid sciences and above all, that of morality. This is what great care is taken to do in all colleges, in all boarding schools, and what has been done in all civilized centuries . . .

> Adjecere bonae paulo plus artis Athenae,
> Scilicet ut possem curvo cognoscere rectum,
> Atque inter sylvas Academi quaerere verum.
> Horat. Epist. 2, L.II. v. 43[131]

I know children must be kept busy . . . and not what they ought to forget.[132] The author is right, and this is what is done by both teachers, and above all fathers and mothers who have the education of the children at heart as they ought to. But if our century is not yet as perfect as it could be: if there is still among us a cause of the corruption of morals, feebleness of the body, softness, it is certainly the passion that reigns here for sedentary games, a passion that we hold principally from the frequentation of frivolous women, who fortunately make up the smallest number, and which is born from our obligingness for this enchanting sex; a passion, which is the daughter of idleness and avarice, and rather a friend of all the other passions; which fills the head with thirty baroque words empty of meaning, and ordinarily at the expense of science, history, morality, and nature which it is made an honor not to know. Such poorly nourished minds have nothing to say to each other except *baste, pontiff, manilla, comet*, etc.[133] Conversations in social circles, so much in use, so esteemed among our fathers and so fit to make talents, good morals appear, and to form them among young people, in these pretty assemblies are either mute, or used to make reflections on all the gew-gaws that decorate these ladies, on all the rare baubles that these gentlemen possess, to recount pretty adventures either invented or at least very much embroidered at the expense of one's neighbor.

> There you always find diverting people,
> Women who have never been able to close their mouths,
> And who shoot a cartridge at their neighbor for you;
> Professional idlers, who always
> Carry home the scandalous taunt of all Paris.
> *The Gambler* of Regnard[134]

The spectacles that are best regulated, most improved, and most fit to inspire morals and taste are sacrificed to this perfidious pleasure; even one's duties and fortune are sometimes sacrificed there. And what is the origin of this remnant of poison that laws that are not severe enough still allow in society? Exercise of the body too neglected, the sciences and the arts still too little cultivated.

* Such was the education of the Spartans . . . to make him good, none to make him learned.[135] Thus the author does not put among the number of sciences that of religion and of morality; for this is what was taught to the children of the Kings of Persia, and what is not neglected to be taught in France even to the last country folk.

Astyages, in Xenophon, asks Cyrus . . . he could persuade me that his school matches that one.[136] The good Montaigne was talking drivel, if he gave us this story as a great marvel. In our schools every day the rod is given to young people who commit smaller injustices than that among them-selves, and less commotion is made about it; no one takes it into his head to make a memorable story of it worthy of finding a place in a book as exalted as that of Xenophon.

Our gardens are adorned . . . even before they know how to read.[137] All this is still exaggerated. The great men of Greece and Rome, their virtu-ous actions, such as the piety of Aeneas, the chastity of Lucretia make up a part of the ornaments of our gardens and our galleries, as well as the Metamorphoses of Ovid; even in the latter are how many allegories of the best morality? And ordinarily it is these subjects that are chosen to be exposed in public.

Moreover these decorations of gardens and galleries are not made for children. Their galleries ordinarily are figures from the Bible, and there is an abundant collection of examples of virtues there.

What brings about all these abuses, . . . of a book if it is useful, but if it is well written.[138] This text is a pure harangue. A man of talent who is not an honest man is not made much of, nor is a well written book if its object is frivolous. For example this discourse would not be esteemed at all, however seductive it might be, if one did not see that the genuine aim of the author is, not to annihilate the cultivation of the sciences and the arts, but to induce those who apply themselves to them not to abuse them, and to be even more virtuous than learned.

Rewards . . . none for fine actions.[139] The proposition is not exactly true. In France there are many rewards, many crosses of knights, pen-sions, titles of nobility, etc., for noble actions. In spite of this, like the author, I find that there are not yet enough of them, and that in fact there ought to be prizes for practical morality as there are prizes for physics, eloquence, etc. Why not make all these sciences proceed to-gether, as they do naturally, and as they are practiced in small schools, in the education given in the parents' home. It will be said to the honor of this century, that virtue is more common than talents; that the whole world has integrity, and does only what it ought to. What I know is that the whole world prides itself on this.

But let someone tell me . . . the revival of the sciences and arts has only too well confirmed.[140] Again the author lacks exactness here. We agree that pleasing talents are caressed a little too much in France; for example that a pretty voice at the opera will often be more celebrated than a physicist of the academy. I admit that there is too much regard for another sort of pleasing men who are even much less useful, not to say completely useless, even harmful to society. I want to speak about this part of the fashionable world, idle, lacking in application, ignorant, whose merit consists in the science of good grace, *airs, manners and fashions*; which would believe itself to be dishonored to examine some useful, serious science deeply; which makes wit consist *of flitting over matters of which it takes only the flower*; which puts all its study into playing the role *of a likable, lively, frivolous, playful, amusing man, the delight of society, a fine speaker, a pleasing mocker*, etc.,(*5)[141] and never that of a man occupied with the public good, of a good citizen, of an essential friend. If one looked at the Frenchman only on this bad side, as our neighbors have had the goodness to do sometimes, one could say with Mr. Gresset . . .

> That our arts, our pleasures, our wits, make it a pity;
> That nothing remains to us but superficial knowledge,
> Barbs, jargon, sad jokes,
> And by dint of with and petty talents,
> In a while we could very well have no more good sense.
>   *The Wicked Man*, Comedy of Mr. Gresset.[142]

But it must be admitted that these futile men, who are such only because they neglect the cultivation of the sciences, are much more rare in France than our rival nations believe; and that in general they are little esteemed . . .

> Without friend, without rest, suspect and dangerous,
> The frivolous and vague man is already unhappy.

says the same Mr. Gresset. Finally all Europe renders this justice to France, that every day one sees useful, necessary talents rewarded there with dazzling rewards. The preceding remark already proves it; but what is more fitting to convince disbelievers of this than those benefits of the king strewn upon the most industrious members of the Academy of Sciences of Paris, those public schools, those demonstrations of anatomy and surgery founded in the principal cities of France? those titles of nobility given to persons distinguished in the art of healing? Is there some country in the universe whose sovereign gives more attention to rewarding and encouraging useful and virtuous men?

*5. The Frenchman in London

We have physicists . . . we no longer have citizens.[143] There is a little ill humor in this. Can there be better citizens than men who pass their life sometimes even impairing their health in research useful to society, such as physicists, geometers, astronomers? Poets and painters recall to men the memory of virtue and its heros and expose the precepts of morality, those of the arts and the useful sciences, in a manner more fit to make them appreciated . . .

> Soon resuscitating the heros of past ages,
> Homer animated courage for great exploits.
> In his turn, Hesiod by useful lessons,
> Hastened the harvest of too lazy fields.
> In a thousand famous writings, wisdom traced
> Was announced to mortals by the aid of verses;
> And everywhere these victorious precepts of wit,
> Introduced by the ear enter into hearts.
>
> Boileau

The musician diverts us from our labors, so that we can return to them with more ardor; and often he celebrates either the greatness of the Supreme Being or the noble actions of great men; at least this is his genuine object. Thus all these arts cooperate for the public good and to make us more virtuous and better.

Or if a few of them are left, . . . and who give milk to our children are reduced, and such are the sentiments we have for them.[144] Doubtless there are a great number of honest people in the country; but it is nevertheless true to say that it is there that are found in the greatest number false witnesses, tricky pettifoggers, cheats, robbers, murderers. Our prisons contain unanswerable proofs of this.

I admit, however . . . and the sacred trust of morals.[145] The policy of these Sovereigns of choosing learned men to form a society destined to remedy the disorders of morals caused by the sciences would be very bad if the thesis of our author were good. Ignoramuses, peasants, country folk would be necessary to make up these academies.

Trusts which these societies protect by the attention . . . they admit.[146] The academies have this in common with all the bodies of a civilized State, and they certainly have little need of these precautions; so much do the sciences and good morals have the custom of going together.

> Friend of good, order, and humanity,
> True wit walks with goodness.
> Mr. Gresset, *ibid.*

These wise institutions—but also salutary teachings.[147] Men of letters and the academies very much owe thanks to the author for the good opinion that he has of the former and the advice that he gives to the latter. But it seems to me that if he reasoned consistently with his principles, the genuine curb on men of letters, on people applied to the arts that deprave morals, ought not to be the hope of entering an academy which will augment even more their ardor for the sources of their depravation; but it ought to be the opposite, ignorance and the abandonment of letters and academies. By indicating to these societies the objects of morality which they ought to make the subject of their prize, the author tacitly agrees that this is one of the principal objects of letters; that thus up to now he has been flying out against only the abuses that are foreign to the genuine destination and ordinary practice of belles lettres.

Do not, therefore, raise an objection . . . for nonexistent evils.[148] This is a little enigmatic. According to me the evils that exist are ignorance and the unregulated passions with which men are born. The remedies employed are teachings, schools, academies.

Why must . . . direct minds toward their cultivation.[149] What becomes, then, of the compliment made to our academies on the preceding page? I suspect that our orator is sorry for having given it: it was not among his principles.

It seems, to judge by the precautions—that a lack of philosophers is feared.[150] It is a little rare to see country folk enter our academies. It is more common to see them leave the plow to come to be lackeys in cities, and to add to the number of useless ignorant people and slaves of luxury there.

I do not want to attempt . . . it would not be tolerated.[151] It would be tolerated wonderfully, but it would not be favorable to the author. Agriculture is not more necessary for drawing excellent products from the earth than philosophy is for making man perform good actions and for making him virtuous.

I shall only ask . . . among ourselves any of your followers.[152] Our author here calls *great philosophers* what the whole world calls monsters. If his thesis needs such a resource, I cannot help pitying the one who upholds it.

Such are the marvelous men . . . immortality was reserved after their death.[153] Such are the men who have been execrated by their fellow citizens, and who have escaped the vigilance of the law courts only by their flight and retirement in climates where unbridled license reigns.

Such are the wise maxims . . . to age to our descendants.[154] I have too good an opinion of our Orator to believe that he thinks what he says here.

Has Paganism . . . the extravagances of the human mind had not yet been invented.[155] Its wisdom was also not made eternal; and since the good things perpetuated by printing infinitely surpass the bad ones, it is beyond all doubt that this invention is one of the finest and most useful that the human mind has ever engendered.

But thanks to typography . . . Hobbes and Spinoza will remain forever.[156] And their refutations also, which are as solid and as edifying as the monstrous errors of these writers are mad, and worthy of the name *reveries*.

*Considering the awful disorders . . . it would be perhaps the finest deed in the life of that illustrious Pontiff.[157] The decision made by the Turks is worthy of the sectaries of Mohammed and of his Koran. Such a ridiculous religion can, doubtless, maintain itself only by ignorance. Learning is the triumph of the true religion. Origen showed this to the pagans very well; and Arnauld, Bossuet to the heretics.[158] The Gospel is the first among all books, doubtless,; but it is not the only necessary one, and Gregory the Great would have lost his name if he had been capable of such a stupidity.

Go, famous writings . . . corruption of morals in our century.[159] It has been seen above that the former centuries were much more corrupt. It is true that they say nothing about their corruption to posterity: but the almost general practice of the vices passed from race to race as if by tradition. Can one compare this overflowing and universal torrent of unregulated passions of barbaric centuries with some libertine poets whom our century still allows to slip away?

And together carry . . . are precious in thy sight.[160] Let omnipotent God remove enlightenment and talents from those who abuse them, let him annihilate the *arts fatal* to virtue; let him give poverty to those who make a bad use of riches: but let him strew abundantly enlightenment, talents and riches upon those who know how to employ them usefully. This is the prayer of a good citizen and a reasonable man.

But if the development of the sciences . . . of strength for those who might be tempted to learn?[161] Since the major premise of this argument is false, these authors are worthy of all the gratitude of the public, and even of the author of the discourse who has profited more than others from their labors.

What shall we think . . . populace unworthy of approaching it.[162] Does the word *Sanctuary* suit a place where, according to the author, one goes to corrupt one's morals and taste. I would have expected a completely different expression, and in this case what does the author understand by that *populace unworthy of approaching it*? The most unworthy of approaching a place of corruption are those who are the most capable of carrying this corruption very far; those who are the most capable of distinguishing themselves in this pretended sanctuary; for example, those who have more aptitude for the sciences, more sagacity, more genius; for all these people will become from this all the more bad, all the more dangerous to the rest of society, according to the principles of the author; unless here the truth slips out from him in spite of himself, and he renders to the sciences only the homage that he owes them in so many respects. This last conjecture is very likely.

Whereas it would be preferable . . . Those whom nature destined to be her disciples needed no teachers.[163] Oh! Here my conjecture becomes more than likely. The author formally acknowledges the dignity and excellence of the sciences; he wishes to admit to them only those who are really fit for them, and at the bottom he is right. This abuse in the vocations is real according to good principles and ordinary principles. But 1. the Citizen of Geneva does not reason consistently with his thesis; for since the sciences are pernicious to morals, the more those who cultivate them are spiritual, subtle, the more they will be evil and to be feared; and in this case, for the good of society, only stupid people ought to be destined for the sciences. 2. This author has forgotten here that he wraps up the arts as well as the sciences in his anathema, and that this cloth maker is a minister of luxury. Let him go plow the earth. What good is cloth? *The good man is an athlete who likes to compete in the nude.* We will resemble virtue better in this simplicity; and why would the rest of the body not bear the injuries of the seasons as well as the face and hands? This would be the means of having *warriors capable of bearing the excess of work* and of resisting the *rigor of the seasons and bad weather.*

Verulam, Descartes, Newton . . . the immense space they covered.[164] First, it is not at all true that Verulam, Descartes, Newton did not have any teachers. These great men had them at first like everyone else and began by learning all that was known during their times. In the second place, from the fact that transcendent geniuses, like these and so many others that Antiquity has not named, have been capable of inventing the sciences and arts, the author wants all men to learn by themselves, and without teachers, in order to discourage those who will not be transcendent like these first ones: but what is possible for geniuses of this caliber, is not so for everyone; and if the sciences are good, these great men have deserved very much from society for having communicated their enlightenment to it, and those who light the way for other men participate in this action. If, on the contrary, the sciences are pernicious, these men are not worthy of the admiration of the author. They are monsters who must be stifled as early as the first *efforts* that they made to *traverse the immense space they covered.* Now, this last choice would have added the finishing touch to extravagance and barbarism: and the author is right to regard these divine men as the worthy *preceptors of the human race.* One is charmed to see that the truth breaks through here, unknown to the orator; it is regrettable only that it is not at all in accord with the rest of the discourse.

If a few men must be allowed . . . to the glory of the human mind.[165] The sciences and the arts are thus monuments raised to the glory of the human mind. Then the author no longer thinks that they are the source of the depravation of our morals; for surely in that case they would deserve to be regarded as the monuments of its shame, and they only tear from the author a completely opposite admission because they are the sources of enlightenment and rectitude which make the honest man and the true citizen.

But if we wish . . . encouragement they need.[166] This, it seems to me, is much epigrammatic praise in favor of geniuses destined to spoil our innocence, our integrity.

The soul gradually adapts itself . . . Chancellor of England.[167] Eloquence, according to the author, draws its origin from ambition, hate, flattery, and falsehood; physics from a vain curiosity, moral philosophy even from human pride, all the sciences and arts from our vices. These are fine sources for consuls and chancellors, at present the objects of the admiration of the author. Either Rome and England were then in very bad hands, or the principles of the orator are very strange.

If the one had held only a chair in some university and the other obtained only a modest pension from an Academy, can it be believed . . . the art of leading people is more difficult than that of enlightening them: [168] This whole page is of the greatest beauty, as it is of the most exact truth, and it is unfortunately in perpetual contradiction with the rest of the work.

As if it were easier . . . the People will continue to be vile, corrupt and unhappy.[169] Thus here the author has returned to the truths that we established in our first remarks. Enlightenment and wisdom thus go together; the learned possess both, since it is only a question of giving them power for them to undertake and do great things. Thus science does not degrade morals and taste. Thus the position the orator has taken is not just nor his discourse solid.

As for us common men, . . . we do not need to know more than this.[170] The cares that the education of children cost prove only too much the pains and the contrivance, and I add, the stratagems that must be put into use to inculcate the principles of morality in men and to form their morals. Not that the theory of that morality, of that education is so thorny; but its practice is among the most difficult, and still one often fails with certain characters with all the art that this enlightened century has imagined for succeeding in this.

Are not your principles engraved . . . in the silence of the passions.[171] The assumption of the silence of the passions is charming; but who will impose silence on these passions for them? if not very lively enlightenment about their perversity, about their fatal consequences, about the means of subduing or even avoiding them; by raising the soul to objects more worthy of it, finally by becoming philosophers and learned people.

That is genuine philosophy . . . that the one knew how to speak well, the other to act well.[172] Why would it be forbidden to deserve these two crowns at the same time? To act well and think well are inseparable, and it is not difficult for someone who thinks well to speak well; but since one does not act without thinking, without reflecting, the art of thinking well ought to precede that of acting well. Whoever aspires, then, to acting well, ought, to be more certain of success, to have *enlightenment and wisdom* on his side, which only the cultivation of the sciences, of philosophy, can give him. "If you wish, says Cicero, to form rules of a solid virtue for yourself, it is from the study of philosophy that you ought to expect them, or there is no art at all able to procure them for you. Now, it would be a capital error, and a lack of reflection, to say that there is no art for acquiring the most sublime, the most essential talents, while there are arts for the more subordinate ones. If then there is some science which teaches virtue, where will you seek it, if not in philosophy?"

Sive ratio constantiae, virtutisque ducitur: aut haec ars est (Philosophia) aut nulla omnino, perquam eas assequamur. Nullam dicere maximarum rerum artem esse, cum minimarum sine arte nulla sit; hominum est parum considerate loquentium, atque in maximis rebus errantium. Si quidem est aliqua disciplina virtutis, ubi ea quaeretur, cum ab hoc discendi genere discesseris. Cicero, *de Offic.* l. II, p. 10. de l'Edit. de Glasgow.[173]

ADDITION To the Preceding Refutation
Dijon, October 15, 1751

Sir,

I just received from Paris a brochure, in which Mr. Rousseau replies to a reply made to his discourse by means of the *Mercury*.[174] This reply has several main points in common with our remarks, and consequently the reply is of interest to us. Our refutation of the discourse will become complete by joining to it the refutation of this reply that I send to you, and I hope that there will still be enough time for it to be placed after our remarks.

I have the honor of being, etc.

P.S. You have found it singular that it has been raised as a question . . . *Has the restoration of the sciences and arts tended to purify morals* . . . The French Academy authentically confirms your opinion, Sir, by proposing for the subject of the prize of eloquence for the year 1752 the establishment of this truth . . . *Love of Letters inspires love of virtue* . . . . It is the right and the duty of sovereign courts, Sir, to redress the decisions hazarded by other jurisdictions. Mr. Rousseau has felt all the force of the authority of this program published by the foremost academy in the world in the matter of letters; he has attempted to weaken it by saying that *for this occasion that wise company doubled the time it previously allotted to authors, even for the most difficult subjects* . . . . But this circumstance in no way invalidates the judgment that this supreme tribunal gives against the thesis of the citizen of Geneva. It can only make it thought that this subject demands much erudition, reading, and consequently time; which is true. Moreover, *this wise company* follows the practice of all academies when it proposes in 1751 the subject of the prize it ought to give in 1752. There are even several which put the interval of two years between the publication of the program and the distribution of the prize.

Letter by Jean-Jacques Rousseau of Geneva About a New Refutation of His Discourse by a Member of the Academy of Dijon

[Named Lecat, Surgeon in Rouen] [1]

Sir, I have just seen a Brochure entitled *Discourse which won the prize of the Academy of Dijon in 1750, accompanied by the refutation of this Discourse by a Member of the Academy of Dijon who denied it his vote*, and in skimming through this Writing I thought that instead of stooping to be the Editor of my Discourse, the Academician who denied it his vote ought to have published the work for which he voted. That would have been a very good way to refute mine.

So here we have one of my Judges who does not disdain to become one of my adversaries, and who finds it very bad that his colleagues honored me with the Prize. I admit that I was very amazed by that myself. I had tried to deserve it, but I had done nothing to obtain it. Besides, although I knew that Academies do not adopt the sentiments of the Authors to whom they give prizes, and that first Prize is awarded not to the person they believe has upheld the best cause, but to the one who has expressed himself best, even if I assumed I were in that position, I was far from expecting from an Academy that impartiality in which the learned take no pride whenever their interests are at stake.

But if I was surprised by the equity of my judges, I admit that I am no less so by the indiscretion of my adversaries. How do they dare display so publicly their ill humour about the honor I received? How can they not perceive the irreparable harm that does to their own cause? Let them not flatter themselves that anyone is deceived about the subject of their chagrin: it is not because my Discourse is badly written that they are angry to see it awarded the prize. Equally bad ones are awarded prizes daily and they don't say a word. It is for another reason which is more closely related to their profession, and which is not hard to see. I knew very well that the sciences corrupted morals, made men unjust and jealous, and made them sacrifice everything to their interest and vainglory. But I believed I perceived that it was done with a little more decency and skill. I saw that people of letters [2] talked endlessly about equity, moderation, virtue, and that it was under the sacred safeguard of these beautiful words that they yielded with impunity to their passions and vices. But I would never have believed they had the impudence to blame the impartiality of their Colleagues publicly. Everywhere else, it is the glory of Judges to pronounce according to equity against their own interest. Only the sciences make integrity a crime in those who cultivate them. That is truly a beautiful privilege they have.

I dare state it: in doing much for my glory, the Academy of Dijon has done much for its own. One day to come, the adversaries of my cause will take advantage of this Judgment to prove that the cultivation of Letters can be associated with equity and disinterestedness. Then the Partisans of truth will reply to them: there is a particular example that seems to work against us. But remember the scandal this Judgment caused at the time among the crowd of people of Letters, and the manner in which they complained about it, and draw from that a just conclusion about their maxims.

It isn't, in my opinion, any less imprudent to complain because the Academy posed its topic in the form of a question. I set aside the unlikely possibility that with the universal enthusiasm prevailing today, someone would have the courage voluntarily to renounce the Prize by coming out in favor of the negative. But I don't know how Philosophers dare find it bad to offer them avenues of discussion: beautiful love of truth, that trembles lest there be an examination of the pro and con! In Philosophic research, the best method to make a sentiment suspect is to exclude consideration of the opposite sentiment. Whoever goes about things that way certainly has the air of a man of bad faith, who is unsure of the goodness of his cause. All France is eagerly awaiting the essay that will be awarded the prize this year by the French Academy;[3] not only will it most certainly obscure my Discourse, which will hardly be difficult, but there is no doubt that it will be a masterpiece. However, what will that do for the solution of the question? Nothing at all. For after reading it, everyone will say: *This discourse is very fine. But if the Author had had the freedom to take the opposite sentiment, he might have written one that is even finer.*

I glanced through this new refutation, for it is yet another one of them, and I don't know by what fate my adversaries' Writings bearing that very decisive title are always those where I am the most badly refuted. I glanced through this refutation, then, without the least regret about the resolution I made not to respond to anyone anymore. I will be content to cite a single passage, by which the Reader will be able to judge whether I am wrong or right. Here it is.

I will agree that one can be an honest man without talents. But is one pledged in society only to be an honest man? And what is an honest man who is ignorant and without talents? a useless weight, a burden even to the earth, etc.[4] I will not reply, surely, to an Author capable of writing in that way. But I believe he can thank me for it.

There is hardly any way, either, without wanting to be as diffuse as the Author, to reply to the extensive collection of Latin passages, verses of LaFontaine, Boileau, Molière, Voiture, Regnard, Mr. Gresset, nor to the story of Nimrod, nor to that of the peasants of Picardy. For what can one say to a philosopher who assures us that he is ill-disposed toward ignorant people because his tenant farmer in Picardy, who is not a Scholar, pays him precisely what is owed, but doesn't give him enough money for his land? The Author is so preoccupied with his land that he even talks about mine. My land! Jean-Jacques Rousseau's land! I truly advise him to slander* me more skillfully.

If I were to reply to some part of the refutation, it would be to the personal remarks with which this criticism is replete. But since they have no bearing on the question, I will not deviate from the consistent maxim I have always followed to stay within the subject I am discussing, without mixing in anything personal. The true respect one owes the Public is to spare it not the sad truths that may be useful to it, but rather all the petty peevishness of Authors** with which polemical Writings are filled and which are good only to satisfy a shameful animosity. It is alleged that I took a word of Cicero's from Clenard;*** So be it. That I have made sole-

---

*If the Author does me the honor of refuting this letter, no doubt he will prove through a fine and learned demonstration, upheld by very serious authorities, that it is not a crime to own land. Indeed, it may not be one for others, but it would be one for me.[5]

**One can see in the Discourse of Lyons[6] a very fine model of the manner in which it suits Philosophers to attack and fight without personal remarks and without invectives. I flatter myself that one can find in my reply, which is in press,[7] an example of the manner in which one can defend what one believes to be true, with all the strength of which one is capable, without bitterness toward those who attack it.

***If I said that such a bizarre citation quite certainly comes from someone to whom the Greek method of Clenard[8] is more familiar than Cicero's *Offices* and who, consequently, seems to volunteer rather freely as a defender of Literature; if I added that there are professions, such as Surgery for example, which use so many words derived from Greek that those who practice them are obliged to have some elementary notions of that Language, I would be assuming the tone of the new adversary and responding as he would have done in my position. I myself can reply that when I risked using the word *Investigation*, I wished to do a service to the Language, by trying to introduce a gentle, harmonious term, whose meaning is already known, and which has no synonym in French. I believe those are all the conditions required to sanction that salutary freedom:

> Ego cur, acquirere pauca
> Si possum, invideor; cum lingua Catonis et Enni
> Sermonem Patrium ditaverit.[9]

Above all I wanted to render my idea exactly. I know, it's true, that the first rule of all our Writers is to write correctly and, as they say, to speak French. That is because they have pretensions, and they want to pass as correct and elegant. My own first rule, with no regard

cisms, well and good; that I cultivate Literature and Music, despite the ill I think of them. I will admit if you wish that I ought to bear at a more reasonable age the punishment for the amusements of my youth. But what difference does all that really make both to the public and to the cause of the Sciences. Rousseau may speak bad French, but that does not make Grammar more useful to virtue. Jean-Jacques may behave badly, but that doesn't make the behavior of Learned men better. That is all I shall respond and I believe all I ought to respond to the new refutation.

I will end this Letter, and what I have to say about a subject so long debated, with a word of advice to my adversaries, which they will certainly scorn and which nonetheless would be more advantageous than they think to the side they want to defend. It is not to heed their zeal so much that they neglect to consult their strength, and *quid valeant humeri*.[10] Doubtless, they will say that I should have followed this advice myself, and that may be true. But there is at least the difference that I was the only one on my side whereas since theirs was the side of the masses, the last to come seemed either dispensed from entering the fray or obliged to do better than the others.

For fear that this advice might appear rash or presumptuous, I add here a sample of the reasoning of my adversaries, from which the accuracy and strength of their criticisms can be judged: *The Peoples of Europe*, I said, *lived a few centuries ago in a condition worse than ignorance. A nondescript scientific jargon, even more despicable than ignorance, had usurped the name of knowledge, and opposed an almost invincible obstacle to its return. A revolution was needed to bring men back to common sense.*[11] Peoples had lost common sense not because they were ignorant but because they were foolish enough to believe they knew something with the big words of Aristotle and the impertinent doctrine of Raymond Lulle.[12] A revolution was needed to teach them that they knew nothing, and we have great need of another to teach us the same truth. Here is the argument of my adversaries concerning this: *This revolution is due to letters. They restored common sense, by the author's admission. But also, according to him, they corrupted morals. Therefore a people must renounce common sense in order to have good morals.* Three writers in a row repeated this fine reasoning. I ask them now which they prefer I accuse: their mind for not having been able to fathom the very clear meaning of this passage, or their bad faith, for having feigned not to understand it? They are people of Letters, so

---

for what will be thought of my style, is to make myself understood. Every time that with the help of ten solecisms I can express myself more forcefully or more clearly, I will never hesitate. As long as the Philosophers understand me well, I gladly let the purists chase after words.

their choice will not be in any doubt. But what shall we say about the amusing interpretations our latest adversary takes pleasure in attributing to the figure in my Frontispiece? I would have believed I was insulting my readers and treating them like children by interpreting such a clear allegory for them—by telling them that Prometheus's torch is that of the sciences, created to inspire great geniuses; that the Satyr who, seeing fire for the first time, runs to it and wants to embrace it, represents common men, seduced by the brilliance of letters, who surrender indiscreetly to study; that Prometheus who cries out and warns them of the danger is the Citizen of Geneva. This allegory is just, beautiful, I dare believe sublime. What is to be thought of a Writer who meditated about it and could not attain an understanding of it? It can be thought that that man would not have been a great scholar among his friends the Egyptians.

I take the liberty, then, of proposing to my adversaries, and to the last one above all, this wise lesson of a Philosopher on another subject: know that there are no objections that can do as much harm to your side as bad replies. Know that if you have said nothing worthwhile, people will disparage your cause by doing you the honor of believing that there was nothing better to say.

I remain, etc.

Disclaimer of the Dijon Academy On the Subject of the Refutation Falsely Attributed to One of Its Members and Taken from the Mercury of France, August 1752 [1]

The Academy of Dijon has seen with surprise in a letter printed by Mr. Rousseau that a brochure has appeared entitled: *Discourse which won the prize of the Academy of Dijon in 1750, accompanied by a refutation of this discourse by an academician of Dijon who denied it his vote.*

The Academy knows perfectly well that its decisions, like those of the other academies of the kingdom, come under the jurisdiction of the tribunal of the public. It would not have taken up the refutation that it disclaims if its author—more occupied with the pleasure of criticizing than with the care of making a good critique,—had not thought, by disguising himself under a name that is not due him, to interest the public in a quarrel which has only lasted too long; or at least to let it catch a glimpse of some seed of division in this society, whereas those who compose it, solely occupied with the search for truth, discuss it without bitterness and without giving themselves over to those partisan hatreds that are usually the results of literary disputes.

They know all the respect that is due to the matters judged, the strength they ought to have among themselves, and how indecent it would be in an assembly of people of letters, for one private individual to take it upon himself to refute in writing a decision passed contrary to his opinion.

It seemed, from Mr. Rousseau's letter, that this pretended academician of Dijon does not have the first notion *about the locality* of an academy in which he claims he occupies a place, when he talks about his land and his farmers in Picardy, because in fact it is false that any academician of Dijon possesses an inch of land in that province. Thus, the academy formally disclaims the *pseudonym* author, and his refutation attributed to one of its members with a falseness unworthy of a man who makes a profession of literature, and whom nothing obliges to mask himself.

But, from whatever pen this work comes, whatever could have been the plan of the one who composed it, it will always do honor to the discourse of Mr. Rousseau, who using the freedom of open questions—the only way suited for clarifying the truth—had enough courage to maintain its side and to the academy which had enough good faith to give it first prize.

Petit, Secretary of the Academy of Sciences of Dijon

At Dijon, June 22, 1752

Preface
to a Second Letter
to Bordes [1]

Forced by new attacks to break the silence I had imposed on myself during this long dispute, I pick up without scruple the pen I had set down. If in the opinion of the Wise I can shed new light on the important maxims that I have established, it matters little to me whether the Public is bored with seeing the same question debated for so long. For even if the fault is not with the aggressors, I am not of a disposition to sacrifice my zeal for the truth to the care of my reputation, and I do not see why I would be so afraid of boring Readers whom I worry so little about displeasing.

I believe I have discovered great things, and I stated them with rather dangerous frankness, without there being much merit in all that. For my independence caused all my courage, and long meditations were my substitute for Genius. A solitary person who enjoys living with himself naturally acquires the taste for reflection, and a man who is keenly interested in the happiness of others without needing them to make his own, is excused from being careful of their false sense of delicacy in the useful things he has to say to them. Moreover, because such a situation is rare and because I have the good luck to find myself in it, I believe I am obliged to take advantage of it in favor of truth, and to state it without scruple every time it appears to me that the innocence and happiness of men are at stake. If I made a mistake in committing myself inappropriately to silence, I ought not to make a greater one by insisting on keeping my word against my duty, and it is to remain consistent with my principles that I want to be quick to abandon my errors as soon as I perceive them.

I am going to pick up the thread of my ideas, then, and continue to write just as I have always done, as an isolated Being who desires and fears nothing from anyone, who speaks to others for them and not for himself, like a man who values his brothers too much not to hate their vices, and who wishes they would learn for once to see themselves as wicked as they are in order at least to desire to make themselves as good as they could be.

I know very well that the trouble I am taking is useless, and in my exhortations I don't have the chimerical pleasure of hoping for the reformation of men. I know they scoff at me because I love them and at my maxims because they are profitable for them. I know they will be no less avid for Glory and money when I have convinced them that these two passions are the source of all their ills, and that they are wicked because of one and unhappy because of the other. I am very sure they will treat as an extravagance my disdain for these objects of their admiration and their labors. But I prefer to endure their jesting than to share their mistakes, and whatever may be true about their duty, mine is to tell them the truth or what I take for the truth. It is for a more powerful voice to make them love it.

I have peacefully endured the invectives of a multitude of authors to whom I never did any harm except to exhort them to become good people. They entertained themselves at their ease at my expense. They made me as ridiculous as they wished. They lashed out publicly against my writings and even against my person without my ever trying to repel their insults other than through my behavior. If I deserved these insults, I could not have avenged myself except by seeking to give them back the same, and far from enjoying myself in such an odious war, the more truths I found to say the sadder my heart would have been. If I don't deserve their insults, it is only to themselves they have said them: perhaps their animosity will have difficulty bringing about in the Public the effect they seek and about which I scarcely care. Extreme passion is often clumsy, and is a warning to be wary. Perhaps, based on their own writings, I will be thought to be better than I really am, when it is seen that even with such ardor to blacken me, the greatest crime they have found with which to reproach me is having allowed a famous artist to paint my portrait.

I am far from being capable of the same Composure toward those who, putting aside my person, attack with some skill the truths I have established. This sad and great System, fruit of a sincere examination of the nature of man, his faculties, and his destiny, is dear to me even though it humbles me. For I feel how important it is to us that pride not cause us to be led astray about what should cause our genuine greatness, and how greatly it is to be feared that by dint of wanting to rise above our nature, we will fall beneath it. In any case, it is useful for men if not to know the truth at least not to be in error, and it is one of the most dangerous of them to fear error less than ignorance, and to prefer—in a forced alternative—to be vicious and wretched rather than poor and coarse.

My sentiment has been combatted with wrath, as I had predicted, by a multitude of Writers. I have answered up to now all those who seemed worth the effort of doing so, and I am very determined to proceed in the same way in the future, not for my own glory, for it is not J. J. Rousseau whom I wish to defend. He must have often made mistakes. Every time he appears to me in this situation, I will abandon him without scruples and without difficulty, even when he is right, as long as it involves only himself. Thus, as long as one limits oneself to reproaching me for having published bad works, or for reasoning badly, for making grammatical mistakes or historical errors, or for writing badly or being temperamental, I will not be very angry about all these reproaches, I will not be surprised by them, and I will never respond to them. But with regard to the System I have upheld, I will defend it with all my strength as long as I remain convinced it is the system of truth and virtue, and that it is because they abandoned it inappropriately that the majority of men, degenerated from their primitive goodness, have fallen into all the errors that blind them and all the miseries that overwhelm them.

Having so many interests to contest, so many prejudices to conquer, and so many harsh things to state, in the very interest of my Readers, I believed I ought to be careful of their pusillanimity in some way and let them perceive only gradually what I had to say to them. If the Discourse of Dijon alone excited so many murmurs and caused so much scandal, what would have happened if I had from the first instant developed the entire extent of a System that is true but distressing, of which the question treated in this Discourse is only a Corollary? A declared enemy of the violence of the wicked, I would at the very least have passed for the enemy of public tranquillity; and if the zealots of the opposite party had not labored charitably to ruin me for the greater glory of philosophy, it is at least beyond doubt that, discussing an unknown man, they would easily have succeeded in turning to ridicule the work and its author, and that beginning by ridiculing my System, this method validated by much experience would have dispensed them from the inconvenient effort of examining my proofs.

Some precautions were thus at first necessary for me, and it is in order to be able to make everything understood that I did not wish to say everything. It was only gradually and always for few Readers that I developed my ideas. It is not myself that I treated carefully, but the truth, so as to get it across more surely and make it useful. I have often taken great pains to try to put into a Sentence, a line, a word tossed off as if by chance the result of a long sequence of relections. Often, most of my Readers must have found my discourses badly connected and almost entirely rambling, for lack of perceiving the trunk of which I showed them only the branches. But that was enough for those who know how to understand, and I have never wanted to speak to the others.

This method has put me in the position of having to reply often to my adversaries, whether to resolve objections, to extend and clarify ideas that needed it, or to finish developing all the parts of my System insofar as the approbation of the Wise assured me of public attention. It is true I thought I had sufficiently attended to all those things by my previous replies, at least for the Readers I had in view. But seeing from the second Discourse of the Academician of Lyon that he still did not understand me, I prefer to accuse myself of clumsiness than to accuse him of bad will. I will try, therefore, to explain myself better, and since it is time to talk openly, I am going to conquer my disgust at last and for once write for the People.

The work I propose to examine is full of pleasant sophisms which, having more brilliance than subtlety and seducing through a sort of colorful style and the ruses of a clever logic, are doubly dangerous for the multitude. I will adopt the very opposite methods in this analysis, and following the Author's reasonings step by step with as much exactitude as possible, in this discussion I will use uniquely the simplicity and zeal of a friend of truth and humanity, who finds all his glory in paying homage to one and all his happiness in being useful to the other.

Preface to Narcissus: Or the Lover of Himself[1]

I wrote this Play at the age of eighteen,[2] and I refrained from presenting it as long as I had some regard for reputation as an Author. At last I felt enough courage to publish it, but I will never have enough to say anything about it. Therefore the issue here is not my play but myself.

In spite of my repugnance I must speak about myself; I must either acknowledge the wrongs attributed to me, or I must vindicate myself against them. I sense very well that the weapons will not be evenly matched, because I will be attacked with jokes and I will defend myself with nothing but reasoning: but as long as I convince my adversaries, I care very little about persuading them.[3] While working to deserve my own esteem, I have learned to forego that of others, who, for the most part do very well without mine. But even if it hardly matters to me whether I am well or ill thought of, it does matter to me that no one has the right to think ill of me, and it matters to the truth I have maintained that its defender not be justly accused of having lent his aid to it only out of caprice or vanity without loving and knowing it.

The side that I took in the question I examined several years ago did not fail to make me a multitude of adversaries* who were perhaps more

*I am assured that several people find it bad that I call my adversaries my adversaries, and that seems to me rather believable in a century in which one no longer dares to call anything by its name. I learn also that each of my adversaries complains that I am wasting my time fighting against chimeras when I reply to objections other than his own; which proves to me something I already rather suspected, namely that they don't waste their time in reading or listening to each other. As for myself, this is a trouble that I believed I ought to take and I have read the numerous writings they have published against me, from the first reply with which I was honored to four German sermons one of which begins in roughly this manner: *My brothers, if Socrates returned among us and saw the flourishing state in which the sciences are in Europe, do I say Europe: in Germany; do I say in Germany? in Saxony; do I say Saxony, in Leipzig; do I say in Leipzig? in this University. Then seized with astonishment and penetrated with respect, Socrates would sit down modestly among our schoolboys, and receiving our lessons with humility; with us he would soon lose that ignorance about which he complained so justly.*[4] I have read all that, and have made only a few replies to it; perhaps I have already made too many, but I am very pleased that these Gentlemen have found them agreeable enough to be jealous about preference. For the people who are shocked by the word *adversaries*, I gladly consent to abandon it for them provided they will be so good as to indicate to me another by which I can designate not only all those who have fought my sentiment, whether by writing or, more prudently and more at their ease in the circles of women and wits, where they were very sure that I would not go to defend myself, but also those who today pretend to believe that I do not have adversaries, who at first had found

attentive to the interest of men of letters than to the honor of literature. I had foreseen this and I had rather suspected that their conduct on this occasion would bear witness in my favor more than all my discourses. In effect, they have disguised neither their surprise nor their chagrin at the fact that an Academy showed its integrity so inopportunely. They have not spared against it either indiscreet invective or even falsehoods* to attempt to lessen the weight of its judgment. Nor have I been forgotten in their declamations. Several have undertaken to refute me openly: the wise have been able to see with what force, and the public with what success they have done it. Others who were more clever, knowing the danger of directly combatting demonstrated truths, have skillfully deflected onto my person an attention that should have been given only to my reasons, and the examination of the accusations they have brought against me have caused to be forgotten the more serious accusations that I have brought against them myself. Therefore it is to these that I must reply once and for all.

They claim that I do not believe a word of the truths that I have maintained, and that while demonstrating a proposition I did not fail to believe the opposite. That is to say that I proved such extravagant things that it can be affirmed that I could maintain them only as a game. This is a fine honor they pay to the science which serves as the foundation of all the others; and one should believe that the art of reasoning serves very much for the discovery of the truth when one sees it used successfully to demonstrate follies!

They claim that I do not believe a word of the truths that I have maintained. Without a doubt this is a new and convenient way to respond to unanswerable arguments on their part, to refute even the demonstrations of a Euclid, and everything in the universe that has been demonstrated. It seems to me that those who so rashly accuse me of speaking in contradiction with my thought do not themselves have many scruples about speaking in contradiction with theirs: for they have assuredly found nothing in my Writings or in my conduct which ought to have inspired them with this idea, as I will soon prove; and it is not permissible for them to ignore that as soon as a man speaks seriously, one ought to think that he believes what he says, unless his actions or his

---

the replies of my adversaries to be unanswerable, then when I replied, have blamed me for having done so because, according to them, I hadn't been attacked at all. While waiting, they will allow me to continue to call my adversaries my adversaries, for, in spite of the politeness of my century, I am as crude as the Macedonians of Philip.

*One can see in the *Mercury* of August 1752, the disclaimer of the Academy of Dijon on the subject of some writing or other.[5]

discourses belie it. Even that is not always enough to prove that he believes nothing of it.

Thus they can shout as much as they want that while declaring myself against the sciences I spoke against my sentiment. To such a rash assertion, stripped equally of proof and likelihood, I know only one reply. It is short and energetic, and I ask them to consider it as made.

They also claim that my conduct is in contradiction with my principles, and it must not be doubted that they use this second charge to establish the first one; for there are many people who know how to find proofs for what is not. Thus they will say that when one writes music and poetry, it is ungracious to denigrate the fine arts, and that in literature which I pretend to despise, there are a thousand occupations more praiseworthy than that of writing Plays. It is necessary also to reply to this accusation.

First, even if this were granted in all its strictness, I say that it would prove that I behave badly, but not that I do not speak in good faith. If it were permitted to draw from the actions of men the proof of their sentiments, it would be necessary to say that the love of justice is banished from all hearts and that there is not a single Christian on the earth. Show me men who always act consistently with their maxims, and I will pass sentence on mine. Such is the lot of humanity, reason shows us the goal and the passions divert us from it. Even if it were true that I did not act in accordance with my principles, from this alone one would not be right to accuse me of speaking in contradiction to my sentiment, or to accuse my principles of falsehood.

But if I wished to pass sentence on this point, it would suffice for me to compare the periods of time to reconcile things. I have not always had the good fortune to think as I do. Seduced for a long time by the prejudices of my century, I took study for the only occupation worthy of a wise man, I looked at the sciences only with respect and scientists[6] only with admiration.* I did not understand that one can go astray while always demonstrating, or do wrong while always speaking about wisdom. It is only after having seen things from close up that I learned to esteem them for what they were worth; and although in my inquiries I always found, *satis loquentiae, sapientiae parum*,[7] I needed much reflection, much

---

*Every time I think of my former simple-mindedness, I can't keep myself from laughing. I didn't read a book of Morality or of Philosophy without thinking I saw in it the soul and the principles of the Author. I considered all these serious Writers as modest, wise, virtuous, irreproachable men. I formed angelic ideas of their relations with each other, and I would only have approached the house of one of them as if it were a sanctuary. Finally I saw them, this childish prejudice was dissipated, and it is the only error of which they cured me.

observation and much time to destroy the illusion of all that vain scientific pomp. It is not surprising that, during those times of prejudices and errors when I so much esteemed the quality of being an Author, I sometimes aspired to obtain it for myself. It is in this way that Poems and the majority of other Writings that issued from my pen and among others this little Play were composed. Perhaps it would be harsh to reproach me today for the amusements of my youth, and at least it would be wrong to accuse me of having thereby contradicted principles that were not yet mine. For a long time I have no longer laid any sort of claim to all these things; and to risk giving them to the Public in these circumstances, after having had the prudence to keep them for such a long time, is to say clearly enough that I disdain equally the praise and the blame that they might deserve; for I no longer think as did the Author whose work they are. They are illegitimate children whom one still caresses with pleasure while blushing to be their father, to whom one says the last farewell, and whom one sends to seek their fortune without worrying much about what they will become.[8]

But this is to reason too much according to chimerical assumptions. If I am accused without reason of cultivating literature which I despise, it is not necessary for me to defend myself; for if the fact were true, there would be no inconsistency in it at all. This is what remains for me to prove.

To do so I will follow, according to my customary practice, the simple and easy method that suits the truth. I will establish the state of the question anew, I will set out my sentiment anew, and I will wait to be shown how, based on that exposition, my actions belie my discourses. On their side, my adversaries—who possess the marvelous art of disputing the pro and con on all sorts of subjects—will not remain without a reply. They will begin, according to their customary practice, by establishing a different question according to their whim; they will make me resolve it as it suits them. In order to attack me more conveniently, they will make me reason, not in my manner but in theirs. They will skillfully turn the eyes of the Reader away from the essential object to fix them to the right and to the left; they will battle a phantom and claim to have vanquished me: but I will have done what I ought to do, and I begin.

"Science is good for nothing, and never does anything but harm. It is no less inseparable from vice than ignorance is from virtue. All literate peoples have always been corrupt; all ignorant peoples have been virtuous. In a word, there are no vices except among the learned, nor any virtuous man except one who knows nothing. Therefore there is a way for us to become decent people again; that is to rush to proscribe science and the learned, to burn our libraries, to close our Academies, our Colleges, our Universities, and to plunge back into all the barbarism of the first centuries."

That is what my adversaries have refuted very well. However I never said nor thought a single word of all that, and nothing can be imagined more opposed to my system than this absurd doctrine which they have the goodness to attribute to me. But the following is what I did say and what has not been refuted at all.

The issue was whether the restoration of the sciences and arts tended to purify our morals.⁹

By showing, as I did, that our morals have not been at all purified* the question was more or less resolved.

But it implicitly contained another more general and more important question about the influence that the cultivation of the sciences must have on the morals of peoples on all occasions. It is this question, of which the first is only a consequence, that I proposed to examine carefully.

I began with the facts, and I showed that morals have degenerated among all the peoples in the world to the extent that the taste for study and letters has spread among them.

This was not enough; for without being able to deny that these things have always proceeded together, one could deny that the one brought about the other. Thus I applied myself to showing this necessary connection. I showed that the source of our errors on this point comes from the fact that we mistake our vain and deceitful knowledge for the sovereign

* When I said that our morals were corrupted, by that I did not claim to say that those of our ancestors were good, but only that ours were even worse. Among men there are a thousand sources of corruption, and while the sciences are perhaps the most abundant and the most rapid, it is hardly the case that this is the only one. The ruin of the Roman Empire, the invasions of a multitude of Barbarians, have made a mixture of all the peoples which must necessarily destroy the morals and customs of each of them. The crusades, commerce, the discovery of the Indies, navigation, long voyages, and other additional causes that I do not want to cite, have continued and augmented the disorder. Everything that facilitates communication among the various nations carries to some, not the virtues of the others but their crimes, and among all of them alters the morals that are proper to their climate and the constitution of their government. The sciences have therefore not done all the evil, they have only done their good part of it; and above all what specifically belongs to them is to have given our vices an agreeable color, a certain honest appearance that prevents us from being horrified by them. When the Play, the Wicked Man¹⁰ was performed for the first time, I remember that it was not considered that the leading role corresponded to the title. Cleon seemed only to be an ordinary man; he was, it was said, like everybody. This abominable scoundrel, whose well developed character should have made all those who have the bad fortune to resemble him tremble within themselves, seemed a total failure as a character, and his wickedness passed for an engaging manner because those who thought themselves very honest men recognized themselves trait for trait.

intelligence which sees the truth of everything at a glance. Taken in an abstract manner, science deserves all of our admiration. The mad science of men is worthy only of scorn and disdain.

Among a people the taste for letters always proclaims a beginning of corruption which it very promptly accelerates. For this taste cannot be born in this way in a whole nation except from two bad sources which study maintains and increases in its turn, namely idleness and the desire to distinguish oneself. In a well-constituted State, each citizen has his duties to fulfill; and these important concerns are too dear to him to allow him the leisure to attend to frivolous speculations. In a well-constituted State all the citizens are so very equal, that no one can be preferred to the others as the most learned or even as the most skillful, but at most as the best: even this distinction is often dangerous; because it makes for cheats and hypocrites.

The taste for letters which is born from the desire to distinguish oneself necessarily produces ills that are infinitely more dangerous than all the good that they do is useful. In the end it makes those who surrender to it very unscrupulous about means for succeeding. The first Philosophers made a great reputation for themselves by teaching men the practice of their duties and the principles of virtue. But soon these precepts having become common, it was necessary to distinguish oneself by opening up contrary routes. Such is the origin of the absurd systems of Leucippus, Diogenes, Pyrrho, Protagoras, Lucretius. Hobbes, Mandeville and a thousand others have pretended to distinguish themselves among us; and their dangerous doctrine has borne such fruit, that although we still have some true Philosophers ardent to recall the laws of humanity and virtue to our hearts, one is surprised to see to what point our reasoning century has pushed disdain for the duties of man and of citizen in its maxims.[11]

The taste for letters, philosophy and the fine arts destroys love of our primary duties and of genuine glory. Once talents have seized the honors due to virtue, everyone wishes to be an agreeable man and no one concerns himself with being a good man. From this is born still this additional inconsistency that men are rewarded only for qualities that do not depend on them: for our talents are born with us, our virtues alone belong to us.

The first and almost the sole cares given to our education are the fruits and seeds of these ridiculous prejudices. In order to teach us to read one torments our unfortunate youth: we know all the rules of grammar before having heard about the duties of man: we know everything that has been done up to the present before we have been told a word about what we ought to do; and as long as we practice babbling no one cares whether we know how to act or think. In a word we are urged to be learned only in things that cannot be of any use to us; and our children are reared precisely as were the ancient athletes of the public games, who, dedicating their robust limbs to a useless and superfluous exercise, kept themselves from ever using them in any profitable work.

The taste for letters, philosophy and the fine arts softens bodies and souls. Work in the study renders men delicate, weakens their temperament, and the soul retains its vigor with difficulty when the body has lost its vigor. Study uses up the machine, consumes spirits, destroys strength, enervates courage, and that alone shows sufficiently that it is not made for us. It is in this way that one becomes cowardly and pusillanimous, equally incapable of resisting pain or the passions. Everyone knows how unfit the inhabitants of cities are to sustain the toils of war and the reputation of men of letters on the score of bravery is not unknown.* Now nothing is more justly suspect than the honor of a coward.

So many reflections about the weakness of our nature often serve only to turn us away from generous undertakings. From meditating about the miseries of humanity, our imagination crushes us with their weight, and too much foresight deprives us of courage by depriving us of security. It is very much in vain that we claim to arm ourselves against unforeseen accidents, "if by trying to arm us with new defenses against natural inconveniences, science has imprinted on our fancy more deeply with their magnitude and weight, than with its own reasons and vain subtleties to protect us from them." [12]

The taste for philosophy loosens in us all the bonds of esteem and benevolence that attach men to society, and this is perhaps the most dangerous of the ills engendered by it. The charm of study soon renders any other attachment insipid. Further, by dint of reflecting on humanity, by dint of observing men, the Philosopher learns to appreciate them according to their worth, and it is difficult to have very much affection for what one holds in contempt. Soon he concentrates into his person all the interest that virtuous men share with their fellows: his contempt for others turns to the profit of his pride: his amour-propre increases in the same proportion as his indifference to the rest of the universe. For him, family, fatherland become words void of meaning: he is neither parent, nor citizen, nor man; he is a philosopher.

---

*Here is a modern example for those who reproach me for citing only ancient ones: The Republic of Genoa, seeking to subjugate the Corsicans more easily found no surer method than to establish an Academy among them. It would not be difficult for me to lengthen this Note, but to do so would insult the intelligence of the only Readers about whom I care.

At the same time that the cultivation of the sciences as it were withdraws the heart of the philosopher from the crowd, in another sense it involves in it that of the man of letters and in both instances with equal prejudice to virtue. Every man who occupies himself with agreeable talents wants to please, to be admired, and he wants to be admired more than others. Public applause belongs to him alone: I would say that he does everything to obtain it if he did not do still more to deprive his rivals of it. From this is born on the one side the refinements of taste and politeness; vile and base flattery, seductive, insidious, puerile efforts, which eventually shrivel the soul and corrupt the heart; and on the other side, jealousies, rivalries, the much renowned hatreds of artists, perfidious calumny, cheating, treachery, and everything most cowardly and odious belonging to vice. If the philosopher holds men in contempt, the artist soon makes himself held in contempt by them, and at last both cooperate to render them contemptible.

There is more; and of all the truths I have proposed for the consideration of the wise, this is the most surprising and the most cruel. Our Writers all regard as the masterpiece of the politics of our century the sciences, arts, luxury, commerce, laws, and the other ties which, by tightening among men the ties of society* from personal interest, put them all in mutual dependence, give them reciprocal needs, and common interests, and oblige each of them to cooperate for the happiness of the others in order to be able to attain his own. Doubtless these ideas are fine, and are presented in a favorable light. But in examining them attentively and impartially, one finds much that should be taken with a grain of salt in the advantages that they seem to present at first.

Thus it is a very marvelous thing to have made it impossible for men to live among themselves without being prejudiced against, supplanting, deceiving, betraying, mutually destroying each other! Henceforth we must beware of letting ourselves be seen as we are: for two men whose interests agree, a hundred thousand can be opposed to them, and there is in this case no other means to succeed than to deceive or ruin all these people. This is the deadly source of violence, treachery, perfidy, and all the horrors necessarily demanded by a state of things in which each— pretending to work for the fortune and reputation of the others—seeks only to raise his own above them and at their expense.

What have we gained by this? Much babble, some wealthy people,

---

* I complain that Philosophy relaxes the bonds of society that are formed by esteem and mutual benevolence, and I complain that the sciences, the arts, and all the other objects of commerce tighten the bonds of society based on personal interest. The fact is that one cannot tighten one of these bonds without the other being relaxed by the same amount. There is therefore nothing contradictory in this.[13]

and some argumentative people, that is to say, enemies of virtue and common sense. On the other hand, we have lost innocence and morals. The crowd crawls in misery; all are slaves of vice. Crimes not committed are already at the bottom of hearts and only the assurance of impunity is lacking for their execution.

What a strange and deadly constitution in which accumulated wealth facilitates the means of accumulating more, and in which it is impossible for those who have nothing to acquire something; in which the good man has no means of escaping from misery; in which the greatest rogues are the most honored, and in which one must necessarily renounce virtue to become an honest man! I know that the declaimers have said all this a hundred times; but they say it while declaiming, and I say it based on reasons; they have perceived the evil, and I have discovered its causes, and above all I have shown a very consoling and very useful thing by showing that all these vices do not belong so much to man as to man poorly governed.*

Such are the truths that I have developed and that I have attempted to prove in the diverse Writings that I have published on this matter. Here now are the conclusions that I have drawn from them.

Science is not at all made for man in general. He ceaselessly goes astray

---

*I notice that there now reigns in the world a multitude of petty maxims that seduce the simple by a false appearance of philosophy, and which, besides that, are very convenient for ending disputes with an important and decisive tone without any need for examining the question. Such is this one: "Everywhere men have the same passions: everywhere amour-propre and self-interest lead them; therefore everywhere they are the same." When Geometers have made an assumption that from reasoning to reasoning leads them to an absurdity, they go back on their steps and thus demonstrate the assumption to be false. The same method, applied to the maxim in question, would easily show its absurdity: but let us reason differently. A Savage is a man, and a European is a man. The semi-philosopher concludes immediately that one is not worth more than the other, but the philosopher says: In Europe, government, laws, customs, self-interest, all put individuals in the necessity of deceiving each other mutually and incessantly; everything makes vice a duty; it is necessary to be wicked in order to be wise, for there is no greater folly than to create the happiness of the cheaters at the expense of one's own. Among the Savages, personal interest speaks as strongly as among us, but it doesn't say the same things: love of society and the care for their common defense are the only bonds that unite them: this word of property, which costs so many crimes to our honest people, has almost no sense among them: among them they have no discussions about interest that divide them; nothing carries them to deceive one another; public esteem is the only good to which each aspires, and which they all deserve. It is very possible for a Savage to commit a bad action, but it is not possible that he take on the habit of doing evil, for that wouldn't be of any good for him. I believe that one can make a very just estimation of men's morals by the multitude of business they have among each other: the more commerce they have together, the more they admire their talents and industry, the more they trick each other decently and adroitly, and the more they are worthy of contempt. I say this with regret; the good man is the one who does not need to fool anyone, and the Savage is that man.[14]

> *Illum non populi fasces, non purpura Regum*
> *Flexit, et infidos agitans discordia fratres;*
> *Non res Romanae, perituraque regna, Neque ille*
> *Aut doluit miserans inopem, aut invidit habenti.*[15]

in its quest; and if he sometimes obtains it, it is almost always to his detriment. He is born to act and think, and not to reflect. Reflection serves only to render him unhappy without rendering him better or wiser: it makes him regret the good things of the past and prevents him from enjoying the present: it presents him the happy future to seduce him by the imagination of it and to torment him through desires and the unhappy future to make him feel it in advance. Study corrupts his morals, impairs his health, destroys his temperament, and often spoils his reason: if it teaches him something, I would consider him very poorly compensated.

I admit that there are some sublime geniuses who know how to pierce through the veils in which the truth is enveloped, some privileged souls, capable of resisting the stupidity of vanity, base jealousy, and other passions that engender the taste for letters. The small number of those who have the good fortune to combine these qualities is the light and honor of the human race; it is fitting for them alone to exert themselves in study for the benefit of everyone, and this exception even confirms the rule; for if all men were Socrates, science would not be harmful to them, but they would have no need of it.

Every people which has morals, and which consequently respects its laws and does not at all want to refine its ancient practices, ought to secure itself against the sciences, and above all against the learned, whose sententious and dogmatic maxims would soon teach it to despise its practices and its laws; which a nation can never do without being corrupted. The smallest change in customs, even if it is advantageous in certain respects, always turns to the disadvantage of morals. For customs are the morality of the people; and as soon as it ceases to respect them, it no longer has any rule except its passions nor bridle but the laws, which can sometimes hold back the wicked, but never make them good. Moreover if philosophy has once taught the people to despise its customs, it soon finds the secret of eluding its laws. Thus I say that it is the case for the morals of a people as it is for the honor of a man; it is a treasure that must be preserved, but that is no longer recovered once it has been lost.*

---

* I find in history a unique but striking example that seems to contradict this maxim: it is that of the foundation of Rome made by a troop of bandits, whose descendants became in a few generations the most virtuous people that has ever existed. I would not have any difficulty explaining this fact if this was the place to do so; but I will content myself with remarking that the founders of Rome were less men whose morals were corrupted than men whose morals were not yet formed; they did not scorn virtue, but they didn't know it yet; for these words *virtues* and *vices* are collective notions that are only born with frequentation among men. Moreover, from this objection one would derive a point against the sciences, for the two first Kings of Rome, who gave a form to the Republic and instituted its customs and its morals, one was occupied only with wars and the other only with sacred rites; the two things in the world that are the most distant from philosophy.16

But once a people has been corrupted to a certain point, whether the sciences have contributed to this or not, is it necessary to banish them or protect the people from them to render it better or to prevent it from becoming worse? This is another question about which I have positively declared for the negative. For first, since a vicious people never returns to virtue, it is not a question of rendering good those who no longer are so, but of preserving as such those who have the good fortune of being so. In the second place, the same causes which have corrupted peoples sometimes serve to prevent a greater corruption; it is in this way that someone who has spoiled his temperament by an indiscreet use of medicine, is forced to continue to have recourse to doctors to preserve his life; and it is in this way that the arts and sciences, after having hatched the vices, are necessary for keeping them from turning into crimes; at least they cover them with a varnish which does not permit the poison to find a vent so freely. They destroy virtue, but leave its public simulacrum* which is always a fine thing. They introduce into its place politeness and the proprieties, and for the fear of appearing wicked they substitute that of being ridiculous.

Thus my opinion is, and I have already said it more than once, to allow to exist and even to support carefully Academies, Colleges, Universities, Libraries, Theatres, and all the other amusements which can give some diversion to the wickedness of men, and keep them from occupying their idleness with more dangerous things. For in a country in which it is no longer a question of honest people nor of good morals, it would be better to live with rogues than with brigands.

Now I ask where the contradiction is in myself cultivating the tastes whose progress I approve? It is no longer an issue of bringing peoples to do good, it is only necessary to distract them from doing evil; it is necessary to occupy them with foolishness to turn them away from bad actions; it is necessary to amuse them instead of preaching to them. If my Writings have edified the small number of good people, I have done them all the good that depends on me, and it is perhaps still to serve them usefully to offer objects of distraction to the others which will keep them from thinking about them. I would consider myself only too happy to have a Play to be hissed every day, if at this cost I could keep in check the bad plans of a single one of the Spectators, and save the honor of the

---

*This simulacrum is a certain softness of morals that sometimes replaces their purity, a certain appearance of order that prevents horrible confusion, a certain admiration of beautiful things that keeps the good ones from falling completely into obscurity. It is vice that takes the mask of virtue, not as hypocrisy in order to deceive and betray, but under this lovable and sacred effigy to escape from the horror that it has of itself when it sees itself uncovered.

daughter or the wife of his friend, the secret of his confidante, or the fortune of his creditor. When there are no longer any morals, it is necessary to think only of public order; and it is known well enough that Music and Theatre are among its must important objects.

If some difficulty remains for my justification, I boldly dare to say that it is with regard neither to the public nor my adversaries; it is with regard to myself alone: for it is only by observing myself that I can judge if I ought to count myself in the small number, and if my soul is in a condition to undergo the burden of literary endeavors. I have felt their danger more than once; more than once I have abandoned them with the plan of no longer taking them up, and renouncing their seductive charm, for the peace of my heart I have sacrificed the only pleasures that gratify it. If in the languors that weigh me down, if at the end of a difficult and painful career, I have dared to take them up again for a few moments to relieve my ills, I at least believe that I have put into this neither enough interest nor enough pretension to deserve the just reproaches that I have made to men of letters in this regard.

I needed a test to complete my self-knowledge, and I took it without hesitating. After having recognized the situation of my soul in literary success, it remained for me to examine it in the reverse. Now I know how to think about it, and I can put the worst before the public. My Play had the fate that it deserved and that I had foreseen; but, aside from the boredom it caused me, I left the performance much more content with myself and more justly so than if it had succeeded.

Thus I advise those who are so eager to seek reproaches to make to me, to study my principles better and to observe my conduct better before they accuse me of inconsistency in them. If they ever perceive that I am beginning to court the favor of the public, or that I become vain from having written pretty songs, or that I blush at having written bad Plays, or that I seek to damage the glory of my rivals, or that I pretend to speak ill of the great men of my century in order to try to raise myself to their level by lowering them to mine, or that I aspire to position in an Academy, or that I go to pay court to the women who set the tone, or that I flatter the stupidity of the Great, or that ceasing to wish to live from the labor of my hands,[17] I hold in ignominy the trade that I have chosen and take steps toward wealth, in a word if they notice that the love of reputation makes me forget that of virtue, I beg them to warn me about it, and even publicly, and I promise them instantly to throw my Writings and my Books into the fire, and to concede all the errors with which they will be pleased to reproach me.

While waiting, I will write Books, compose Poems and Music, if I have the talent, time, strength and will to do so: will continue to say very frankly all the evil that I think about letters and about those who cultivate them,* and will believe that I am not worth any less for that. It is true that it will be possible to say some day: This professed enemy of the sciences and arts, nevertheless composed and published Theatrical Plays; and this discourse will be, I admit, a very bitter satire, not on me, but on my century.

*I wonder at how much most men of letters have gone astray in this affair. When they saw that the sciences and the arts were attacked, they thought that they were being attacked personally, while without contradicting themselves they could all think like me that, whereas these things have done a great deal of evil to society, it is very essential to use them today as a medicine for the evil they have caused, or like those harmful animals that must be crushed on top of their bite. In a word, there is not a man of letters who, if in his conduct he can pass the test of the preceding passage, couldn't say in his favor what I say in my own, and this way of reasoning seems to me to suit them all the better because, among us, they care very little about the sciences provided that they continue to place the learned in honor. It is like the priests of paganism, who only supported religion as long as it made them respected.

Notes

Bloom	Jean-Jacques Rousseau. *Émile*. Edited by Allan Bloom. New York: Basic Books, 1979.
Collected Writings, I	Jean-Jacques Rousseau. *Rousseau Judge of Jean-Jacques, Dialogues. Collected Writings of Rousseau*, Vol. 1. Edited by Roger D. Masters and Christopher Kelly. Hanover, N.H.: University Press of New England, 1991.
Havens	Jean-Jacques Rousseau. *Discours sur les sciences et les arts*. Edited by George R. Havens. New York: Modern Language Association of America, 1946.
Launay	Jean-Jacques Rousseau. *Oeuvres complètes*. Vols. 1–2. Paris: Editions du Seuil [Collection l'Intégrale], 1967–1971.
Masters, I	Jean-Jacques Rousseau. *First and Second Discourses*. Edited by Roger D. Masters. New York: St Martin's, 1964.
Masters, II	Jean-Jacques Rousseau. *Social Contract, with Geneva Manuscript and Political Economy*. Edited by Roger D. Masters. New York: St Martin's, 1978.
Pléiade	Jean-Jacques Rousseau. *Oeuvres complètes*. Vols. 1–5. Paris: NRF-Editions de la Pléiade, 1959ff.
Vaughan	Jean-Jacques Rousseau, *The Political Writings of Rousseau*. Vols. 1–2. Edited by C. E. Vaughan. Cambridge: Cambridge University Press, 1915.

NOTES TO INTRODUCTION

1. It is not possible to review completely the vast secondary literature on Rousseau. For bibliographical surveys, see Peter Gay's Introduction to Ernst Cassirer, *The Question of Jean-Jacques Rousseau* (New York: Columbia University Press, 1954), 3–30, and Alfred Cobban, *Rousseau and the Modern State* (London: George Allen and Unwin, 1934), chapter 2. Many of the more useful secondary works are cited in the footnotes to this introduction. A useful bibliography of recent works can be found in *Jean-Jacques Rousseau*, ed. Harold Bloom (New York: Chelsea House Publishers, 1988) 289–98.

2. *Rousseau Judge of Jean-Jacques*, Dialogue III (Pléiade, I, 934); *Collected Writings of Rousseau*, I, 213.

3. Robert Wokler has argued that Rousseau worked out and developed his views in response to critics of the *First Discourse*: see Wokler, "The Discours sur les sciences et les arts and Its Offspring: Rousseau in Reply to His Critics," in *Reappraisals of Rousseau: Studies in Honour of R. A. Leigh* (Manchester: Manchester University Press, 1980) and *Social Thought of J. J. Rousseau* (New York: Garland Publishing, 1987). This argument runs counter to Rousseau's own claim that he had foreseen all of the criticisms of the *Discourse* in advance (see p. 110 below). It is also sometimes asserted that Rousseau changed his position fundamentally between writing the *First Discourse* and the publication of the *Second Discourse* in 1755 or of the *Social Contract* and *Emile* in 1762 (e.g., Vaughan, I, 80—81). For other scholars, Rousseau's works are "inconsistent" or "incoherent"—and hence do not form a system because they rest on fundamental confusions: e.g., John Charvet, *The Social Problem in the Philosophy of Rousseau* (London: Cambridge University Press, 1974).

Since a number of recent commentators, including Wokler, have argued that many of the presumed contradictions in Rousseau's thought are not contradictions at all, two distinct interpretive questions need to be posed: first, did Rousseau have a "system" that he developed consistently in his works; and second, if so, did he give a consistent or systematic expression to his thought from the *First Discourse* onward. Based on extensive evidence (much of it in replies to critics that are included in this volume) that Rousseau's major writings are guided by a consistent system of thought, we answer both questions in the affirmative. However, this does not mean that his works, written under different guises and for different purposes, form a systematic expression like the *Encylopedia* of Hegel. On this issue, see Arthur Melzer, *The Natural Goodness of Man* (Chicago: University of Chicago Press, 1990). In one of his replies to critics of the *First Discourse—Observations on the Response* (below, pp. 45–46)—Rousseau treats "esoteric" doctrine as widespread among philosophers; he thus knew of the technique of "disguising" the truth in philosophic writing from the outset of his career. On the possibility that he himself used this technique, see *Reveries*, Promenade IV (Pléiade, I, 1025–1032); Leo Strauss, *Persecution and the Art of Writing* (Glencoe, Ill.: The Free Press, 1952), especially chapter 1; and Heinrich Meier's excellent critical edition (with German translation) of the *Second Discourse* [*Diskurs über die Ungleichheit*] (Paderborn: Schoningh, 1984), which provides evidence that Rousseau used the technique. For an admission that Rousseau did not reveal his thought completely in the *First Discourse*, see his *Confessions*, Book VIII (Pléiade, I, 388).

4. Letter to M. de Malesherbes, January 12, 1762 (Pléiade, I, 1135–1136). Compare *Confessions*, VIII (Pléiade, I, 351). Jean-Jacques himself thus describes all of his mature writings as based on a single "principle" resulting from the "illumination of Vincennes." For further evidence that the main outlines of Rousseau's position did not change over time, see the "Preface to a Second Letter to Bordes," written in 1753–1754 (Pléiade, III, 106, and below, p. 214), and *Confessions*, VIII (Pléiade, I, 388), as well as Roger D. Masters, *Political Philosophy of Rousseau* (Princeton, N.J.: Princeton University Press, 1968), 206–207.

5. The *Preliminary Discourse* of the *Encyclopedia* appeared just after the publication of the *First Discourse,* and although Rousseau was among those who wrote for it, he ultimately broke with Diderot and most of his friends. For a useful account of the *philosophes,* see Peter Gay, *The Enlightenment: An Interpretation* (New York: Knopf, 1966–1969).

6. This essay won the Prize of the Academy of Dijon in 1750, and was published late in that year or early in 1751. For the history of the work, see the Introduction in George R. Havens's critical edition (Havens, pp. 1–88).

7. This work, whose full title is *Discourse on the Origin and Foundations of Inequality among Men,* was written for another prize competition of the Academy of Dijon and published in 1755 (Vaughan, I, 118–23).

8. *First Discourse,* p. 7 below. (All citations indicated by page alone refer to the translations in this volume.)

9. See below, p. 7.

10. A passage from Plato's *Apology*—Socrates' defense before the Athenian jury—is cited by Rousseau to substantiate his argument, providing a striking example of his use of incorrect or incomplete quotations to serve his purposes. In the present example, Rousseau omits Socrates' reference to the ignorance of politicians and substitutes artists for artisans, thereby redirecting the Socratic criticism to the particular targets central to his topic. Compare *Apology,* 22a–23b (the passage critical of artisans that Rousseau cites) with the *First Discourse,* p. 21 (where Rousseau praises artisans). In effect, he makes Socrates more of a citizen and less of a philosopher. In *Socrate devant Voltaire, Rousseau et Diderot* (Paris: Minard, 1967), Raymond Trousson has shown that in all likelihood Rousseau relied on Diderot's translation of the *Apology* for the term "artists" rather than "artisans." While it is thus not possible to establish a deliberate substitution in this word, the rearrangement of this quotation, like that of many others elsewhere in Rousseau's works, follows a pattern that is too contrived to be entirely a product of carelessness or chance.

In any event, it is clear that Rousseau uses the Socratic passage to make a point that is very different from the one made by Socrates. Whereas Socrates clearly attacks artisans, Rousseau does not. In eighteenth-century usage, "art" can refer to any systematic body of knowledge, and this is the meaning given the term in the *Encyclopedia.* Although this meaning encompasses artisans under the term "artists," Rousseau's examples in the *Discourse* focus on the fine arts and touch on artisans only as they cater to luxury through ornamentation. The spirit of Rousseau's usage can be indicated with a remark from *Émile*: "These important fellows who are called artists rather than artisans, and who work solely for the idle and rich, set an arbitrary price on their baubles. Since the merit of these vain works exists only in opinion, their very price constitutes a part of their merit, and they are esteemed in proportion to what they cost" *Émile,* Book III (Pléiade, IV, 457; Bloom, p. 186). And, of course, Rousseau trains Emile to be a carpenter.

11. This praise of the academies, it should be noted, is almost certainly ironic: an academy like that of Dijon included precisely the kind of "indiscreet" "compilers of books" whom Rousseau attacks in the sequel.

12. Here we see one reason why the substitution of "artists" for "artisans"

in the quotation from Plato's *Apology* suited Rousseau's purposes. See above, note 10.

13. See below, p. 22.

14. See below, p. 4.

15. For a fuller analysis of the reasoning outlined in the following discussion, see Leo Strauss, "On the Intention of Rousseau," *Social Research*, 14 (December 1947): 455–487, and *Natural Right and History* (Chicago: University of Chicago Press, 1953), chapter 6 (A).

16. *Republic* V.472–473.

17. Ibid., V.519–520.

18. Ibid., VI.495, for example.

19. *First Discourse*, p. 14. Among recent interpreters of Rousseau, Bertrand de Jouvenel has been perhaps the most insistent in emphasizing Rousseau's reliance upon the ancients. See "Rousseau the Pessimistic Evolutionist," *Yale French Studies*, 28 (Fall–Winter, 1961–1962): 53–96, and "Essai sur la Politique de Rousseau," in Jean-Jacques Rousseau, *Du Contrat Social* (Genève: Les Editions du Cheval Ailé, 1947), 13–165.

20. *First Discourse*, p. 21.

21. See below, p. 27.

22. See below, p. 30.

23. See below, p. 37.

24. *Confessions*, Book VIII (Pléiade, I, 366).

25. See below, p. 37.

26. See below, p. 53.

27. See below, p. 53.

28. See below, pp. 55–57.

29. See below, p. 98.

30. Perhaps equally important, Rousseau felt—as he was to put it later—that Bordes' "Discourse" was "a very fine model of the manner in which it suits Philosophers to attack and fight without personal remarks and without invectives" (*Letter to Lecat*, p. 177, note).

31. "Preface to a Second Letter to Bordes," p. 183. Bordes, in responding to Rousseau's "Final Reply" with a "Second Discourse," said that he had at first regarded Rousseau's *Discourse on the Arts and Sciences* as a frivolous paradox but that Rousseau's replies had revealed his "system."

32. See below, p. 184.

33. See below, pp. 184–185.

34. Compare note 3, above.

EDITORIAL NOTES TO THE
Discourse on the Sciences and Arts (First Discourse)

1. From Ovid's *Tristia*, Book V, Elegy X.37: "Here I am the barbarian, because no one understands me." Since Rousseau considered the epigraph the clue to an entire work (see *Rousseau Judge of Jean-Jacques*, Dialogue III [*Collected Writings*, I, 218; Pléiade, I, 941]), it is wise to look up the source of his preliminary

quotations and compare them to the works they introduce. This quotation apparently symbolizes Rousseau's expectation that few men of his time will understand the thesis proposed in the *First Discourse*. The epigraph is, however, subtler than that: even though the arts and sciences appear to be generally condemned in the *First Discourse*, Rousseau identifies himself with the poet Ovid from the very outset.

2. This foreword was added by Rousseau in 1763, when he was preparing a collected edition of his writings. It is not certain which works Rousseau includes in this unfavorable comparison—see Havens, pp. 169–170. Although Rousseau admitted elsewhere that the *First Discourse* was poorly written (*Confessions*, Book VIII [Pléiade, I, 352]), he included it, together with the *Second Discourse*, among his "principal writings" (letter to Malesherbes, Jan. 12, 1762, Pléiade, I, 1136).

3. When the Parlement of Paris, on June 9, 1762, condemned Rousseau's *Émile* and ordered him seized, Rousseau was forced to flee the French capital. Later that month, both the *Émile* and the *Social Contract* were condemned and burned in Geneva, where Rousseau's arrest was also ordered. Having taken refuge at Yverdon, he was forced to move early in July by a decree of the government of Berne, and he settled in Motiers (where this foreword was written). In September 1765, Rousseau fled Motiers after his house was stoned; the remaining years of his life were punctuated by repeated displacements, which Rousseau often believed were necessary to avoid what he considered to be a plot against him.

4. The League (or Holy League) was an organization of French Catholics that attempted to suppress Protestants in France during the wars of religion in the sixteenth century. Formed in 1576, it ceased to be important after the victories of Henry IV and his abjuration of Protestantism in 1593.

5. There has been much disagreement concerning the location of these additions. See Havens, pp. 175–176 and Pléiade, III, 1240. Perhaps the most plausible hypothesis concerns two sentences praising the Academy of Dijon for its prize competition (p. 19) since these remarks would have been base flattery in a contest entry.

"We are deceived by the appearance of right" (Horace, *On the Art of Poetry*, v. 25).

7. Note that in restating the question, Rousseau changes it. The French word *moeurs*, here translated as "morals," poses a most difficult problem for a translator. Allan Bloom has suggested "manners [morals]" as a means of conveying the combination of an ethical assessment and a description of habits implicit in the term; see his *Politics and the Arts* (Ithaca, N.Y.: Cornell University Press, 1968), pp. 149–150. We have decided against this translation in part because Rousseau uses the expression "morals (*moeurs*) and manners" (p. 51 of this volume). Although the phrase "way of life" is perhaps the best single equivalent for *moeurs*, it is awkward and does not always capture the specific nuance intended; in addition, it could be confused with the phrase *manière de vivre*, which occurs several times in Rousseau's *Second Discourse*. The range of meanings of the term can be illustrated with examples from Rousseau's contemporaries. The article "*Moeurs*" in Diderot's *Encyclopedia* gives a straightforward definition: "free actions of men, natural or acquired, good or bad, susceptible to rule and direction." In his *De la manière d'etudier et de traiter l'histoire naturelle*, published in 1749, the great natu-

ralist Buffon speaks of the need to study the *moeurs* of animals. In this use, *moeurs* clearly means something like characteristic ways of behaving. The best account of the meaning of the term can be found in the *Considerations sur les moeurs de ce siècle*, published in 1751 by Rousseau's close friend Charles Duclos. Duclos begins his book by referring to the various meanings of this word, which has no synonyms. He says that its most general sense is "natural or acquired habits for good or for bad." He goes on to distinguish *moeurs* from morality (*la morale*). The latter is a set of rules for governing behavior, while *moeurs* are these rules put into practice badly or well. Thus, "good *moeurs* are practical morality." In his article "Moeurs" for his *Dictionary of Music*, Rousseau argues that the ancient Greek concern with the *moeurs* of music was a concern with reducing to rules "what is decent (*honnete*), suitable (*convenable*) and seemly (*bienseant*)." Throughout the present translation the following conventions will be adopted: when possible, *moeurs* will be rendered as "morals." Only on occasions when this clearly is inaccurate as English usage, another term, such as "customs," will be used. The adoption of different English words to translate a given French term is virtually inescapable and is justified by the following remark of Rousseau:

I have a hundred times in writing made the reflection that it is impossible in a long work always to give the same meanings to the same words. There is no language rich enough to furnish as many terms, turns, and phrases as our ideas can have modifications. The method of defining all the terms and constantly substituting the definition in the place of the defined is fine but impracticable, for how can a circle be avoided? Definitions could be good if words were not used to make them. In spite of that, I am persuaded that one can be clear, even in the poverty of our language, not by always giving the same meanings to the same words, but by arranging it so that as often as each word is used, the meaning given it be sufficiently determined by the ideas related to it and that each period where the word is found serves it, so to speak, as a definition. (*Émile*, II, Bloom, 108n; Pléiade, IV, 345n)

8. Rousseau uses *lumières* in the sense of "natural or acquired intellectual capacity." Except for several places where it is appropriate, "lights" (the literal equivalent) has been avoided as too awkward. Where the emphasis in the text seems to be primarily on man's natural mental faculties, "intellect" has been used; when Rousseau seems to mean primarily acquired intelligence, we have adopted "enlightenment." This should not cause any confusion since the nouns "enlightenment" and "intellect" are used for no other French word (although we do translate the verb *éclairer* by the verb forms of "enlighten").

This sentence has a broad element of irony, as will be seen by comparing the *Second Discourse* (especially Masters, pp. 163–168). For example, note Rousseau's remark that "in relations between one man and another . . . the worst that can happen to one is to see himself at the discretion of the other" (ibid., p. 163). That Rousseau regarded himself a victim of partisan judges is the major theme of the *Dialogues*; see volume 1 of this series.

10. Constantinople was captured by the Crusaders in 1203 and by the Turks in 1453 (see Havens, p. 180).

11. The word translated as *fatherland* is the French word *patrie*. This word

poses some problems for translation because the most literal translation, "father-land," is not of very common usage in English, while *patrie* is very common in French. Generally, on most occasions in which *patrie* would be used in French, "country" would be used in English. Thus, in English, "country" is used to describe a geographical area and an object of political loyalty or patriotism. In French, *pays* would be used for the former. That Rousseau distinguishes between the two is shown clearly by a statement in *Émile*, "he who does not have a fatherland (*patrie*) at least has a country (*pays*)" (*Émile*, Bloom, V, p. 473). Thus, *patrie* indicates a stronger civic attachment or obligation than does *pays*. In the dedication to the *Second Discourse*, Rousseau also indicates that, in the best cases, political allegiance is to a group of fellow citizens rather than to a place. He says that he would wish to have been born in a place "where that sweet habit of seeing and knowing one another turned love of the fatherland into love of the citizens rather than love of the soil" (Masters, I, p. 79). Also in Book I, chapter 9 of the *Social Contract*, he contrasts ancient kings who "considered themselves leader of men" with modern kings who cleverly call themselves "masters of the country (*pays*)" (Masters, II, p. 57). In short, for Rousseau a *patrie* is an object of strong obligation, is formed of a group of citizens, and involves a politics based on leadership rather than mastery. On the other hand, a *pays* is either merely a place or a political object inspiring limited obligation, not involving a strong sense of shared citizenship, and compatible with despotism. That Rousseau uses a word connected with the word *father* is noteworthy, although it should also be noted that *patrie* is a feminine noun in French. This connection comes from the traditional passing of citizenship by descent from the father rather than the mother. In addition, Rousseau clearly wishes to suggest that feelings of patriotism can be as intense as family ties.

12. "The art of disputation on all things, without ever taking a stand other than to suspend one's judgment, is called Pyrrhonism" (Pierre Bayle, *Dictionnaire historique et critique*, 3rd ed. [Rotterdam: Michel Bohm, 1720], III, 2306). Compare Bayle's footnote B on that page with Rousseau's "Profession de foi du vicaire Savoyard" in Book IV of *Émile* (in the Bloom edition, pp. 266–313, esp. pp. 267–269).

13. With an oratorical flourish, Rousseau alludes to the discovery, first widely accepted in the eighteenth century, that the tides are determined by the position of the moon (Havens, p. 189).

14. This citation is from Montaigne's essay "On the Art of Conversing," *Essays*, Book III, chapter 8. For an English translation, see the edition of Donald Frame (Stanford, Calif.: Stanford University Press, 1958). The exception is generally assumed to have been Diderot, then Rousseau's closest friend (Havens, pp. 187–88).

15. Although several Egyptian kings had this name, the Sesostris said to have conquered the world is apparently legendary (see Havens, p. 190).

16. Cambyses II, king of Persia, successfully invaded Egypt in 525 B.C. (Havens, p. 190).

17. King Philip of Macedonia conquered the main Greek city-states in 338 B.C. (Havens, p. 191).

18. The great Athenian orator (385?–322 B.C.) was a leading opponent of Macedonian hegemony in Greece.

19. Ennius (239 to c. 170 B.C.) was an early Latin poet, and Terence (194 to 159 B.C.) was a famous author of comedies (Havens, p. 192). Thus, Rousseau dates the beginning of the fall of Rome near the beginning of the second century B.C.

20. According to Tacitus, *Annals* XI. 18, this title ("elegantae arbiter") was given to Petronius, satiric author and courtier of Nero. Since Petronius lived in the first century A.D., the "fall" of Rome under the "yoke she had imposed on so many peoples" cannot be the capture of Rome by the barbarian general Odoacer in A.D. 476. Although this event is traditionally called the "fall of Rome," it would appear that the "yoke" Rousseau has in mind is one-man rule—that is, the establishment of the Roman Empire by Augustus in the years following the Battle of Actium (31 B.C.). If this conjecture is correct—and it seems inescapable, since Rousseau speaks of the "fall" of Rome as coming before the day on which Petronius was called "Arbiter of Good Taste"—this passage serves as a carefully guarded equation of monarchy with subjection or slavery. Indeed, if one considers Rousseau's examples carefully, it will be seen that states with healthy morals were often republics, whereas the corrupt societies he names were mainly (though not exclusively) empires and monarchies.

21. Xenophon's *Cyropaedia* (Havens, p. 196).

22. Tacitus (c. A.D. 55 to c. 117), especially in his *De moribus Germanorum* (Havens, p. 197).

23. The reference is to Montaigne's "Of Cannibals," *Essays*, Book I, chapter 31 (Frame, 159). Havens identifies this and other references to Montaigne in his notes.

24. Compare Montaigne, "Of Experience," *Essays*, Book III, chapter 13 (Frame, 116).

25. Pisistratus, tyrant of Athens from 554 to 527 B.C., was reputed to have been the first to transcribe and organize the poetry of Homer, the "prince of poets" (Havens, pp. 200–201).

26. Compare Thucydides, *History of the Peloponnesian War*, I, x:

For I suppose if Lacedaemon were to become desolate, and the temples and the foundations of the public buildings were left, that as time went on there would be a strong disposition with posterity to refuse to accept her fame as a true exponent of her power. And yet they occupy two-fifths of the Peloponnese and lead the whole, not to speak of their numerous allies without. Still, as the city is neither built in a compact form nor adorned with magnificent temples and public edifices, but composed of villages after the old fashion of Hellas, there would be an impression of inadequacy. Whereas, if Athens were to suffer the same misfortune, I suppose that any inference from the appearance presented to the eye would make her power to have been twice as great as it is. (Everyman's Library [New York: E. P. Dutton, 1910], p. 7).

27. For some of the implications of this paraphrase of Plato's *Apology*, see the Introduction (p. xiv, n. 10).

28. Cato the Elder (234–149 B.C.), Roman statesman known for his efforts to restore what he considered to be the pure morals of the early Republic. Note that Cato was a contemporary of Ennius, identified in note 18.

29. Epicurus (c. 342–270 B.C.) founded the Epicurean philosophic school or sect, and his contemporary, Zeno, founded that of the Stoics; Arcesilaus (316–241 B.C.) was an extreme skeptic who took the position that "nothing was certain" (Havens, p. 203).

30. Havens indicates (p. 203) that Rousseau here transcribes a sentence of Seneca ("Postquam docti prodierunt, boni desunt" [*Letters* xcv. 13]), which had been quoted by Montaigne in "Of Pedantry," *Essays*, Book I, chapter 25 (Zeitlin, I, 122).

31. As Havens points out (p. 207), the reference here is to Plutarch's "Life of Pyrrhus," which describes both Cineas and Fabricius. See Plutarch, *Lives of the Noble Grecians and Romans* (New York: Modern Library, n.d.), 481f. This "prosopopocia" of Fabricius was the first part of the *Discourse* written by Rousseau. See *Confessions*, Book VIII (Pléiade, I, 351).

32. The irony of this rhetorical question is clear if one considers the last sentence of Fabricius' speech: neither King Louis XII nor King Henry IV would have been likely to conclude that "the most noble sight that has ever appeared beneath the heavens" was the Roman Senate.

33. Compare the story told by Socrates in Plato's *Phaedrus*, 274c–275b, concerning the origin of writing.

34. This is almost a word-for-word quotation of the version of the fable given by Plutarch, except that Rousseau neglects to add the remainder of Prometheus' advice to the satyr: "It burns when one touches it, but it gives light and warmth, and is an implement serving all crafts providing one knows how to use it well." See Havens, p. 209, and compare Plutarch, "How to Profit by One's Enemies," trans. Frank Cole Babbitt, *Moralia* (Loeb Classical Library; London: Heinemann, 1928), II, 74. On the fable of Prometheus, compare Plato's *Protagoras*, 320d-322a.

35. Reproduced p. 2.

36. The word translated as "well" can also mean a mineshaft. This saying can be traced back to Fragment 17 of Democritus, although Democritus says that the truth is hidden in the *depths*. In "On the Art of Conversing," which Rousseau cited above (see p. 7), Montaigne refers to the maxim, but renders it as "in the bottom of abysses." Further, Montaigne says that he disagrees with Democritus and suggests that the truth is elevated above us rather than hidden beneath us. Rousseau returns to this maxim in his defenses of the *Discourse*, see p. 89 below. In a comment on this passage, Gautier accuses Rousseau of attempting to reintroduce ancient skepticism (see pp. 77–78 below), and Rousseau's reference in the next paragraph to the traditional skeptical argument that there is no criterion by which the truth can be judged gives some grounds for this. The general tone of the argument at this point of the *Discourse* calls into question the very possibility of real knowledge and certainly suggests that humans have no natural tendency to pursue knowledge. It is, however, not impossible that Rousseau's choice of "well" is meant to indicate the difficulty rather than the impossibility of acquiring knowledge. With this in mind, one can recall the ancient discovery that stars can be observed from the bottom of a shaft or a well even in daytime. This discovery is referred to by Buffon in volume 4 of his *Histoire naturelle*, with which Rousseau was familiar.

37. We are indebted to Professor Joseph Cropsey for the suggestion that, of this list of scientific discoveries due to "illustrious philosophers," the first three refer to the work of Newton, the next two to Descartes' philosophy, and the last two to studies by Bacon. Compare the three philosophers mentioned by name on p. 21. More recently, Victor Gourevitch has suggested that Rousseau refers to Newton, Kepler, Malebranche, Leibniz, Fontenelle, Rèaumur, and Bonnet; see his *First and Second Discourse Together with the Replies to Critics and Essay on the Origin of Languages* (New York: Harper and Row, 1986), 305.

38. Compare Montesquieu, *The Spirit of the Laws*, XXIII, xvii: "Sir [William] Petty supposed, in his calculations, that a man in England is worth what he could be sold for in Algiers. That can only be true for England: there are countries where a man is worth nothing; there are some where he is worth less than nothing" (Paris: Garnier Frères, 1949), II, 114–15. The best English translation is by Anne Cohler et al. (New York: Cambridge University Press, 1989). Montesquieu's reference is to Sir William Petty's *Essay in Political Arthmetick*, published in 1686.

39. In order, Rousseau apparently refers to the conquest of Persia by Alexander the Great (334–330 B.C.); the inability of the Persians to conquer the Scythians (see especially the account of the invasion, led by Darius Hystaspis in 512 B.C., in Herodotus, *Histories* IV. 118–142); Rome's conquest of Carthage in the Three Punic Wars (265–241 B.C., 218–202 B.C., and 150–146 B.C. respectively); the invasion and conquest of Rome by the Goths, Huns, and Vandals, which culminated in the "fall of Rome" to Odoacer in A.D. 476; the conquest of the Gauls by the Franks and the Saxon invasions of Britain in the fifth century A.D.; the victories of the Swiss over the Austrian Hapsburgs Leopold I (1315) and Leopold III (1386) and over Charles the Bold, duke of Burgundy (1476); and finally the successful revolt of the Netherlands against King Philip II of Spain (1566–1579). These historical references are particularly interesting because of the element of exaggeration present in many of them. The first example (the conquest of "The Monarchy of Cyrus" by an army of 30,000 men under a "prince who was poorer than the least significant Persian satrap") can only refer to the ultimate defeat of the Achaemenian dynasty founded by Cyrus the Great because Persia was never conquered during the reign of Cyrus himself (although Cyrus was killed while fighting the Massagetae, a savage tribe east of the Caspian). Rousseau's statement of the event thus tends to mislead the hasty reader, who will not immediately recognize that Alexander the Great had become master of Greece before attacking Persia. Similarly, although Rome was not as wealthy as Carthage prior to its victory in the Punic Wars, the Roman republic was hardly "nothing" at the time; and the "handful of herring-fishers" who defeated Spain were the extremely prosperous Dutch, whose development of commerce and industry formed an indispensable basis for the successful revolt of the Northern Provinces of the Netherlands.

40. The reference is clearly to Plato's *Republic*, especially Book V, 451–457 (where Socrates argues that the education and activities of women must equal those of men in the best city). Rousseau later developed this theme in Book V of *Émile*.

41. Rousseau here complains about the poor taste of French (and especially Parisian) society, with particular emphasis on the growing dislike of the classical dramas of Corneille and Racine, and the refusal to accept—or even listen seriously to—Italian music (see Havens, pp. 244–245).

42. François Marie Arouet (1694–1788), universally known as Voltaire. Rousseau's refusal to cite the most famous author of his time by his pen name is, in this context, hardly accidental; to be famous in eighteenth-century France, Rousseau implies, one must put on a false front. Compare Havens, pp. 225–26.

43. Charles-André ("Carle") Van Loo (1705–1765) and Jean-Baptiste-Marie Pierre (1713–1789) were famous contemporary painters whose works were sometimes criticized by Diderot (Havens, pp. 226–27).

44. Jean-Baptiste Pigalle (1714–1785), French sculptor whose statues were in fashion at the time of the writing of the *First Discourse* (Havens, p. 228). The relative obscurity of these contemporaries named by Rousseau would seem to confirm his point that to gain fame in a corrupted society one must sacrifice those qualities that produce lasting fame.

45. Michel de Montaigne. The preceding two sentences, as well as the remainder of this one, are taken virtually word for word from Montaigne's "Of Pedantry" (Frame, 106).

46. Rousseau thus cites Diderot's anonymous work, *Pensées Philosophiques*, in which the distinction between awe of God and fear of God is made in Pensée 8 (see Havens, pp. 234–236). It should be noted that shortly after its publication in 1746, *Pensées Philosophiques* was condemned and burned by the Parlement of Paris as "scandalous, and contrary to Religion and Morals" (Arthur M. Wilson, *Diderot: the Testing Years* [New York: Oxford University Press, 1957], 55).

47. Rousseau again borrows from Montaigne's "Of Pedantry," *Essays* I:25 (Frame, 106).

48. Montaigne puns here by using the Greek verb "to strike" or "beat" as his example.

49. All of this long note, with the exception of the first and last sentences of the first two paragraphs, is quoted from Montaigne's "Of Pedantry" (Frame, 105, 123–124). Rousseau changes the order of the paragraphs, however, and makes one significant omission.

50. Louis XIV, king of France from 1643 to 1715, founded at least five academies: Académie Royale des Beaux-Arts (1648), Académie des Inscriptions et Belles Lettres (1663), Académie d'Architecture (1671), Académie des Beaux-Arts at Rome (1677), and Académie des Jeux Floraux (1694). The first and most important, however, was the Académie française, formally constituted in 1635 under Louis XIII; *le grand monarque* (as Louis XIV was called) did not originate the institution for which he is praised. This hollow commendation of Louis XIV is paralleled by a similar instance of "damning with false praise" in the *Second Discourse*.

51. It may be suggested that the foregoing sentences allude, respectively, to Berkeley (1685–1753), Spinoza (1632–1677), Mandeville (c. 1670–1733), and Hobbes (1588–1679).

52. Francis Bacon, first Baron Verulam and Viscount St. Albans (1561–1626), who received his title after becoming Lord Chancellor of England in 1618.

53. The reference is to Cicero and Bacon. Note that Rousseau's earlier reference to the latter as "Verulam" is not accidental—compare note 52.

54. This comparison between Sparta and Athens is also drawn from Montaigne's "Of Pedantry" (Frame, 105).

EDITORIAL NOTES TO
"Observations on the Discourse"

1. This notice announcing Rousseau's prize-winning discourse was presumably written by the Abbé Guillaume-Thomas-François Raynal (1713–1790), editor of the *Mercury of France* and a friend of Rousseau. It was published, along with Rousseau's reply ("Letter to Raynal," pp. 25–27), in the June 1751 number of the *Mercury*.

EDITORIAL NOTES TO
"Letter to M. the Abbé Raynal"

1. See *First Discourse*, Second part, p. 14.

2. Since this "expanded work" probably became the *Discourse on the Origin of Inequality*, Rousseau's reaction to the prospective criticisms of his *First Discourse* contradicts the thesis that these attacks led him to change his fundamental principles. (See Introduction, note 3).

EDITORIAL NOTES TO
"Reply to the Discourse . . . by the King of Poland"

1. Originally published anonymously, this reply was later formally attributed to King Stanislaus I of Poland (1677–1766). Rousseau assumed that portions were contributed by a Jesuit advisor, Father de Menou. See *Confessions*, Book VIII (Pléiade, I, 366). The "Reply" appeared in the *Mercury of France* of September 1751.

2. The *First Discourse* was originally published anonymously, with Rousseau identified simply as a Citizen of Geneva.

EDITORIAL NOTES TO
"Observations by Jean-Jacques Rousseau of Geneva"

1. Rousseau's rejoinder to King Stanislaus of Poland appeared in the *Mercury of France*, October 1751. At the time Rousseau wrote it, the king's authorship was still anonymous.

2. Pliny the Younger wrote a "Panegyric" of the Emperor Trajan.

3. See Saint Augustine, *De Doctrina Christiana*, Book II, chapter 40, and *Exod.* 12:35, 33:22

4. Several sources report King Alphonso X of Spain (1252–1284), known as Alphonso the Wise, as having said that if God had consulted him, he could have given him advice about improving creation.

5. Rousseau refers to the "Preliminary Discourse" of Diderot's *Encyclopedia*. The "Discourse" was written by Jean LeRond d'Alembert and was published in 1751.

6. Rousseau does not copy this paragraph accurately. Cf. p. 32 above.

7. Rousseau refers to Molière's play.

8. Tertullian (c. 155–c. 220) was one of the early Church Fathers.

9. "He discarded friendship because it was not favorable either to the ignorant or the learned. . . . He said it is reasonable that the prudent man should not expose himself to dangers by patriotism, that he ought not in fact to renounce this prudence for the benefit of imbeciles. He taught that when it is opportune, the wise man can devote himself to theft and to adultery as well as to sacrilege. Nothing, in truth, is shameful by its nature. It was necessary to root out an opinion born from the popular opinion of fools and simpletons. . . . The wise man could frequent courtesans without becoming suspect because of it" (Diogenes Laertius, *Life of the Philosophers*, "Aristippus").

10. Clement of Alexandria (c. 150–c. 215), another Church Father.

11. Said of Pope Gregory the Great (590–604): see Bayle's *Dictionary*, under "Grégoire I."

12. "Not in the way of Aristotle, but in the way of the Fisherman."

13. In a manuscript, Rousseau added a note naming "the Duke de la Rochefoucauld"; he refers to Maxim 218.

14. Cartouche (1693–1721) was a famous bandit. In the *Social Contract* (IV, 8), Rousseau also accuses Oliver Cromwell (1599–1658) of being an ambitious hypocrite; see Pléiade III, 466.

15. In both the Pléiade and the Intégrale editions, two lines are missing from the text of this note. This error is all the more important because it obscures Rousseau's great subtlety in understanding what would today be called the methodology of crosscultural and historical anthropology and sociology. This omission has been noted by Victor Gourevitch in his translation of *The First and Second Discourses Together with the Replies to Critics and Essay on the Origin of Languages* (New York: Harper and Row, 1986), 314.

16. Stanislaus had just founded the Royal Academy of Sciences and Letters at Nancy.

EDITORIAL NOTES TO
"Refutation of the Observations"

1. This "Refutation" is by Claude-Nicolas Lecat, a professor of anatomy and permanent secretary of the Academy of Rouen; Lecat also wrote the Refutation below (pp. 130–174).

2. See "Observations," above p. 39.

3. Ibid., p. 40.

4. Ibid., p. 38.

5. *First Discourse*, above, p. 4.

6. Ibid., pp. 21–22.

7. "In turn it is the one necessary thing."

8. "Observations," above, p. 38.

9. Ibid., p. 48.

10. The reference is to plays by Molière and Delisle de la Drévetière.

11. *First Discourse*, above, p. 4.

12. "Observations," above, p. 41.

13. Ibid., p. 41.

14. Ibid., p. 47.

15. Nicolas Boileau-Desprèaux (1638–1711) was a prominent poet and critic. Among his most important works are the *Satires*, quoted here, and *The Poetic Art*, also cited by Lecat. Lulli is the original Italian spelling of the last name of Jean-Baptiste Lully (1633–1687), music master of Louis XIV who dominated French music.

16. Ibid., p. 51.

17. Ibid., p. 53.

18. "We have a defendant who has confessed."

EDITORIAL NOTES TO
"Refutation . . . by Mr. Gautier"

1. M. Gautier, a professor at Lunéville, published this refutation in the *Mercury of France*, October 1751.

2. See above, pp. 5–6.

3. See above, p. 6.

4. See above, p. 6.

5. Gautier refers to the Greek historian Herodotus (c. 480–c. 425 B.C., the Roman historian Justan (first century A.D.) and geographer Strabo (13 B.C.–A.D.25). For Rousseau's response, see pp. 85–86 below.

6. Charles Rollin (1661–1741) was the author of *Ancient History*.

7. See above, p. 12.

8. See above, p. 12.

9. See above, p. 12.

10. See above, p. 12.

11. See above, p. 13.

12. See above, p. 13.

13. These are ancient skeptics who denied the possibility of knowledge.

14. See above, p. 13.

15. See above, p. 19.

16. See above, p. 16.

17. See above, p. 17.

18. See above, pp. 18–19.

19. See above, p. 20.

EDITORIAL NOTES TO
"Letter to Mr. Grimm"

1. This letter was published as a brochure in November 1751. In 1763, after Rousseau's break with Grimm, he asked his publisher, Duchesne, to replace

Grimm's name with three asterisks (thereby implying that his friendship at the time was germane to the tone of his rejoinder to Gautier).

See p. 79 above.

3. Carneades (214–129 B.C.) was, as Rousseau implies, a Greek philosopher. He was a skeptic who argued against Stoicism.

4. This passage is from p. 72 above. The last sentence departs from Gautier's version.

5. See pp. 77–78 above.

6. See p. 76 above.

7. "bitter humor."

EDITORIAL NOTES TO
"Discourse on the Advantages of the Sciences and the Arts"

1. Charles Bordes presented this discourse to the Academy of Lyons on June 22, 1751; it was first published in the *Mercury of France* in December of that year. Bordes was an old friend of Rousseau.

2. The French word *savant*, translated here and elsewhere in this discourse as "scientist," has usually been translated as "learned" when rendering Rousseau's texts. In eighteenth-century French, there is no word that means exactly what we mean by "scientist," although the word *savant* is often used with this meaning. For example, in *Considérations sur les moeurs de ce siècle*, published around the time of the *First Discourse*, Rousseau's friend Charles Duclos says, "There is another order of *savants* who are occupied with the exact sciences." Thus, the word is broader than either those learned in the traditional disciplines of scholarship or those devoted to the natural sciences; Rousseau often uses it to encompass both.

3. Bordes is referring to Caligula.

4. Bordes refers, respectively, to Czar Peter I, commonly called Peter the Great, and Frederick the Great.

5. These battles all took place during the War of the Austrian Succession (1740–1748). Montalban occurred in 1744; Lawfelt, in 1747; the retreat from Prague, in the winter of 1742–1743; the retreat from Bavaria, in 1743; and Berg-op-Zoom, in 1747.

6. The first volume of the *Encyclopedia* of Diderot and d'Alembert, to which Rousseau had contributed, appeared in 1751.

7. Lucius Junius Brutus led the revolt that overthrew the Tarquins; he condemned to death his own sons Titus and Tiberinus after they conspired to restore the rule of the Tarquins. Publius Decius Mus, his son and grandson were Romans of the third and second centuries B.C. who pledged themselves to the infernal gods in return for Roman military victories. Lucretia committed suicide after having been raped by Sextus, the son of Tarquin the Proud (510 B.C.). Caius Mucius Scaevola burned his own hand to punish himself for failing to kill King Porsenna during the siege of Rome by the Etruscans (507 B.C.). (See Intégrale, II, 149.)

8. Lucius Quinctius Cincinnatus (born c. 519 B.C.) was twice called from his small farm to be dictator of Rome. Publius Cornelius Scipio Aemilianus Afri-

canus Numantinus (185–129 B.C.), also known as Scipio the Younger, was the destroyer of Carthage and a strong proponent of Greek learning. He was friendly with the playwright Terence and Gaius Laelius, member of an important plebian family. Laelius and Scipio were important characters in Cicero's *De Republics*. For information on Fabricius, see note 31 to the *First Discourse*, p. 11. Titus was emperor of Rome from A.D. 79 to 81, was very learned in Greek, and was known for his generosity.

EDITORIAL NOTES TO
"Final Reply"

1. Rousseau originally intended this reply to Charles Bordes's "Discourse on the Advantages of the Sciences and Arts," published in the *Mercury* in April 1752, to close the debate over his *First Discourse*. Although he ultimately published another defense ("Letter [to Lecat]", pp. 175–179) and, after Bordes published a rejoinder in 1753, started the manuscript of a "Second Letter to Bordes" (below, pp. 182–185), the "Final Reply" is one of the clearest statements of his paradoxical and often misunderstood position. See Pléiade, II, 1270–1271, 1283 and compare *Confessions*, Book VIII (Pléiade, I, 366).

2. In 1761, Rousseau explained that he had used the words "Citizen of Geneva" only "on those works that I think will do honor" to the city (*La Nouvelle Héloïse*, Second Preface [Pléiade, II, 27]); hence, this self-identification indicates the importance he attached to the "Final Reply." Such an interpretation is not contradicted by the fact that, on a copy of his text intended for a corrected edition of his *Collected Writings*, Rousseau later deleted the words "of Geneva" (Plèiade, I, 1270). These corrections are subsequent to the condemnation of Rousseau's work by Geneva in 1762 and include a similar deletion on the title page of the *First Discourse* (Pléiade, I, 1240).

3. "We must no longer remain silent for fear that silence seem to be dictated by weakness rather than by discretion" St. Cyprian (c. 210–258) was bishop of Carthage.

4. Plutarch, "On Tranquillity of Mind," 4; *Moralia*, 466D; Loeb Classical Library, trans. W. C. Helmbold (London: Heinemann, 1939), VI, 177.

5. Plutarch, "On Envy and Hate," 5; *Moralia*, 537D; Loeb Classical Library, trans. Philip H. De Lacey and Benedict Einarson (London: Heinemann, 1959), VII, 101. This same text had been cited, without an attribution to a Spartan king, by Montaigne, *Essays*, III, xii, *ad finem*. In the manuscript of corrections (see note 2 above), Rousseau added: *quod malos boni oderint, bonos oportet esse* ("That good men hate the wicked is the proof of their goodness). Cf. Plutarch, "On Moral Virtue," 12; *Moralia*, 451E (Loeb ed., VI, 81).

6. Note that, as in the text of the *First Discourse*, Rousseau speaks of "artists" where Plato had referred to "artisans": cf. *Apology*, 23e and *First Discourse*, p. 10 and Introduction, note 10.

7. In the manuscript corrected when preparing republication of his works, referring to the legal prosecution to which he had been subject, Rousseau added the note: "It will be remarked that I said this as early as the year 1752" (Pléiade, III, 1272; Intégrale, II, 142).

8. On Cyrus and Alexander, see Plutarch, "Of Curiosity," 13; *Moralia*, 521F–522A (Loeb ed., VI, 509). On Scipio, Rousseau seems to refer to a saying attributed to Scipio the Elder when he captured Carthage as a man of twenty-five; Plutarch, "Sayings of the Romans," *Moralia*, 196B (Loeb ed., III, 163).

9. There was a refutation of Rousseau, in the form of a dialogue in Latin, at the graduation ceremonies of the College of Geneva on May 23, 1751. Actually, however, it appears that the sixteen-year-old Jean-Alphonse Turrettini praised Rousseau's position, and the condemnation was presented by the Pastor Jacob Vernes (Pléiade, III, 1273; Intègrale, II, 143).

10. See p. 94 above.

11. See p. 93 above.

12. See pp. 95–97 above.

13. This note and the immediately following paragraph in the text show that there is no sharp break between the *First* and *Second Discourses*.

14. Cf. Cicero, *On Divination*, I, xli; Diodorus of Sicily, II, xxiv; III, lx; I, xciv; Strabo, III, 39.

15. See p. 93 above.

16. Three Athenian generals: Miltiades (died 489 B.C.); Aristides (540–468 B.C.); Themistocles (525–460 B.C.). Socrates lived from 467 to 400/399 B.C.; Plato, from 429 to 347 B.C.

17. See p. 94 above.

18. See p. 94 above.

19. Cicero's famous orations against Catiline and the Catilinarian conspiracy of 63 B.C. were traditional models of rhetoric. For the texts, see Cicero, *Selected Political Speeches,* trans. Michael Grant (Baltimore: Penguin, 1969), 71–145.

20. See pp. 94–95 above.

21. Cf. Thucydides, *History of the Peloponnesian War,* I, 89–93 (New York: Modern Library, n.d.) 51–54.

22. See pp. 94–95 above.

23. A variant reads: "Open your eyes and leave your blindness."

24. Cf. Plato, *Gorgias,* 515a.

25. See p. 104 above.

26. Plato, *Republic,* 613a–b. Cf. *Phaedo*, 63b–c, 80d–84b, 114d–115a.

27. See p. 100 above.

28. Montaigne, *Essays,* I, xxxvii, "Of Cato the Younger."

29. Plutarch, "Sayings of the Romans," *Moralia*, 194 F (Loeb ed., III, 155).

30. Rousseau explicitly raises this question in *Émile*, (Bloom, p. 463). Cf. *Social Contract,* III, i: "the larger the state grows, the less freedom there is."

31. "It is a spectacle worthy of the gaze of God, who watches over the work of his hands: the spectacle of a quasi-divine battle that pits a brave man against bad fortune. I see nothing, I say, that seems nobler to Jupiter's eyes when he deigns to contemplate it than this spectacle of Cato who, his faction in complete defeat, remains standing among the ruins of the State" (Seneca, *On Providence*, II).

32. See p. 107 above.

Plutarch, "Publicola," *Lives of the Illustrious Men,* trans. J. Langhorne and W. Langhorne (London: Bohn, 1855), I, 115.

34. Emperor from A.D. 79 to 81.

35. "Both as a private citizen and later as his father's colleague, Titus had been not only unpopular but venomously loathed. However, this pessimistic view stood him in good stead: [as soon as everyone realized that here was no monster of vice but an exceptionally noble character], public opinion flew to the opposite extreme" (Suetonius, "Titus," *Lives of the Twelve Caesars*, 1, 7; trans. Robert Graves [Baltimore: Penguin Books, 1957], 287, 290). Rousseau combines two separate sentences, omitting the phrase in brackets.

36. "So the Spartan, when he was asked what he effected by his teaching, said, 'I make honorable things pleasant to children'" (Plutarch, "Can Virtue Be Taught," 2, *Moralia*, 439F [Loeb ed., VI, 9]). Cf. "On Moral "Virtue," 12; *Moralia*, 452D (ibid., 87).

37. See p. 107 above.

38. Montaigne, *Essays*, III, vi, "Of Coaches."

39. See p. 105 above. In his revision of the manuscript (see above, note 2), Rousseau inserted here the sentence: "So that a man who was amusing himself at the side of a highway by shooting at the passers-by could say that he was keeping busy during his leisure to protect himself from idleness."

40. See p. 101 above.

41. Cf. *Second Discourse*, Part 1 (Masters, I, p. 110): "If nature destined us to be healthy, I almost dare affirm that the state of reflection is a state contrary to nature and that the man who meditates is a depraved animal."

42. As Victor Gourevitch has noted in *The First and Second Discourses Together with the Replies to Critics and Essays on the Origin of Languages* (New York: Harper and Row, 1986), 321, these words are incorrectly italicized in the *Pléiade* and *Intégrale* editions.

43. Rousseau lists artisans in style in the middle of the eighteenth century: Hebert was a jeweler who worked for the court at Versailles; the brothers Martin were cabinetmakers; Lafrenaye was the model of the character Frenicol in Diderot's *Les Bijoux Indiscrets* (Intégrale, II, 151).

44. See p. 99 above.

45. "A good mind does not need a broad literary culture" (Seneca, *Moral Letters*, cvi; cited by Montaigne, *Essays*, III, xii). Cf. Charon, *De la Sagesse*, III, xiv.

46. See p. 105 above.

47. Plato, *Phaedrus*, 274b–278b.

48. "Whether he is a Trojan or a Roman" (Virgil, *Aeneid*, X, 108). Jupiter declares that he will have no preference for one or for the other.

49. Perhaps the projected "Second Reply to Bordes," of which only the preface was written. See below, pp. 182–185.

50. See *First Discourse*, Part 2 (p. 18).

51. See p. 102 above.

52. See p. 104 above.

53. See p. 106 above.

54. Jean François Melon (1680–1738), author of the *Essay politique sur la commerce* (1734), which applied the principles of Sir William Petty, the English economist who had been indirectly criticized in Part 2 of the *First Discourse* (p. 14 and editorial note 36).

EDITORIAL NOTES TO
"Refutation . . . by an Academician of Dijon"

1. This "Refutation" was the work of Claude-Nicolas Lecat who was also the author of the "Refutation" above, pp. 55–69. He was, in fact, not a member of the Dijon Academy as he pretends to be in this work. This "Refutation" appeared in late 1751 along with a reprint of the *First Discourse*.

2. *First Discourse*, p. 21.

3. "Here I am the barbarian, because no one understands me," from Ovid's *Tristia*, Book V, Elegy X.37, is the epigraph of the *First Discourse*. See editorial note 1 to the *Discourse*.

4. "To sum up, the wise man is inferior to Jove alone, free, honored, beautiful, and in short king of kings" (Horace, *Epistles*, Book I, Letter 1).

5. "We are deceived by the appearance of right" (from Horace, *On the Art of Poetry*, v. 25) is the second epigraph of the *First Discourse*.

6. "In sum there are certain limits fixed, on this or that side of which the right cannot stand" (Horace, *Satires*, I, 1, 106–107). We would like to thank Jay Freyman of the Ancient Studies Department of the University of Maryland Baltimore County for locating this passage.

7. Lecat cites the opening paragraph of the *Discourse*, see *First Discourse*, p. 4.

8. "We are mere numbers, born to consume the fruits of the earth" (Horace, *Epistles*, I, 2, 27).

9. "But if you could you only lay aside the frigid poultices of cares, / you would go where heavenly wisdom led you / Let us, both high and low complete this work, this application, quickly, / if we wish to live, loved by our country, by ourselves."

10. Lecat cites the beginning of the second paragraph of the Discourse, *First Discourse*, p. 4.

11. *First Discourse*, p. 4.

12. *First Discourse*, p. 4.

13. *First Discourse*, p. 4.

14. *First Discourse*, p. 4.

15. *First Discourse*, p. 4.

16. *First Discourse*, p. 4.

17. *First Discourse*, pp. 4–5.

18. *First Discourse*, p. 5.

19. *First Discourse*, p. 5.

20. *First Discourse*, p. 5.

21. *First Discourse*, p. 5.

22. *First Discourse*, p. 5.

23. *First Discourse*, p. 5.

24. *First Discourse*, p. 5.

25. *First Discourse*, p. 5.

26. *First Discourse*, pp. 5–6.

27. *First Discourse*, p. 6.

28. "Either virtue is an empty word, or the experienced man rightly strives after honor and reward" (Horace, *Epistles* I, 17, l. 41–42).

29. *First Discourse*, p. 6.

30. *First Discourse*, p. 6.

31. *First Discourse*, p. 6.

32. *First Discourse*, p. 6.

33. "Everything suits Aristippus, show, position, fortune" Horace, *Epistles*, I, 17, l. 23.

34. *First Discourse*, p. 6.

35. On Nimrod, see *Gen.* 10:8–10.

36. Anthropophagi are cannibals.

37. Cartouche, Nivet, and Raffiat were notorious highwaymen. Cartouche, whose real name was Louis-Dominique Bourguignon (1693–1721), is discussed later in this essay. See also p. 50 above.

38. "Do not do to another what you would not have done to you."

39. *First Discourse*, p. 6.

40. *First Discourse*, p. 6.

41. *First Discourse*, p. 6.

42. "The beginning of wisdom is fear of the Lord." *Prov.*, 1:7.

43. *First Discourse*, p. 6.

44. *First Discourse*, p. 6.

45. *First Discourse*, p. 6.

46. *First Discourse*, pp. 6–7.

47. Molière, *Misanthrope*, Act I, Scene 1.

48. It is in fact Philinte who delivers this response to Alceste, the Misanthrope.

49. *First Discourse*, p. 7.

50. *First Discourse*, p. 7.

51. *First Discourse*, p. 7.

52. *First Discourse*, p. 7.

53. *First Discourse*, pp. 7–8.

54. *First Discourse*, p. 8.

55. *First Discourse*, p. 8.

56. *First Discourse*, p. 8.

57. *First Discourse*, p. 8.

58. The Parcae are the Roman versions of the three fates.

59. Vincent Voiture (1598–1648) was a French poet and academician.

60. *First Discourse*, pp. 8–9.

61. *First Discourse*, p. 9.

62. Astrea, sometimes identified with Diké (Justice) lived among humans during the Golden Age. See Ovid, *Metamorphosis*, I, 150.

63. This remark occurs at the beginning of Fontenelle's *Digression sur les Anciens et les Modernes*, published in 1686. Rousseau cites it in Book IV of *Émile*, Bloom edition, p. 343.

64. "The brave are created from the brave and good. . . . But learning increases innate life, and just culture stengthens the heart."

65. In the text, Lecat gives a rough translation of a passage from Cicero's *Pro Archia Poeta*.

66. "Thus each demands the other's help, and unites in an oath of friendship."

67. *First Discourse*, p. 9.

68. This story is in Plutarch's life of Aristides.

69. *First Discourse*, p. 9.

70. Alexander the Great.

71. Christian Wolff (1679–1754) was living under Frederick the Great at the time Lecat was writing.

72. *First Discourse*, p. 9.

73. "O the times, O the morals!" This is Cicero's famous exclamation over the corruption of his age; it occurs in numerous places in his works, perhaps most famously in *In Catilinam*, I.1,2.

74. *First Discourse*, p. 10.

75. *First Discourse*, p. 10.

76. *First Discourse*, pp. 10–11.

77. *First Discourse*, p. 11.

78. *First Discourse*, p. 11.

79. *First Discourse*, pp. 11–12.

80. *First Discourse*, p. 12.

81. *First Discourse*, p. 12.

82. *First Discourse*, p. 12.

83. *First Discourse*, p. 12.

84. *First Discourse*, p. 12.

85. "And the pious poets whose words were worthy of Phoebus, or those who embellished life refinement by the arts. All these have their brows encircled with bands as white as snow." The lines are in fact, Virgil, *Aeneid,* VI, 662, 663, and 665. Lecat leaves out the line, "And they who by their good deeds won the gratitude of others." He also begins the quotation after other members of the list who receive the highest honors although they did not practice the arts and sciences.

86. On the frontispiece, see *First Discourse*, p. 12.

87. *First Discourse*, p. 12.

88. As the Pléiade editors have noted, Rousseau's word *feuilletter* is an unusual word and had a variety of senses at the time Rousseau used it, ranging from examining a book lightly to studying with application (Pléiade III, n.1 to p. 17).

89. *First Discourse*, p. 12.

90. *First Discourse*, p. 12.

91. *First Discourse*, p. 12.

92. *First Discourse*, p. 12.

93. *First Discourse*, p. 12.

94. *First Discourse*, p. 12.

95. *First Discourse*, p. 12.

96. *First Discourse*, p. 12.

97. *First Discourse*, pp. 12–13.

98. *First Discourse*, p. 13.

99. *First Discourse*, p. 13.

100. *First Discourse*, p. 13.
101. Clenard was a professor at the University of Louvain who wrote a Greek primer. For Rousseau's response to this point, see below, p. 177.
102. *First Discourse*, p. 13.
103. *First Discourse*, p. 13.
104. *First Discourse*, p. 13.
105. *First Discourse*, p. 13.
106. *First Discourse*, pp. 13–14.
107. *First Discourse*, p. 14.
108. *First Discourse*, p. 14.
109. *First Discourse*, p. 14.
110. *First Discourse*, pp. 14–15.
111. *First Discourse*, p. 15.
112. *First Discourse*, p. 15.
113. *First Discourse*, p. 15.
114. *Belle nature*, the term translated as "beautiful nature," is one of the key terms in seventeenth- and eighteenth-century thought about the beautiful. It is meant to show how art can be confined to the imitation of nature and also to the beautiful. Thus, art imitates, not nature as such, but *la belle nature*.
115. Jean Baptiste Louis Gresset (1709–1777) was a French poet and playwright. His best known work is *The Wicked Man*, from which comes this line.
116. Followers of Aristotle. Lecat speaks of the modern revolt against ancient and Christian Aristotelianism that took place in the seventeenth century.
117. *First Discourse*, p. 15.
118. *First Discourse*, pp. 15–16.
119. Lecat refers to the leading sculptors of the day, Jean-Baptiste LeMoyne (1704–1778); Edme Bouchardon (1698–1762); the Adams brothers, Lambert Sigisbert (1700–1759), Nicholas Sebastien (1705–1778), and Francois Gaspard Balthazar (1710–1761); and Rene Michel (or Michel Ange) Slodtz (1705–1764).
120. *First Discourse*, p. 16.
121. *First Discourse*, p. 16.
122. *First Discourse*, p. 16.
123. *First Discourse*, p. 16.
124. *First Discourse*, pp. 16–17.
125. *First Discourse*, p. 17.
126. *First Discourse*, p. 17.
127. *First Discourse*, p. 17.
128. *First Discourse*, p. 17.
129. *First Discourse*, p. 17.
130. *First Discourse*, pp. 17–18.
131. "Good Athens added a little more to my art, namely that I might be able to distinguish the straight from the crooked and to seek the truth in the groves of the Academy."
132. *First Discourse*, p. 18.
133. These are all terms from card games. They refer, respectively, to the ace of clubs, ace of hearts, nine of diamonds, and nine of clubs.

134. Jean Francois Regnard (1655–1709). *The Gambler* (*Le Joueur*) is probably his best known piece. It was first performed in 1696.

135. *First Discourse*, p. 18.

136. *First Discourse*, p. 18.

137. *First Discourse*, p. 18.

138. *First Discourse*, p. 18.

139. *First Discourse*, pp. 18–19.

140. *First Discourse*, p. 19.

141. *The Frenchman in London* was written by Louis Boissy (1694–1758).

142. See note 115 above.

143. *First Discourse*, p. 19.

144. *First Discourse*, p. 19.

145. *First Discourse*, p. 19.

146. *First Discourse*, p. 19.

147. *First Discourse*, p. 19.

148. *First Discourse*, pp. 19–20.

149. *First Discourse*, p. 20.

150. *First Discourse*, p. 20.

151. *First Discourse*, p. 20.

152. *First Discourse*, p. 20.

153. *First Discourse*, p. 20.

154. *First Discourse*, p. 20.

155. *First Discourse*, p. 20.

156. *First Discourse*, p. 20.

157. *First Discourse*, p. 20.

158. Origen (c. 185–c. 254) was a prolific writer in defense of Christianity. Antoine Arnauld (1612–1694) was a Jansenist theologian who wrote *The Perpetuity of the Catholic Faith Concerning the Eucharist* against Calvinism. Jacques Bossuet (1627–1704) was the most prominent theologian of his time and wrote *History of the Variations of the Protestant Churches* against Protestantism.

159. *First Discourse*, pp. 20–21.

160. *First Discourse*, p. 21.

161. *First Discourse*, p. 21.

162. *First Discourse*, p. 21.

163. *First Discourse*, p. 21.

164. *First Discourse*, p. 21. As noted in the context of Rousseau's passage, Verulam is Sir Francis Bacon.

165. *First Discourse*, p. 21.

166. *First Discourse*, p. 21.

167. *First Discourse*, p. 21.

168. *First Discourse*, pp. 21–22.

169. *First Discourse*, p. 22.

170. *First Discourse*, p. 22.

171. *First Discourse*, p. 22.

172. *First Discourse*, p. 22.

173. This is the Latin translated by Lecat above.

174. The "Reply" by Stanislaus.

EDITORIAL NOTES TO
"Letter by Jean-Jacques Rousseau to Lecat"

1. This reply was published in 1752.
2. Rousseau's term (*gens de lettres*) carries the sense of what has since come to be called "the intellectuals," though this word was not in use in his time.
3. The topic of the prize competition of the French Academy in 1752 was "Love of Letters Inspires Love of Virtue." See above, p. 39.
4. See "Refutation," above, p. 133.
5. This note could be cited as added confirmation that Rousseau's "system" of thought was developed by the time he published the *First Discourse*. While owning private property would not have been contrary to Rousseau's criticism of the arts and sciences, it is surely difficult to reconcile with the attack on property (especially at the beginning of Part 2 of the *Discourse on Inequality*. Cf. the editor's Introduction, note 3, with the "Preface to a Second Letter to Bordes," below p. 184.
6. Rousseau refers to the "Discourse on the Advantages of the Sciences and Arts" by Charles Bordes (pp. 93–109).
7. Rousseau's "Final Reply" (pp. 110–129).
8. Nicholas Clenard was a professor of Greek and Hebrew who wrote *Institutiones in linguam graecam* and *Nouvelle Méthode*.
9. "Why, if I can gain a little something, should I abstain from it, when the speech of Cato and Ennius enriched the language of the homeland" (Horace, *On the Art of Poetry*, 55–57).
10. "what their shoulders can bear" (Horace, *On the Art of Poetry*, 40).
11. *First Discourse*, p. 4.
12. Spanish theologian and mystic (1235–1315).

EDITORIAL NOTES TO
"Disclaimer by the Dijon Academy"

1. Lecat made a response to this disclaimer (see Launay, pp. 176–180) in which he defended himself for having disguised his identity in writing his "Refutation."

EDITORIAL NOTES TO
"Preface to a Second Letter to Bordes"

1. This is the beginning of a response to the *Second Discourse on the Benefits of the Sciences and Arts*, published by Charles Bordes in August 1753 in reply to Rousseau's "Final Reply." Rousseau never finished the "Second Letter to Bordes" and did not publish this preface; instead, he turned his attention to his own *Discourse on the Origin of Inequality*. Rousseau's draft manuscript, dating from 1753, is nonetheless extremely important because it indicates clearly the plan Rousseau followed in the publishing works based on his "system." See editors' Introduction, note 3, and Masters, *Political Philosophy of Rousseau*, (Princeton, N.J.: Princeton University Press, 1968), pp. x–xv.

EDITORIAL NOTES TO
"Preface to Narcissus"

1. *Narcissus* was performed on December 18, 1752. For an account of its reception see *Confessions*, Book VIII (Pléiade, I, 387–388). In this context Rousseau says, "In the Preface which is one of my good writings, I began to expose my principles a little more than I had done until then." It was published in 1753. The play itself is of importance for showing Rousseau's early reflections on the issues of vanity and love.

2. In the *Confessions*, Rousseau says that, in fact, he wrote it several years later. See *Confessions*, Book III (Pléiade, I, 120). Before its performance it was touched up by Marivaux.

3. Throughout his works Rousseau very consistently distinguishes between "convincing," which produces agreement through rational argument, and "persuading," which produces agreement by an appeal to feelings or passions. For example, in Book II, chapter 7, of the *Social Contract*, he argues that the legislator must persuade the people to accept his laws because they are in no condition to be convinced by rational argument. Rousseau makes the same distinction in chapter 4 of the *Essay on the Origin of Languages* when he discusses the emotional power of the earliest human languages which could "persuade without convincing."

4. This is a paraphrase of the beginning of a speech by Johann Friedrich Burscher given in 1752.

5. See above, pp. 180–181. Note Rousseau's disingenuous implication that he was otherwise unaware of Lecat's attack, to which he had already responded.

6. Elsewhere this word is usually translated as "the learned." See note 2 to p. 96 above.

7. "Enough talking, not enough wisdom." This is Rousseau's correction. The original addition read *eloquentiae* instead of *loquentiae*, eloquence instead of talking. This original reading is a citation from Sallust's *Catiline Conspiracy*, V, 4.

8. This remark can be considered as of particular importance for considering Rousseau's abandonment of his illegitimate children because it was written only a few years after he first began to reflect seriously on this abandonment. Cf. *Confessions*, Book VIII (Pléiade, I, 356–358).

9. Compare the the formulation of the question posed by the Academy of Dijon. See p. 1 above.

10. *The Wicked Man* is a play by Gresset, first performed in 1747.

11. Leucippus and Protagoras lived during the fifth century B.C.; Diogenes the Cynic, during the fourth; Pyrrho, during the fourth and third; and Lucretius, during the first. They were atomists, skeptics, or atheists. Thomas Hobbes (1588–1679) was the author of *Leviathan*. Bernard Mandeville (1670–1733) was the author of *The Fable of the Bees*. Rousseau discusses him in the *Second Discourse*. The fact that these thinkers lived in rather separated periods indicates that Rousseau is not arguing for a simple historical decline. Furthermore, the emphasis on the consequences of the doctrines of Hobbes and Mandeville indicates that the modern project of publicizing doctrines has more widespread effects than the

mere existence of comparable doctrines in antiquity. On this point see p. 20 above.

12. Montaigne, "Of Physiognomy," *Essays*, III, 12. The word *vain* is Rousseau's addition.

13. This passage bears a striking resemblance to Burke's attack on the substitution of artificial bonds (private interest, law, and terror) for natural ones in his *Reflections on the Revolution in France*. Ironically, Burke includes Rousseau among the philosophers he holds responsible for such pernicious artifice.

14. This note outlines the core of the argument of the *Discourse on the Origin of Inequality*.

15. "He is not swayed by the fasces of the people, nor by the King's purple, nor by the discord setting faithless brothers against each other; Nor by Roman affairs, nor realms doomed to perish. Nor does he pity in his misery the poor or envy the rich" (Virgil, *Georgics*, II, 495–499). Rousseau omits verse 497, which reads, "nor by the Dacian sweeping down from his confederate Danube."

16. See *Social Contract*, IV, ii ff., and Masters, *The Political Philosophy of Rousseau* (Princeton, N.J.: Princeton University Press, 1968), 365–367.

17. This is a reference to Rousseau's profession as copyist of music.

Index

UNIVERSITY PRESS OF NEW ENGLAND publishes books under its own imprint and is the publisher for Brandeis University Press, Brown University Press, University of Connecticut, Dartmouth College, Middlebury College Press, University of New Hampshire, University of Rhode Island, Tufts University, University of Vermont, and Wesleyan University Press.

Library of Congress Cataloging-in-Publication Data
Rousseau, Jean-Jacques, 1712–1778.
    [Discours sur les sciences et les arts. English]
    Discourse on the sciences and arts : (first discourse) and
polemics / Jean-Jacques Rousseau ; edited by Roger D. Masters and
Christopher Kelly ; translated by Judith R. Bush, Roger D. Masters,
and Christopher Kelly.
      p. cm. — (The Collected Writings of Rousseau ; vol. 2)
    Translation of: Discours sur les sciences et les arts.
    Includes bibliographical references and index.
    ISBN 0–87451–580–7
    1. Rousseau, Jean-Jacques, 1712–1778—Translations into English.
I. Masters, Roger D. II. Kelly, Christopher, 1950– . III. Bush,
Judith R. IV. Title. V. Series: Rousseau, Jean-Jacques,
1712–1778. Works. English. 1990 ; vol. 2.
    [PQ2040.D63E5]
    848'.509 s—dc20
    [194]   91–50820

∞